BORN IN A TRUNK...

Just outside
the center door fancy

Best To you
Billy Toby Choate

a memoir by
BILLY *"TOBY"* CHOATE

First Edition
First Printing • December 1994

ISBN 1-885591-42-X

Printed in the USA by

𝓜ORRIS
PUBLISHING

3212 E. Hwy 30
Kearney, NE 68847
800-650-7888

OUTLINE

PART I
THE TENT SHOWS

PART II
CHOATE'S COMEDIANS - THE EARLY YEARS

PART III
THE GOLDEN YEARS - 1902-1929

PART IV
THE DEPRESSION YEARS - 1929-1942

PART V
MY WAR YEARS - 1943-1945

PART VI
BISBEE'S COMEDIANS AFTER THE WAR

PART VII
THE CANVASMEN

PART VIII
MAGICIANS WHO TROUPED ON BISBEE
COMEDIANS

PART IX
BAD LUCK

PART X
POPCORN, SNOW CONES, AND CANDY

PART XI
DON'T LAUGH

PART XII
STORMY WEATHER - BLOW DOWNS AND TEAR UPS

THE TOBY SHOW

Yesterday--a vacant lot,
  quiet without a sound.
Today--a busy beehive,
  the Toby show's in town.
The canvas top is billowing out,
  the side walls are in place.
The quickly laid out stake line,
  displays a certain grace.
At evening when the shadows form,
  and sunbeams start their laggin'.
You see the line begin to form,
  before the ticket wagon.
The farms, the shops, the stores they
    leave,
  making straight for the tent show
    door.
Happy to be here again this year,
  for they've seen a Toby show before.
The house lights are killed, the curtain
    goes up,
  the actor steps out with his line.
And the background is set for a
    wonderful play,
  produced to tickle your spine.
From beyond the wings you hear a tune,
  chanted in a voice that's rare.
And an entrance is made from center
    stage,
  that brings you up from your chair.
A tousled mop of red hair on his head,
  freckled face set off with a grin.
Checkered pants, yellow coat, shoes too
    big,
  lets you know Toby's in town again.

If you've read the heralds around the
    town,
  you know the show is quite cricket.
It may be "John Slater Awakens,"
  or Bob LaThey's "Meal Ticket".
There are many acts to amuse you,
  with comedy bits in between.
There are hoofers, vent acts and
    magicians,
  all add to the color and sheen.
Now the Bill for tonight is ended,
  the curtain comes down on the finale.
And the crowd slowly troopes from the
    tent,
  to the tune of the orchestras bally.
Then as you slowly drive home in the
    night,
  there's one thing you'd like to know.
Wouldn't it be a wonderful thing,
  if life was a Toby show.

WRITTEN BY W. V. MATTHEWS
FORDSVILLE, KENTUCKY
A BISBEE FAN FOR MANY YEARS

This book is dedicated with humble and grateful appreciation to those thousand of fans who braved the wind, rain, mud and sat on hard folding chairs to see Bisbee's Comedians. And especially to my kids: Welby Charles, Cherita and LaMar LaThey.

PREFACE

This book is a part of America's past, a part of Americana. The repertoire show, otherwise known as a tent show, Rep show or Toby show. At one time, there were over four hundred of these type shows on the road touring the West, Southwest, South and Southeast. It is said with good authority these shows employed more actors and actresses than Broadway and the Legitimate theatre combined.

To the 90's generation, the thought of acting likely brings to mind stardom, big bucks, and Hollywood or Broadway. But somewhere at the foundation of arts and entertainment, lies a handful of true theatre stars. People who grew up around the tent shows and groomed their skills under the rawest and often impromptu conditions.

They came from a time when there were no second takes or free rides. They put up the scenery, set the stage, put on their own makeup, and quietly pulled up their own bootstraps when performances didn't fly.

I came from that era and this book is about two tent shows I am well acquainted with: Choate's Comedians and Bisbee's Comedians. I was born and raised on the Choate show and spent most of my adult life owning and operating the Bisbee show. This book is also about "TOBY", the lovable character I had the pleasure of playing for 12 years.

The late Joe Creason, long time Louisville Courier Journal staff writer and friend of mine, said in one of his many stories on the Bisbee show and TOBY, "The show had been on for four or five minutes when a loud voice that twanged like a lost guitar string was heard off stage." The audience came to life as the owner of the voice, a freckled faced party wearing a red wig and clothes that fit like they wanted nothing to do with him, bounded in front of the footlights. "My name is Toby T. Ticklebush," he announced to no one and all, "and I'm on my way to Chicago to sell a load of hawgs." The crowd howled in wild abandon as Toby followed that announcement immediately by letting the villain have it with one of the oldest gags known to man. "I didn't sleep a wink last night," he reported, "the window shade was up." "Why" the heavy bit, "didn't you pull it down?" "Because," he replied, looking out over the crowd with a look that had "vacancy" stamped all over it, "I couldn't reach across the street." As far as the audience was concerned, the show started that moment.

Yes, the tent shows are gone now. Once there were hundreds of them playing towns from Canada to Mexico. They well deserve a page in the history of show business in America. Long before the days of wide angled screens and television, tent shows were bringing live theatre to small towns a thousand miles from Broadway. They did more, they served as a proving ground for the budding talents for many performers whose names later hung in shimmering greatness, names like Clark Gable, Jennifer Jones, Buddy Ebson, Red Skelton, Milburn Stone, Lyle Talbert and many more.

Here is the route of Bisbee's Comedians. The show played these towns for 42 years and very few times was the route changed. The show opened in April and played the spring Tennessee towns, jumped into Kentucky for the summer months and then into the West Tennessee cotton towns for the fall months closing at Collierville, Tennessee in November.

The show always opened in Lexington, Tennessee then moved to Parsons, Linden, Hohenwald, Dickson, Waverly, Camden, Bruceton, McKenzie, then jumped to Murray, Kentucky, Benton, Fulton, Clinton, LaCenter, Smithland Kuttawa, Eddyville, Marion, Morganfield, Princeton, Dawson Springs, Calhoun, Owensboro, Livermore, Hartford, Fordsville, Leitchfield, Morgantown, Greenville, Russelville, Elkton, Hopkinsville, Cadiz and then back to Tennessee playing Union City, Martin, Dresden, Dyer, Obion, Dyersburg, Halls, Ripley, Covington, Brownsville, Whiteville, Somerville, Moscow, and finally closing in Collierville.

Playing the same towns year after year Bisbee's Comedians made many friends. We never did but we could have billed as "the show with a million friends." Some became personal friends, some became more like family. You will meet many of these friends in this book.

PART I
THE TENT SHOWS

I grew up on a dramatic institution known as a repertoire tent show. This institution, though it has now ceased to exist, was once the most popular branch of the American theatre. In the 1920's, there were over 400 of these type shows on the road. They employed more people than Broadway and Hollywood combined. Two shows I am well acquainted with are Choate's Comedians and Bisbee's Comedians. My young life was spent growing up on the Choate show, and most of my adult life was on the Bisbee show. But before preceding, it might be helpful to consider the shows more generally, for there are few people under the age of thirty who have ever seen a tent show.

Most of the shows opened in the spring and played continuously until late fall. The Bisbee show opened at Lexington, Tennessee the first of April and closed at Collierville, Tennessee the last of October. Most of the shows played either a three day or a week stand.

Although there was variation in size and cost of equipment, the basic layout for all tent theatres was similar. There was both reserved and general admission seating, a stage with scenery, and backstage dressing rooms, The entrance, designated by a separate

2

tent or marquees, served to enhance the tents appearance as well as a lobby where tickets were sold and where "bally boards" displayed pictures of the actors. Seating was divided between the bleachers and folding chairs. Bleachers, called "blues" because they were always painted with blue paint, were general admission seats. Boards twelve feet in length were placed over stringers and held erect over wooden jacks. The boards were held in place by ropes laced to the jacks. To make them safe and secure, a stake or "toe pin" was driven at the base of each stringer. Still, on soft and muddy lots there was always the danger of the seats falling apart while loaded with spectators. In the early spring of 1935, Choate's Comedians was playing Alto Pass, Illinois. It was opening night and the house was full and the blues were packed. Grandpa came back and told Dad he thought they should move the people off the "blues" on account of the soft ground. Before this could be done, six sections of the "blues" went down, injuring a number of people. No suits were brought against the company, but the doctor bills were paid by the Choate's.

In the fall of 1941, Bisbee's Comedians was playing Whitesville, Tennessee. As a concert feature, they did a short version of Dr. Jekyll and Mr. Hyde. Thayer Roberts, a very fine actor and makeup artist, was playing the title role. At the climax, Rod Brasfield, who was doing the comedy and Toby that year, would jump off the front of the stage, run up the center aisle, and out the front door with Thayer in hot pursuit. On this particular night, Thayer with his grotesque made up face, stopped in front of the blues, raised his arms, and lunged toward the people making a terrible sound with his voice. The people yelled, screamed, fell off, and jumped off those "blues." It was as if someone had taken a broom and swept them clean. Two people had to be taken to the hospital. Needless to say, that was the last time Thayer and Rod ran through the audience.

Folding chairs were used for reserved seats. Tickets for these seats were sold inside the tent at the entrance to the section. The chair seats and the "blues" were separated by a canvas fence called a "bally line."

The stage area was designed to accommodate the play, and the specialties between the acts of the play. A canvas proscenium hung the full width of the tent. On the Bisbee show the stage was 28 X 16. There was a front curtain as well as a "specialty', "olio" or a "street drop" curtain used for the vaudeville and specialty acts. The area behind the stage was reserved for dressing rooms and storage. The Bisbee show had two dressing rooms, one

4

for men and one for women, placed on ground level. The men's was behind the stage and the women's was at the left of the stage and curtained off for privacy. The Choate show found it advantageous to use truck vans that were driven into place alongside the stage; this eliminated loading and unloading the wardrobe trunks and the actors could dress at stage level.

Scenery was stored in the remaining space backstage. Both the Choate and Bisbee show carried their own furniture, including ceiling pieces, practical doors and windows, and flat scenery. In 1927, John Finch, of Grayville, Illinois, a well known scenic artist, painted seven sets of flat scenery for Choate's Comedians. Bisbee's Comedians used painted 4 X 8 plywood panels that could be changed quickly and took up very little storage space. Jess Bisbee was a very fine artist and painted the scenery on his show. His front curtain and street drop were masterpieces.

Tent theatres varied in size. Many managers took pride in their tents and were constantly adding new twists and innovations. In the 1920's, Choate's Comedians was using a large circus tent that seated 3,000 people. As I remember the outfit in the 1930's, the tent was 55 X 120. In the early years, the show moved by wagons. In the early 1900's, the show moved by rail and owned their own private baggage car. Finally, the show used trucks for their moves from town to town. The Bisbee tent was a 60 X 140 dramatic end. It seated 1,500 people and moved on six semi-trailer trucks. Some of the tent repertoire companys during the 1920's were very elaborate. William L. Slout tells in his book Theatre in a Tent, about Texas manager Charles Harrison, who had a passion for large outfits. After World War II, his show was so heavy it took a day to tear down and three days to set up. Roy Garrett, boss canvasman for the W.I. Swain show, and with Bisbee's Comedians for many years, told me it took 10 hours to tear down the Swain outfit and 20 hours to set it up. I have also heard the story of the Paul English Players touring Louisiana carrying a rising orchestra pit. The show also carried an ornate water fountain displayed by colored lights, located at the entrance of the tent. One season, Harley Sadler who operated a show in Texas, used a tent designed with a fly loft over the stage, allowing the scenery to rise out of sight as in the permanent theatre buildings. However, managers who framed their shows too elaborately often found themselves in financial difficulty.

Bisbee's Comedians played three day and weeks stands. The outfit would be set up early Monday morning and the show would be presented that evening at 8:00. The performance consisted of an orchestra, a three act comedy drama play, and vaudeville specialties between the acts of the play.

The show began each evening with a 30 minute concert by the orchestra. They played old standards and popular songs of the day. After the orchestra, the play began. A comedy or comedy drama divided into three or four acts. Between the acts of the play various specialties were featured, magicians, song and dance teams, ventriloquists or jugglers. After the main show a concert or after show was presented. This consisted of a musical opening with bits, black outs, and specialties. There was an extra charge for the concert.

However, the most important feature of the tent show was the play. The plots, predictable enough, reflect small town values and tastes in every detail. The farmer, for example, is an important fixture in many shows. He is portrayed as the ideal man--simple, honest, independent, industrious, healthy and happy. Many of the undesirable characters-----the gossips, the hypocritical deacons, and the ruthless bankers are, for one reason or another, out to ruin him. Yet he never loses his integrity, and circumstances always turn out well for him in the end. Another feature of the many plays is the contrast between the country and the city, a contrast that is as old as the theatre itself. The country life always represents the ideal; the city life always represent corruption and deceit. In addition to the plot, the dress of the characters often makes this point. The city characters are usually elaborately dressed, but their dress is a little too elaborate, or too "high falooting" as the country characters might say. It seems to say the city folks need a fancy outside to cover up a not so fancy inside. The country characters, on the other hand, are plainly dressed, often sporting a straw hat, and boots-----typical "hayseed" as the city folk might say. But this plainness seems to represent an innocence and a simplicity that is to be admired.

In fact, it is surprising to note how little the cast changes from one show to another. All the plays are characterized by clearly defined characters. The good characters are always rewarded in the end; the bad characters are always punished. The villain, referred to as the "heavy" is ordinarily patterned after the black-coated scoundrels of the old melodramas, possessing the same vengeful, sneaking, self-centered qualities. Yet, unlike the melodramas, he is frequently good looking and cannot always be recognized for the scamp he is. The hero and heroine, known as the "leads" are, on the other hand, nearly perfect, possessing all the rugged individualism, flag waving patriotism and moral scrupulousness that any small town audience could ask for. The main plot usually focuses upon the heavy's attempts to undermine the financial stability or virtuous reputation of one or both of the leading characters.

The character man and woman were the Dad and Mom, of the leading man or the leading woman. Some of the best parts were written for these characters.

Supplementing the nucleus of the cast are the two younger characters----- the juvenile and the ingenue. The juvenile is a young male character. The ingenue is the attractive young lady with whom he is in love. They remain relatively minor characters whose flirtation merely adds a little extra spice to the main plot.

The other character type that should be mentioned here is the general business actor which varies from play to play more than any other type. The importance of the general business performers should not be underestimated, for they were often required to display more versatility than anyone else in the cast. They were just as apt to be playing a doctor or a hillbilly or, in the case of females, a maid or a socialite.

Finally, there was Toby, the red-haired, freckle faced, country bumpkin, who became in the course of time, not only a night fixture, but a feature attraction. Toby usually has a lot to do with foiling the plots of the villain. Sometimes he even accomplishes the feat single-handedly. But the villain of these shows are not fools: they are shrewd and cunning. Consequently, in order for Toby to be a believable character, he too must have a good deal of wit. The tent shows came to need a feature attraction. They needed something that would assure the audience of a good deal of comedy every night.....Toby came to fill this need very well.

PART II
CHOATE'S COMEDIANS - THE EARLY YEARS

My grandfather, William Carroll Choate, founder of Choate's Comedians, was born in 1863, during the Civil War. His father, also named William, was a young man of twenty-four who had enlisted in the Union army in 1862 and was captured in 1863 about the time of the Battle of Gettysburg. A year later, he died of starvation in the notorious Andersonville, Georgia prison.

Like many families, the Choate's suffered severe economic and emotional hardships after the war. With the head of the household dead, Grandpa was forced to assume more responsibility than was natural or healthy. It is for these reasons perhaps, that Grandpa became so captivated by a broken down Punch and Judy show that rambled through Tunnel Hill, Illinois, in 1878. In fact, he was so taken with the show and it's owner, Tony White, that when the show left Tunnel Hill, he went with it. It would have no doubt staggered the mind of this young fifteen year old to know that he would spend the next sixty-three years of his life on the road with a tent show. Even though Grandpa was soon dissatisfied with the poor quality of Tony White's show, he stayed with it for two seasons. Mostly because he had learned to like the wandering life of a small town showman.

Grandpa was, from first to last, a big talker, and the more people he could come to meet and come to know, the better he liked it.

In the fall of 1880, Grandpa "bought for a song" as he used to say, a bankrupt circus outfit. The winter of 1880-1881 he spent renovating the outfit and preparing to put it on the road in the spring.

In addition to renovating the equipment, the other immediate problem was finding performers for the show. He contacted a couple of tumblers and jugglers who had been with the circus before it went bankrupt, and convinced them to come back for another season. He also talked to a couple of his Johnson County friends, who played banjo and guitar, to join him. Grandpa played violin, or "fiddle" as he called it. The three of them could sing as well as play, and they developed quite a repertoire of novelty numbers.

But even though Grandpa was busy that winter preparing his show for the spring, he evidently found some leisure time. For it was in the winter of 1880-1881 that he began to date a local girl, Mary Webb. Early that spring, Grandpa and Mary were married. A few weeks later, in early May, Grandpa took the show on the road.

For years show people have argued about who had the first tent show on the road. In 1937, Billboard magazine asked it's readers to write in and supply any information that might be helpful in resolving the question. The response was overwhelming but, as one might imagine, it produced more confusion than Illumination. The shows most mentioned for consideration, however, were the Choate show of Southern Illinois, the J.C. Rockwell show from the East, the yankee Robinson show of Northern Illinois, and the John Ginnivan Stock Co. of Northern Indiana. All these shows began, as near as one can determine, in the early 1880's. But one problem with determining which troupe should be regarded as the first is the rather vague definition of the term "tent show." The term eventually came to refer to shows that consisted of comedy drama plays, music and vaudeville. The Choate show started presenting skits on a stage during the 1890's.

I remember asking Grandpa if he thought he was the first to start a show of this type? He said, "My boy, it really doesn't make any difference. When it is 6:00 P.M. and the lightning is flashing, the thunder is roaring, it is pouring down rain, and we are out grapevining the tent, I like to think Mr. Ginnivan was the start of all this. But when the sun is shining, the grass is green, the house is full and the leading man is not drunk, I like to think I am the one who started such a grand and great institution." The point, I suppose, is not that one show came before another, but that this small group of shows began what was to become a major industry in American theatre.

Grandpa's first summer on the road was modestly successful. He made some money, but most of the profit was used to buy two teams of horses to pull his wagons.

Perhaps the oddest, though most memorable, occurrence of the summer was Grandpa being dubbed with the nickname "Pop". Since he was only eighteen at the time, freckle-faced and a bit "tow-headed," there is some reason to believe that the name originally was meant to be a joke. But, joke or not, the name stuck, and as Grandpa grew older, more respected, and more well known, the name became more and more appropriate. So from his eighteenth birthday on, he was never called anything but "pop".

Late in the year of 1881, Mary gave birth to a baby boy. They named him Edward. Grandpa took the show out in the spring of 1882, and he had a five piece orchestra and had added a couple of more acts. He toured over a slightly larger area that summer, and business improved considerably. It was so good, as a matter of fact, that he was able to buy a farm just outside Tunnel Hill that winter. Shortly after the first of the year, 1883, Grandpa and Grandma had their second child, Claire Ethel.

Things were going good for Grandpa's show. By 1883, he was featuring a seven piece orchestra. In the winter of 1884, Claire Ethel, who had just turned one, died of the whooping cough. The next year, 1885, they had another son, Claude. Two years later, in 1887, their third son, my dad, Arlie, was born.

1888 was undoubtedly the saddest in Grandpa's life. A severe small pox epidemic swept through Southern Illinois killing large numbers of people. Grandpa's business that summer, as one might imagine, was slow. But more importantly, his own family was, in the fall of the year, stricken with the small pox. Claude, then three, contracted the disease first. He died in a matter of days. Then Grandma contracted the disease-----in a short time, she was also dead. Grandpa stayed on the farm that winter, but set out once again with his show in the spring, leaving the boys with his Mother and step-father.

The next year, 1889, Grandpa remarried. He married another Tunnel Hill girl, twenty year old Philenda Burklow. Philenda had never been married and was, as she used to admit later, afraid of being an "old maid". This fear made her less apprehensive, than she would have otherwise been, about taking a husband who came with two

15

little boys. In fact, she seemed delighted at the prospect of having youngsters immediately. So, in the summer of 1890, Philenda gathered up the boys, battened down the hatches on the farm, and struck out with Grandpa for the summer. Grandma never appeared on the stage, but her job was perhaps the most challenging of all-----she cooked the meals in the cook tent. For supplies, Grandpa relied on the local patrons. He traded free passes for such basic staples as eggs, milk, butter, fresh vegetables and meat. He also traded passes for field corn to feed the horses. During these years, Grandpa's show ordinarily stayed in one location for two or three days, making it necessary for him to go out and gather food supplies only once at each stop. This method worked well unless the weather got bad. When the roads got muddy, it was extraordinarily difficult to move the wagons, which were loaded to capacity and beyond. At times, the roads became so murky that both teams of horses had to be harnessed to one wagon and pulled two or three miles. Under those conditions, it sometime took as long as two or three days to get from one town to the other. It also caused supplies to run short. But his good reputation made it possible for him to buy what he needed at reasonable prices. He always used to say that "folks was mighty reasonable when it come to lookin' after the show." The show moved on four farm wagons. Grandpa would tell me how the teams would get stuck when swollen streams had to be forded. At one time, the wagons and horses were swept downstream, the tent was wet, and everything else in the wagons, so they decided to camp there for the night. They spread the tent out to dry and Grandpa said, "If I remember rightly, we caught some mighty fine catfish out of that creek." One year he planned on playing some new towns in Missouri and working his way into Arkansas, but he was afraid he couldn't make it back to Illinois before winter set in.

Grandpa was on the road ten years or so before he got around to naming the show. People had, up to this time, merely referred to it as "Pop Choate's Outfit". But early in the 1890's, the official billing for the show became "The Choate Brothers Show". Why Grandpa chose this name has, and probably always will, remain a mystery. Probably, Grandpa wanted to convey the idea that this was a family enterprise, that it was legitimate and wholesome. Show people of all kinds in those days had to fight against the reputation of being tricksters and ne'er-do-wells. Perhaps Grandpa's show title was a way of combating this perception.

Grandpa told me many interesting stories concerning Peg Leg Jones. Peg Leg had, as his name indicates, lost one of his legs and replaced it with a wooden peg. His act consisted of playing the fiddle and dancing to his own music. His favorite gimmick was doing a fast buck and wing, and turning back flips for a finish. Peg Leg was a crowd pleaser and remained on the Choate show throughout most of the 1890's.

PART III
THE GOLDEN YEARS – 1902-1929

Around the turn of the century, the Choate Brother's show underwent a number of transitions. Grandpa bought a new tent from the Anchor Tent and Supply Company in Evansville, Indiana. In addition, he bought fifty canvas bottom benches, each of which seated four people. The benches were placed down in front of the stage and were used as reserve seats. After paying an admission to get into the tent, the customer, if he chose, pays another admission to sit in the canvas bottomed benches. If he chose not to, he sat in the bleachers or blues, (or in the "chicken roost" as the kids called them).

About this time, Grandpa sold his wagons and horses and began to move the show by railroad. The advantages to this were obvious-----the show could be moved farther, faster, and more economically than ever before. The result was that the Choate Brothers show became not just a Southern Illinois show, but a show that played throughout the South, regularly touring through Southern Illinois and Indiana, Kentucky, Missouri, Tennessee, Mississippi, and Louisiana. It also enabled him to lengthen his season by several weeks because he was in a milder climate. This, in addition to his larger tent,

19

which seated more people, made the show a much more profitable business than ever before. By now, Grandpa could attract more and better performers. Not only could he afford to pay them more, but he could give them more work under better conditions and house them better. His troupe no longer stayed in tents, but in hotels. The performers were no longer expected to handle the job of putting up and tearing down the tent. He hired a crew of canvasmen to do that.

It was at this time that Grandpa dropped the name "Choate Brothers" in favor of "Choate's Comedians".

Grandpa's sons, Ed and my dad Arlie, had grown up on the show, but had developed different ambitions. Uncle Ed had no inclination to appear on the stage. It wasn't until the show was preparing to depart on it's first season by rail in 1902 that Uncle Ed, then twenty-one, met Myrtle Simmons from Marion, Illinois. A year later in December, 1903, they were married. They bought a small farm out side Jeffry, Illinois and settled down. They lived there for many years before moving into Marion, where they lived until their deaths.

Dad's temperament was much different. Uncle Ed was shy, Dad was not. Uncle Ed wanted no part of the stage, Dad most certainly did. In fact, by the time Dad grew into adolescence, the show was presenting dramas and he regularly played the juvenile. When he reached his seventeenth birthday, he took over the leads. He made a particularly good leading man, having a strong voice, an erect posture, curly brown hair, and a handsome face. Even more importantly, he had been around the show long enough to know how to make maximum use of his attributes.

In the summer of 1908, the show played for a week in Pollock, Louisiana. Most of the troupe, including Grandpa, Grandma, and Dad, stayed at the local hotel, which was owned and operated by Charles Jackson and his wife, Amelia. They had a nineteen year old daughter named Mae. Pollock was a small Louisiana town and the inhabitants were, typically enough, skeptical of strangers. The older people, including Mr. & Mrs. Jackson, were not particularly pleased about the town being "overrun with show people" (though, observed Dad mischievously in later years, "they weren't unhappy enough to turn away our business.") The younger people, including May, were delighted by the development.

The Choate troupe, which never performed on Sunday night, spent the evening relaxing in their rooms, with the help of a full moon and a swing on the front porch, Arlie and Mae used the time to get acquainted. Amid such circumstances, it is not surprising that they became friends rather quickly. By

the time the show left town on Saturday
night, Mae and Arlie had exchanged
addresses and promised one another to
write regularly. And write they did.
When the show closed in December, Arlie
went back to Pollack to visit a few days
before heading home to Illinois.

The next season (1909), the show
was back in Louisiana. The result was
that Arlie and Mae began to see one
another more freely. After the show
closed in December, Grandpa, Grandma,
and Dad went to Pollock where Dad and
Mother were married. The wedding took
place on December 14, 1909.

It was at this time that Grandpa
officially made Dad a full partner in
the business.

The 1910 season was, among other
things, devoted to teaching Mother to
act. She was enthusiastic about the
prospect of being a performer and worked
at it diligently, but throughout the
summer she appeared only in bit parts
despite her clamoring for larger roles.
"Take a summer to learn the trade,
dear," Grandpa would tell her, "and from
then on you'll get to work all you
want." But just when Mother was looking
to the 1911 season and beginning to
think in terms of larger roles, a
problem developed-----she became
pregnant.

When the show opened in early May
of 1911, Mother and Grandma stayed in
Johnson City, Illinois, to await the

22

baby. Finally, June 2nd, Mother gave birth to a baby boy. My brother was named Welby Carroll Choate. It was another five weeks before Mother regained enough of her strength to rejoin the show; she spent another week rehearsing. Then on Monday night, July 23, with the show in Ridgeway, Illinois, Mother became an active member of the cast.

For two years (1912-13), things went well. Grandpa and Dad opened the show early, toured over a wide territory, and made good profits, not closing until Christmas in the deep south. There were many factors that created a boom in the tent show industry between 1912 and 1917. One was the improved quality of the plays that were becoming available. In 1916, Choate's Comedians featured a particularly strong week of plays, two of which were the new Charles Harrison plays-----The Awakening of John Slater and Saintly Hypocrites and Honest Sinners. In addition to the increasing number and improved quality of plays becoming available, the tent shows were beginning to capitalize on the crowd pleasing "Toby" as a box office attraction.

War was officially declared the first part of April, in 1917, just before the show opened. Business throughout the 1917 season was good, but even the simplest set up and tear down jobs were troublesome because of the

23

shortage of manpower. Train schedules became more and more unreliable and caused the troupe expensive overnight delays in getting from one town to another.

The 1918 season was worse. The winter of 1917-18 had been extremely severe. Abnormal amounts of snow and prolonged sub-freezing temperatures had caused many farmers to lose much of their livestock and winter wheat. And, as everyone in the tent show business knew, you couldn't make it, if you didn't attract the farmer.

The 1919 season was much more successful than the two previous ones had been. The end of the war alleviated manpower and material shortages and returned transportation schedules back to normal. In fact, the show was on the road a full forty weeks, and enjoyed good business.

The 1920 season is memorable because it was the first season that Ray Zarlinton worked on the show. He was a great "Toby" comedian, but he was equally good in character parts. It wasn't long before he became a favorite of Grandpa and Dad.

At the beginning of the next season, 1921, George and Marie Crawly joined the show. George was, by that time, well known in the tent show business. He was the author of three plays and had made a name for himself as "Toby". Ray and George were experts at their crafts, and it created something of a problem for Grandpa and Dad, who may very well have been the only show on the road at that time employing two first rate Toby comedians-----Ray Zarlington and George Crawly.

One of the hits of the 1921 season was the feature play, Sputters or Girl of the Flying X. This is George Crawley's most well known play, one that he had written a few years earlier in 1916. While he was with Choate's Comedians he wrote, The Girl from Illinois for Mother. On the front of the script he wrote, "For Mae Choate-----the cleverest and most beautiful of leading ladies."

1923 was particularly eventful. On March 5, Mother's Father and my Grandfather, was run over by a car while he was in St. Louis on business. He died five days later on March 10. To complicate matters, I was born four days after the funeral, on March 17. I was named Billy Charles after my Grandfather Choate and Grandfather Jackson.

The events of the spring had left Mother weaker and more unsteady than Dad had anticipated. Because of that, he insisted that Mother not work for several weeks. It was July when she finally appeared on the stage. It was the first absence from the Choate's Comedians stage since the birth of Brother Welby eleven years earlier.

Despite all of the extraordinary

occurrences that took place during the 1923 season, business was good from opening day on.

During the winter of 1923, Dad and Grandpa decided to expand their operation, and put out two shows. By the time the two shows opened in April, Choate's Comedians number one (operated by Dad) employed thirty-three people and Choate's Comedians number two (operated by Grandpa) employed twenty. George Crawley was assigned to play Toby on the number one show while Ray Zarlington was assigned to the part on Grandpa's show.

Also hired to work on Grandpa's show that summer was Bernice Allen. She was given the ingenue and lead roles. This meant, of course, Bernice would spend most of the summer playing opposite Ray, a prospect that excited her a good deal. Whereas the leading lady and the comedian never met with romantic success during a performance, off stage the plot worked differently. Ray and Bernice were in love before the show had been on the road a month. In the fall of 1925, after going together two seasons, Ray Zarlington and Bernice Allen were married, much to the delight of everyone, especially Grandma Choate, who featured herself the chief architect of the match.

The big story on the number one show that year, 1924, was Brother Welby's appearance as a full time performer-----he assumed a full load of juvenile roles. That meant, for the first time in a few years, two members of the Choate family (Mae and Welby) were nightly regulars.

In 1926, Dad bought a new Ford truck with a Mounted Tangley Calliophone. The truck was painted circus style and Dad used it for advertising. Whether or not the calliophone helped business is a questionable matter, but it didn't hurt, and because it was bright, flashy, and melodic, it gave Dad as much satisfaction as any accessory to the outfit possibly could have.

On October 15, the show closed for the season in Providence, Kentucky. Six weeks later, Dad opened a circle stock in southern Illinois with headquarters in Harrisburg. At this time, Jess and Mary Bisbee joined Choate's Comedians as a feature doing their magic act.

PART IV
THE DEPRESSION YEARS – 1929–1942

It wasn't until 1929 that the boom in the tent show industry, which had lasted for nearly a decade, began to disintegrate. Even though the Great Depression did not officially begin until the end of October, when the stock market crashed, business on the show was way off all summer. Even though no one knew it at the time, the bad luck that plagued the show that season was merely a trifle compared to the troubles lurking in the decade ahead.

All things considered, things went well in 1930. Dad and Grandpa had no illusions about turning a big profit during the 1930 season, they merely wanted to hold things together until prospertiy returned. And that, they mistakenly assumed, couldn't be too far away.

In 1932, the show, which had survived two depression years, prepared to open in the midst of yet another one. Each year more and more shows were closing, and those which managed to stay open were merely trying to outlast the depression.

1932 is notable because it is the year Brother Welby chose to get married. Back in 1930, he had met a young girl while the show was playing the Stonefort reunion. Her name was Eva Pankey. Welby and Eva were married on Sunday,

August 7, 1932 in Shawneetown, Illinois. I was nine years old at the time and there are two things I remember about that marriage: one, Mother crying for two days. She told me she was crying because she was happy. I couldn't understand that, and two, the show was playing in Uniontown, Kentucky. Monday, the band was playing their usual concert up town when Welby and Eva drove up. The band immediately broke into "Here Comes the Bride". I was very happy because I had a new sister.

Perhaps the most significant event that occurred in 1933 was the addition of a seasoned tent trouper, Bob LaThey, and his wife Pearle, to the cast. Bob and Pearle were to be on the Choate show every season from then on.

Bob had worked successfully on a number of shows. He made a splendid character actor because he managed to create distinctive and unusual features for each character. Bob was a particular sensation as the title character in The Old Grouch, a play which featured, obviously enough, an old man who makes life difficult for the younger and more likable characters. Whenever Rep. show actors got together, his name always came up, "no one can do the Grouch like Bob LaThey," they would say.

Bob's new wife, Pearle, was a pretty young lady who, though she had all of the physical attributes of an actress, had never been exposed to the stage. But Bob was determined to teach her the trade. No one wanted to mess with training an amateur, especially when it would amount largely to on the job training. For whatever reason, Dad and Grandpa hired Bob and Pearle with understanding that Bob would do character parts and Pearle would play the ingenue. Fortunately, Bob had been right about Pearle's ability. It wasn't long before she was a conspicuous asset to the cast.

No one, except my immediate family, had more influence on me, as a young boy, than Bob LaThey. From the first time Bob and Pearle joined the show, I practically lived with them. Most mornings I would head for their trailer and Pearle would fix our breakfast. They were rabid Cardinal fans and most afternoons were spent listening to the baseball games on KMOX, the popular St. Louis radio station. A number of times we went to old Sportsman Park, in St. Louis, to see the Cardinals play.

I made my first appearance on the stage at the age of six months when my Mother carried me on in place of the doll they had been using. I am told I started crying in the middle of the serious scene. Even at that age I was trying to get in the act, and steal the show. My next appearance took place on opening night when Choate's Comedians were playing Anna, Illinois. Extra

30

wardrobe trunks were stored at the right
of the stage in front of the proscenium.
Just before the curtain went up the
audience started laughing and clapping.
No one back stage could imagine what was
going on. It was I who was causing the
uproar. I had managed to crawl upon the
trunks and I was treating the audience
to a dance like they had never seen
before. I wasn't doing a time step, or
a soft shoe, or even a buck and wing,
but I was doing a lot of shaking and
wiggling, and the audience was eating it
up. Someone came and carried me off and
the audience booed him. I really laid
them in the isles that night. I was
four years old when that incident
happened.

The summer I was six years old the
show was playing Metropolis, Illinois.
There was good and bad in being in
Metropolis that year of 1929. There was
a boy there who had a Shetland pony and
he let me ride it. That was the nice
part of being in that river town that
year. However, something else happened
that I shall never forget. My Dad,
Mother and I went to a restaurant to
have a late afternoon lunch. On the way
back to the Hotel we went in the drug
store. On the counter was a beautiful
bow and arrow set. The more I looked at
it, the more I knew I had to have it. I
could just imaging myself pulling the
string on that bow and letting an arrow
fly. So, I asked Mother if she would

31

buy it for me. She said, "No Billy
Charles, you do not need a bow and arrow
set." Usually I could talk Dad into
letting me have most anything, but not
this time. He agreed with Mother and in
spite of all my crying and screaming, I
didn't get the bow and arrow set. That
night the doors opened and the band
assembled in front of the tent to play
their usual concert. I always enjoyed
hearing them play, so I hurried to the
front, staying next to the side wall so
I wouldn't run into a stake. I wasn't
very old, but I had been around a tent
long enough to know an iron stake hurt
when you hit it with your shin bone. I
listened to the band, along with many
other people waiting to go to the show.
They always closed with Billboard, and
on the last chorus played it as fast as
they could, and I always waited for
that. After the concert I headed for
the back of the tent taking a short cut
through the marquee. As I went behind
the ticket box I noticed Grandpa's big
black grip. Grandpa always sold front
door tickets and he always kept change
and big bills in his grip. I looked at
that money and all I could see was
arrows flying before my eyes. The
temptation was too great, so I reached
in, took a ten dollar bill, and headed
for the drug store. Thirty minutes
later I was behind the tent shooting
arrows at one of the trucks. Grandpa
and Dad approached me, and Dad said,

"Where did you get that bow?" I told him I bought it. Grandpa said, "I am short ten dollars. Did you take ten dollars out of my grip to buy that bow?" "Yes I did," I replied, "and here is your change." Thinking that by giving the change back to him, that would make everything just fine. But, without saying another word, Grandpa grabbed me, grabbed one of my arrows, and proceeded to beat the living day lights out of me. When he got through with me, I didn't want to see another arrow. That was the only time Grandpa ever whipped me, but it taught me a lesson. That was the last thing I stole.

When I was nine or ten years old, I did my first singing specialty. My Dad knew I had a good singing voice and I had been begging him to let me go on. One day, he said to me, "Billy Charles, tomorrow night I want you to do a couple of numbers." I couldn't believe it.....this is what I had been dreaming about. That night when I went to bed I couldn't go to sleep, and when I finally did doze off, I dreamed I was on a Broadway stage or in front of one of the big bands of the day. That afternoon I rehearsed with the orchestra. Everyone was looking forward to my debut. That night I was just a little nervous as I stood in the wings. The orchestra played my introduction, I stepped out on the stage in front of the street drop, the spotlight hit me, and I was on. I

33

opened with an upbeat arrangement of
There Will Be Some Changes Made and
closed with a ballad. There was great
applause and I had to do an encore.
What a thrill!!! When I came off the
stage everyone was slapping me on the
back and rubbing my head. My Mother and
the other women on the show were hugging
and kissing me, and I thought, this is
something else, this is it. This is
what I want to do the rest of my life.
I went to the orchestra leader and said,
"Can I rehearse a couple of new numbers
in the morning?"

Besides being a very fine actor,
Bob LaThey also turned out to be bit of
a playwright. Bob's first play written
in 1935, was entitled, The Singer and
The Fool. A title that was chosen in an
attempt to capitalize on the name of an
Al Jolsen movie, The Singing Fool.
Bob's most notable play is called Meal
Ticket. The lead in this play is a
young man from the city who marries a
country girl. Her family is absolutely
of no account, and they take advantage
of their son-in-law's fortune and good
humor. The Toby part is fresh and
funny. It is not like the Toby part in
The Singer And The Fool, full of
overworked jokes. Meal Ticket was one
of the most popular and most frequently
used plays on the Choate show, and other
repertoire shows during the thirties.

In July of 1937, Choate's
Comedians, were playing Shawneetown,

Illinois. One afternoon, the LaThey's and I drove to Harrisburg to catch a movie Pearle wanted to see. On the way back Bob told me he was writing a new play and he was writing a part for me. I could hardly wait for him to finish it. I had done some bit parts, but this was to a full fledged juvenile and I was thrilled with the idea of becoming an actor at the early age of fourteen. Finally, the play was finished and we immediately started rehearsal. Bob worked with me between rehearsals. He taught me how to enter, he taught me how to walk, to sit, to turn and to project. Finally, it was time to break the show in. Robert LaThey's "Lander's Murder Mystery" had it's first showing in Eldorado, Illinois and, I made my debut as an actor, that night. I remember I was very nervous, but after I made my first entrance, the nervousness left me and I was completely wrapped up in my character.

Between the second and third acts Bob made an announcement, and told the audience I was doing my first part. He brought me out and the audience gave me a standing ovation. What a thrill!!! In later years, whatever ability I attained as an actor, credit must be given to Bob LaThey. When I was a young boy he helped me, gave me direction, and taught me stage presence.

During the depression business fluctuated from one year to another.

1937 was a year when nothing seemed to go well for the Choate show. My breaking into parts was the only highlight of the year. The show opened in Cambria the third week in April and began to work its way through the familiar towns of southern Illinois. Business was way off and the show lost money at every stop.

Bob LaThey began to talk to Grandpa and Dad about taking the show to Texas for the fall season. Bob had lived in Texas and he insisted there were enough good towns down there to keep the show going for some time. The show played Hurst, Illinois the last week in August. On Saturday night after the show, the outfit was torn down, and the next morning the show headed for Texas minus, Grandpa, Grandma, and me. Grandpa and Grandma decided to stay home and I was to stay with them and go to school at Carbondale.

Business for the show was fair in Texas, certainly better than it had been in Illinois. In November, we got out of school for four days for a teachers meeting. I had a model B Ford car, and a friend, Dige Foster, and I decided to visit the show in Texas. Grandpa gave me ten dollars (which was a lot of money back then) and we took off. We arrived in Dekalb, Texas just as the show was over. We went back stage and Mother almost fainted when she saw me. We stayed a couple of days, and then headed

36

back to Illinois.

Business was a good deal more solid in 1938 than it had been in 1937. The show opened in Cambria and had a successful run through southern Illinois, then it moved into Missouri for a few weeks of good business, and in the late fall the show moved into Tennessee. When the show closed in November, Grandpa and Dad had put together another profitable season.

Of all the towns the Choate show played, my favorite was Shawneetown, Illinois. There was a number of reasons for this. First and foremost, I was a good swimmer, and in Shawneetown there was the Ohio river, Big Lake, and Round Pond. All were good swimming places. Then, there was Buck Litsey. He was a river man who owned a fish dock. As a kid I liked to be with Buck. He took me riding in his speed boat and told me wild stories. Probably none of them were true but I enjoyed them.

Last but no means least, there was Rudy Phillips. He had a Bar-B-Q place and made the best Bar-B-Q I have ever tasted. He also had a bevy of good looking girls working for him. His Bar-B-Q was great, but I think the girls also attracted me to his place. Anyway, we became friends and have remained so through the years. Choate's Comedians always played Shawneetown on the 4th of July week. Back at that time, Shawneetown attracted many tourists and

it was a great week for Choate's
Comedians. I had many friends in
Shawneetown and I always looked forward
to playing there. "Hobo Bill" is
another name that pops in my mind when I
think of Shawneetown. This may have
been the name of his boat, anyway, he
had a tug boat and barge and Dad
contracted him to move the show to the
river towns the show was playing the
next few weeks. He moved the show from
Shawneetown to Elizabethtown, then to
Rosiclaire, and from Rosiclaire to
Golconda. Bill let me ride in the cabin
and even let me steer the boat with the
big wheel. What a great thrill! Of
course I had friends in all the towns
the show played, but I especially
remember the Hosicks in Elizabethtown.
The boys name was Junior and the girls
name was Josephine, I believe that was
her name. Their father owned the
funeral home in Elizabethtown, and we
became good friends. The Barrs of
Golconda is another name that comes to
mind. Of course Cambria was Choate's
Comedians winter quarters. It was where
I was born and grew up, and through all
the years I have always referred to it
as my hometown. We had such great
neighbors, and most of them had kids my
age or a little older. The Sargents,
Hestons, Darnells, Greens, Biggs,
Finleys, Hesse, Schoosh, Covers, Whites,
Halls, and Tyners. I won't even attempt
to name the kids. They were my good

friends and I shall always remember them.

Grandpa and Grandma Choate's fiftieth wedding anniversary took place on March 25th. The attendance was enormous. Droves of show people came from all over the south and Midwest. But show people were not the only ones to pay their respects to one of the last genuine pioneers of the tent show industry. Cards and letters came from all over the Choate territory-----cards and letters from people who had seen Pop's show as little children and who had grown up to take their children and sometimes even their grandchildren to his show.

No one knew it at the time, but the massive celebration for Grandpa and Grandma that day turned out to be something of a farewell, not only to them, but to an entire era.

Grandma no longer got around easily, and she was subject to spells of fatigue. The show was scheduled to open in Cambria that second week of April, and Grandma swore she would be well enough to travel by then. But she wasn't. So when the trucks pulled out of Cambria for the summer season, Grandpa and Grandma were left behind. It was the first summer since 1889 that they did not take to the road come spring, but Grandma insisted they would join in a few weeks.

On Sunday, June 7th, Grandma was

admitted to the Herrin Hospital. It was late in the day on June 22, with her family gathered around her, Grandma Choate passed away peacefully.

The funeral was held in Tunnel Hill at the Webb Cemetery. Hundreds of people came. Rather than have the funeral in the church, as had been planned, it was decided to have it out in back on the edge of a small grove of trees. Brother Wilburn Sutton preached and Bob Ferganson sang. Bob was on the show and had also been with the Muny opera in St. Louis for a couple of seasons. He had a beautiful baritone voice and when he finished singing In the Garden, his voice echoing throughout those hills, there was not a dry eye in the hundreds of people gathered there that day. I have never felt such emotion.

After the funeral, the show opened in Carmi, where it had been sitting idle for a week. Grandpa joined the show in Carmi, but had lost a good deal of his vitality. From that time forward, Grandpa toured with the show only sporadically.

1939 was a sad year for the Choate family. However, the show Dad organized was one of the best and business was excellent. One of the features of the show was the Dixieland band. I had become a pretty fair bass fiddle player, brother Welby was a good drummer, and there was three young and stylish trumpet players - Larry Barnes, Bill Webb, and Tommy Lawson-----a great piano player-----Marine Barnes (Larry's wife)-----a big-toned tenor sax man name Bill Pue, the result was the band was a good drawing card. It was especially appealing to the young people. Almost every night the first eight or ten rows were filled with teenagers.

The show closed the 1939 season the second week in October in Kenton, Tennessee. As was the custom, we joined Ray and Berniece and Audra and Virginia Hardesty and played several weeks in theatres around southern Illinois. Later on I joined the Bill Hummel band out of Kansas City. We played a string of one nighters to Florida. Finally we went on a location job at a private club in Tallahassee. We had been there a couple of weeks when a sax player, Rudy Expado, approached me about going to Daytona Beach. I didn't like the club where we were and the band played the same stock arrangements over and over, and by this time I was sick of them, so I said "Let's go." We arrived in Daytona Beach by Grayhound that afternoon. Broke, hungry, and no job. Rudy stayed with the instruments while I looked for a job. I found a small rundown club. They had a piano player and drummer and could use us. Scale at that time was one dollar an hour. We were to play five nights a week, twenty dollars a week. Doesn't sound like much of a salary, but remember, this was 1940 and many people were working for thirty dollars a month. We found a cheap dirty room, and we were set. We would stay in bed until 12:00 so we wouldn't have to eat breakfast. Then, we would head for the beach, watch the girls all afternoon, and then at 8:00 P.M. we would start playing at the club. Really, not a bad life. Rudy started dating a woman much older than he was. He was a good looking fella, dark complexion, black eyes, and black curly hair. She fell madly in love with him. One night he came to the room and told me he was going to marry this woman. He said he didn't love her, but she was rich and because of all her wealth, he thought he could learn to love her. They were leaving the next afternoon for New York, where she lived, and would be married there. I never heard from Rudy again.

A week later, I left Daytona Beach and went to Deland to see Chic and Stella Palettee. They had been on Choate's Comedians for a number of years and were getting ready for the 1940 season. After a few days with the Palettee's, I headed for Illinois and the coming tent season.

The show rehearsed at Cambria and opened there the second week in April. Again, Dad had organized a very good show. Some of the members of the cast were: Johnnie and Connie Spaulding,

42

Robert and Pearle LaThey, Ollie and Lucille Locktee, Larry and Maurine Barnes, Jerry and Pauline Mansell, Dick and Hazel Butler and Berniece, Jimmie Reynolds, Bill Webb, Bill Pue, Chic and Stella Pallette, and the Choate's. The 1940 season was underway. Even though the weather was uncomfortably cool through the first part of May, business was considerably better than average-----and it stayed that way. Everyone had come to believe that the depression was finally over. Business throughout Illinois had resembled the profitable years of the twenties.

In late August, Kay Brothers Circus, a well known Eastern show, moved into Illinois. This show was owned by Mr. and Mrs. Frank Ketrow and their two sons. They had a big beautiful outfit. The tent was a 90 X 200 bail ring and all the trucks were new. Mr. Ketrow talked to Dad about putting a Rep. show under his outfit. A partnership was formed and the first town played under this arrangement was Vienna, Illinois. The Ketrow's had an elephant named Ted, and two baby elephants. Also, a number of other animals. All the animals were shipped back to their winter quarters, except Ted. He was kept on the show to help put up and tear down the outfit.

It was Saturday night. The show was over and the boys had the outfit down and loaded on the trucks for the move to Cape Girardeau, Missouri. As I

43

walked to the trailer where my bunk was,
I noticed what a beautiful night it was.
There was a full moon, a smell of
honeysuckle and I saw Ted staked out at
the end of the lot. I thought to
myself, what a beautiful, peaceful
night. Two hours later it was not so
peaceful. I was awakened by a shrill
noise, a noise I had never heard before.
I looked out my window and saw Ted
rampaging down the middle of the lot.
His trunk was high and the sound he made
as he trumpeted was frightening. Al
Moody, the trainer, was out trying to
calm him down, to no avail. Ted put his
head against one of the big loaded
semi-trucks, and had it off its wheels.
I thought sure it was going over on its
side. Then, he turned and went to the
end of the lot. There was a board
fence, but that didn't stop Ted. He
tore through that fence like it was not
there, and he was off into the night.

Al knew he would be hard to find in
the dark and that the elephant could
travel many miles in a short time. The
main worry was that some farmer would
shoot him. Al went to the sheriff's
office to tell them about Ted and to get
the word out, the elephant was not
dangerous. About 6:00 A.M. the show
moved off the lot for Cape Girardeau,
leaving Al, a couple of boys, and the
elephant trailer to haul Ted when he was
found. At 10:00 A.M., eleven miles from
Vienna, in a woods, they found Ted.

44

They said he was as glad to see Al as Al was to see him. He had a couple of cuts but no serious injuries. The rest of the season was uneventful, business remained good and the show closed the last week in October at Paragould, Arkansas.

By the time spring arrived in 1941, the war in Europe was expanding and the United States was becoming more and more involved. Dad and Grandpa had both vowed in 1919 that they would never again try to run a tent show in the midst of a war. But the United States was not involved in the fighting by March, and Dad decided to open the show as usual.

The show opened in Cambria the first of May, with the same personnel that was with the show in 1940, except Dick, Midge, and Peggy Lanham was added to the cast. As had been the case the previous year, business was big. The show moved along its familiar southern Illinois route, and made money at every stop. From DuQuion to Elkville to Carbondale to Cobden to Anna to Dongola to Ullin, everyone seemed to be bustling with excitement and money. When the show reached Anna and packed the house on opening night in a down pour of rain, it became clear that the attitudes which had prevailed during the depression were beginning to change.

The cotton crop was not good in Tennessee so Dad decided to play a few

45

towns in Kentucky. The show closed the
last week in September at Mayfield,
Kentucky. I knew the Bisbee show had a
few more weeks to run, so I wired Jess
and told him I was at liberty. He wired
back to join at once, which I did. The
show played its familiar West Tennessee
towns and closed Thanksgiving week in
Collierville, Tennessee. Rod and Elinor
Brasfield were having Thanksgiving
dinner at a restaurant in Memphis and
invited me to go with them. At dinner,
Rod told me he was joining his Brother
Boob, who had a show in stock, at a
theatre in Gadston, Alabama. Rod said,
"Billy, I talked to Boob last night and
told him about you. He can use you, if
you are interested, and will pay you
twenty-seven dollars a week." It didn't
take me long to decide. Twenty-seven
dollars was a lot of money in 1941.
There were men working on the WPA for
forty dollars a month. So, after the
show closed Saturday night, Rod, Elinor
and I drove to Hohenwald where Elinor's
folks lived and they owned a house. The
following Friday, Rod and I headed for
Gadsden, Alabama. We arrived late in
the afternoon and checked in the Leak
Hotel, and got a room for three dollars
a week, a nice room with a private bath.
Also, the dining room was fabulous,
"pitch till you win" family style meals
for only thirty-five cents. I took a
bath, changed clothes, and Rod and I
headed for the theatre. I was a bit

apprehensive in meeting Boob Brasfield for the first time. I had heard many stories about him, not all of them good. He was supposed to be tough and a perfectionist. I had also heard he was an alcoholic who stayed drunk all the time.

We got to the theatre just as the first show was over. After the introductions, Boob took me to his private dressing room. As I walked in I noticed an ice chest setting in the corner full of beer. He told me of his plans and what was expected of me. He was opening a show in Georgia, a circle stock, which was to play six towns (no show on Sunday), and was to headquarter in Cartersville. I was to do straight parts and singing specialties. The show would do bits, black outs, scenes, specialties with a band, along with a line of chorus girls. I was looking forward to going in Cartersville and working on this show. Besides the good money I would be making, I would be working with a remarkable cast of performers and gaining experience that could not be bought.

We moved to Cartersville, rehearsed two days and opened in the Cartersville Theatre Monday night to a packed house. Besides Boob, Rod and myself, others in the cast were: Les and Opal Lyle, Bill and Marigold Armand, Jerry Dexter, Ralph Blackwell, Toots Hodge, Bob Fisher, Happy Lawson, and a line of girls and I

47

must not forget Bonnie Brasfield. Bonnie was Boob and Neva's daughter. She was a very clever girl, good talking woman, had a great stage appearance, and could belt out a song with the best of them, and kick as high as any of the girls.

I took a liking to Happy Lawson. He was a good piano player and did singing specialties. He also wrote many songs. He wrote <u>Melancholy Baby</u> and sold it for $25.00. I asked why he did such a thing and he said, "Hell, I was hungry." He did a song in his specialty called <u>Any Time</u>. It was a great song and Happy said he had a copyright on it and a number of other songs he had written. I just knew that song was going to be a hit. And sure enough, a number of years later, Eddy Arnold recorded it, along with a number of other artists, including Eddie Fisher. Happy made thousands and thousands of dollars off of <u>Any Time</u>, however, of the hundreds of other songs he wrote, <u>Any Time</u> was the only hit.

Things were running very smooth. Our jumps were short. We would usually leave at noon for the town we were playing that night, have a rehearsal and do two shows and them make the drive back to Cartersville. We had a good show and it was a privilege to work with Boob Brasfield. Some of the stories I had heard about Boob were true. He was tough and a perfectionist, but what I had heard about him being drunk all the time was just not true. He did drink a lot of beer, but I never saw him drunk. On the stage, he was an artist. His timing was unbelievable. Rod was a very funny comedian, but Boob was two or three notches ahead of him. I worked with Rod, Boob and Ray Zarlington. What made these men so great as comedians, was their ability and timing. All three would steal the show in character parts, and were equally good in serious scenes. Everyone who knew them would not agree with me I am sure, but in my opinion, Boob was the cleverest, most talented, ingenious, quick-witted comedian to play on any stage anywhere.

It was the evening of Sunday, December 7, 1941. There were many people in the lobby gathered around the radio listening to President Roosevelt when I came downstairs. I asked Ralph Blackwell, "What's going on?"

"Japan has bombed Pearle Harbor and we are at war," he said. I didn't know where Pearle Harbor was located, but not wanting to appear dumb, I didn't ask. Anyway, I thought to myself, it wouldn't take but a few months for America to whip those Japanese, and the war would be over before I would have to go. Little did I realize, and it would have staggered my mind, if I had known at that moment I was destined to spend three years in the Army, and many months of combat. Not fighting the Japanese, but the Germans in the European Theatre of War.

In February I had a letter from Dad informing me he and Grandpa had decided not to open the show for the 1942 season. They gave strong consideration to opening in the spring. But the harder they worked to putting a show together, the more stumbling blocks they came up against. Many of the young performers were being enticed away from the shows by the high salaries being paid at defense plants. Also, gasoline and tires were being rationed. So rather than take out an inferior show and face the troubles of running a tent show with a war going on, they decided not to open, hoping the war would be over quickly. This was an earth shaking decision they made. Grandpa was now eighty-one years old and had spent sixty-three years of his life trouping. Dad was fifty-seven and had spent all his life on Choate's Comedians. I was told Mother and Welby took this news the hardest. But they both adjusted to life off the road. As for me, I had made up my mind I was going back to the Bisbee show. Boob wanted me to stay on his show in Gadston. It was tempting but I had been raised on a tent show and I loved it, even though it was hard work. Also, Jess and Mary were so good to me and treated me like a son. So, I was looking forward to the 1942 season, though I was sad that Choate's Comedians would not be on the road.

Rehearsals started in early April. We rehearsed two weeks, getting up in six shows and opening at Lexington, Tennessee. If Jess and Mary and the other people on the show had known all the trouble, and trials and tribulations we were to encounter that summer, we would have closed the opening week.

Bisbee's Comedians roster that 1942 season included: Rod and Elinor Brasfield, Leo and Maxine Lacey, Joe and Georgia Hoffman, Tom and Barbara Brooks, Ossie and Lola Johnson, Les and Opal Lyle, Mac and Gladys McWhorter, Howard Johnson, Loyed Gilbert, Thayer Roberts, Cliff and Mabel Malcomb and myself.

Business was good and everything was running smooth until we played Russelville, Kentucky. On Friday night with a packed house and during the second act of the show, a couple of drunks started a disturbance. Jess was on the front door and told two of the working boys to see if they couldn't quiet them down. They not only couldn't quiet them down, a real knock down bloody fight developed. In the process of getting a bad beating, one of the drunks picked up a chair, meaning to hit one of the canvasman, instead hit a pregnant woman. All hell broke loose, there was shouting, screaming and general confusion. The ambulance came and took the lady to the hospital, and the police came and took the four combatants to jail. We finally continued the show cutting everything that could be cut. Everyone was upset and wanted to get it over with, even the audience.

The next morning the sheriff was down bright and early. The woman's husband had sworn out a warrant for Jess Bisbee's arrest, and had also attached the outfit and equipment. Jess left with the Sheriff but in less than one hour was back along with the two canvasman who had been in jail over night. Jess gave the order to tear down. We blew the Saturday night in Russelville and moved to Hopkinsville, our next date. We heard the pregnant woman was not hurt bad and did not lose her baby. Of course she and her husband sued the show. Jess settled out of court. He never did tell me but I know it cost him a bundle. Like everyone else at that time, he didn't have liability insurance and I know it hurt him and Mary financially, but no one would have ever known it.

There was a lot of dissension on the Bisbee show in 1942. For one thing, too many disliked each other from the opening day. Most of the men started putting on their makeup around 7:00 P.M. This gave them plenty of time as the orchestra did not play until 7:30 and the curtain didn't go up until 8:00. Thayer Roberts was a great actor and makeup artist, but he was also peculiar in many ways. He stayed to himself and in his trailer most of the time. One evening around 6:00 I walked in the dressing room and there was Thayer putting on his makeup. I said, "Thayer, what in the world are you doing making up at this time of the day?" He read me the riot act, finally saying, "It is none of your damn business what time I make up." I was telling Leo Lacey what happened, and he said, "Well Billy, he dislikes Tom Brooks and Ossie Johnson so much he can't stand to make up with them." Leo was right, from then on till the show closed, Thayer would come over early, put on his makeup, then go back to his trailer until curtain time. Tom Brooks and Ossie Johnson didn't hit it off together either. They almost came to blows a couple of times. Then one day Ossie was on top of a step ladder painting the top of his trailer. Loyed Gilbert and I were sitting under a shade tree at the back of the tent. Gilley had just remarked, "I hope Ossie doesn't fall off that ladder," when Tom Brooks came out of his trailer carrying a gun. I said, "Is that a gun?" Gilley said, "It sure is, what in the world is he doing with a gun?" We soon found out. Tom walked slowly over to the men's dressing room. The side wall was raised and he had a clear view of Ossie on the step ladder, who at that very moment was leaning over the top of the trailer with a paint brush in one hand and a gallon of paint in the other. Tom took the gun (we later found out it was a bee bee gun), laid it on top of the makeup table and took aim at Ossie's rear end. Gilley said, "My God, he is going to shoot Ossie!" And he did. The bee bee hit Ossie right were it was intended. The paint brush went one way, the bucket of paint went the other and Ossie flew off the ladder. He hit the ground running holding his butt yelling, "Lola, Lola, do something, help me, a bumble bee had stung me." In the meantime, Tom has put the gun in his wardrobe trunk, and is sitting in a chair, bent over laughing. As far as I know, Ossie never did know Tom shot him with the bee bee gun, and I sure wasn't going to tell him.

In July we were playing Murray, Kentucky. We were set up on a lot across from Murray State College. A number of girls from the art class was painting scenes of the tent. As I was visiting and talking to them Jess Bisbee came by in his car and said, "I need to go to Paducah, do you want to go with me?" I replied, "I don't believe, I believe I would enjoy myself more talking to these girls than I would riding with you to Paducah." He laughed and drove away. Little did I know at the time what a wise decision I made. I went up town to Rudy's Cafe to eat lunch and was walking back to the lot when Rod and Elinor stopped and said, very

54

excited, "Jess has been in a wreck. He is in the hospital, get in, we are going there." We met Mary in the waiting room just as a doctor came up. He told Mary Jess had a 50-50 chance of survival. Both his legs and one arm were broken. The doctors were more concerned with his internal injuries than broken bones. They assured Mary, Jess would receive the best of care and there would be no need of moving him to some other hospital. Mary turned to Rod and said, "Rod I want you to take charge of the show. Open the doors as usual tonight. That is the way Jess would want it. Also," she added, "Tell everyone to pray." Later on we found out Jess was on his way back from Paducah. At the little town of Hardin there is a four way stop. For some reason Jess didn't stop and hit another car broadside. The man in the other car was not hurt seriously but Jess was critical when the ambulance finally got him to the hospital. We left Mary at the hospital and when we got to the lot, Rod called a meeting informing everyone that Mary had put him in charge. He said, "The next few weeks are going to be extremely difficult for the show." He continued, "You are all troupers and I expect full cooperation from every one of you. Let's be loyal to the show, and let's be loyal to Jess and Mary." Things did go fairly smooth. Five weeks later the doctors discharged Jess from the

55

hospital.

An ambulance brought Jess from Murray to Cadiz, Kentucky where the show was playing. Jess was still in traction and it took some doing to get him in his custom built trailer. However, with the help of everyone, especially Cliff Malcomb, who was a fine carpenter and did some remodeling, Jess was resting comfortable in his hospital bed a few minutes after arriving. Though he couldn't get up and out, and it would be a few weeks before he could do these things, he was happy to be back with his show.

The afternoon Jess joined the show, a bad electrical storm hit Cadiz and Trigg County. A bolt of lightning hit a main transformer and cut off the power to all of the county. It cleared off after the storm and Red Turner started and checked out the 5KW generator the show carried. The light plant worked perfectly, so the bally band was sent out on the truck informing the town folk Bisbee's Comedians would show and the curtain would go up at 8:00 whether or not the power came on. The people started lining up early and when the curtain went up we were about the only place in the county that had lights, and the tent was packed and jammed. Even had to take the SRO sign down.....there was no standing room.

Things went as well as could be expected on a tent show and Jess improved daily. Jess and Mary's house trailer was pulled by the light plant truck. Mary drove their Buick on the jumps and Jess wanted me to drive the truck pulling him and the trailer. Every time we moved I was apprehensive something would happen. I drove as slowly and as safely as I could knowing every little bump would jar Jess and cause him pain. The doctor from Murray came to see Jess while we were in Obion, Tennessee. After his examination he took Jess out of the traction, and two weeks later he came out of the trailer for a short walk. What a happy day!!! That night after the show Mary had a party for Jess. He made a short speech thanking everyone for keeping the show on the road following his accident.

On a Sunday morning in October, the show moved from Somerville to Moscow, Tennessee. We had one more town to play before closing for the season, which was Collierville. Jess wanted to waterproof the tent before storing for the winter. It was a fair sunny day, so it was a good day for waterproofing. This was the days before Persurvo and other fire proof waterproofing liquids, so gasoline and paraffin was used. The paraffin bars were put in a pot, then put on a stove to melt. It was then mixed with the gasoline and while it was still hot, spread on the canvas with sprinklers. As you can imagine, this made the canvas highly flammable. Moscow was a nice little city with the railroad tracks running through the middle of the business district. There were stores and shops on one side of the tracks and houses on the other side. The show lot was on the side of the tracks where the houses were. In the fall of the year when the nights got cold, the tent was heated by burning coke in fifty drum barrels. These fires were started early in the afternoon to burn the highly toxic gases off the coke. Even though we had covers and stove pipe running through ballast boards to take the fumes out, it was still dangerous if the barrels were carried in too soon. One fall the Choate show was playing Stuttgard, Arkansas. The coke barrels were set in the tent too quickly and that night two people in the audience, and my Mother on the stage, were overcome and had to receive medical attention.

Gilley and I had crossed the tracks to get something to eat. We had finished our supper and were just sitting and talking when a young boy burst into the cafe and yelled, "The show tent is on fire!" We ran out and my heart almost stopped when I saw the fire. All of the tent was blazing. The chair truck was parked next to the tent and I jumped in the cab, the only driveway was at the front of the tent which was impossible to reach. There was a fairly deep ditch to cross to reach the street but I gunned it and made it across. We got all the trucks and trailers off the lot and this was about all that was saved. There were a few folding chairs and a couple of wardrobe trunks left, but that was all. As the tent had just been water treated with gasoline and paraffin it only took a few minutes for the outfit to completely burn. By the time the little fire department arrived, it was all over. My wardrobe trunk was closed so I managed to salvage most of my clothes. I was standing looking at the terrible mess when Jess came up and said, "Well, Billy, this is a tragic end to a hectic season, but this won't stop Bisbee Comedians. However, it is going to be very hard to organize a show next season, with the war and very few young people left. You yourself will no doubt be in the service before too long, so I think I will just lay off the road until this war is over, do some painting and take it easy." And that is what he did. It would be 1946 before Bisbee's Comedians would hit the road again.

The next morning I got up and went down to the lot to say my good bye's. It was a sad day as I stood looking at what was left of the beautiful tent theatre which now lay blackened and smoldering on the ground. Joe and Georgia Hoffman came to say good bye. They had worked on Choate's Comedians a few years before. Joe said, "We were lucky this didn't happen during the performance, many people would have been hurt, or even killed." He also added, "Do you know this is the only time I have been on a show that closed when the song, Old Aung Syne was not played when the curtain went down on closing night. I would play it now but the piano doesn't have any keys left."

After hugs, handshakes and good bye's, Rod and Elinor Brasfield took me to Memphis where I caught a train for Wayne City, Illinois. Dad and Mother had converted a store building into a movie theatre. They had spent quite a bit on the remodeling, it looked very nice and they were doing well and making money.

I made a trip down to Cambria to see some friends and change my draft board from Williamson County to Wayne County. I knew it would only be a matter of days before I would be called, and sure enough, a week later, I received my GREETINGS. I was examined in Chicago along with many other young men. Then, back to Wayne City to await my assignment, which came a week later on January 25, 1943.

One night at the skating rink, I met this very cute girl. Her name was Vera Wanda Thomason. I asked her for a date, she consented and we drove over to Mt. Vernon for dinner. Little did I realize at the time, that I would spend the biggist part of the rest of my life

60

with her, she would later become my wife
and Mother of my children. We had
another date before I left, and though
we had just met, I knew Vera Wanda was
the kind of girl that someday I would
like to marry.

PART V
MY WAR YEARS - 1943-1945

I got my orders to report to Fort Eustes, Virginia where I was to take my basic training. My transition from civilian to Army life wasn't too difficult for me. I had been on the road enough that I didn't know the meaning of the words "home sick". With some of the other boys it was different. Every night when the lights went out, you could hear sobbing and crying. They say there is nothing worse than "home sickness". I was thankful I had never experienced the feeling.

My second week of basic I was called to the captain's office. "Choate," he said, "Sgt. Weaver has recommended you for acting Corporal. Here is your arm band." I left that office on a real high. Many privileges were granted by being promoted to acting Corporal. No guard duty, and best of all, no KP (kitchen police). I am sure I am one of the few who spent twenty-nine months in the Army, and never pulled one day of KP duty.

I had a good strong voice and was good at leading men in close order drill and counting cadence. So, at the end of our thirteen weeks of basic training, they kept me on the cadre and promoted me to the permanent rank of Corporal. This entitled me to a private room, a raise in pay and many other benefits.

The weekend of my promotion, Corporal Brooks and I went to Newport News on a weekend pass. We took in a movie, and after the show, with no place else to go, we went to the USO canteen. When we walked in, a six piece Dixieland band was blaring away to the couples on the crowded dance floor and others standing and sitting at the tables. I am sure the ratio was ten service men to every girl in the place. We were about ready to leave when I noticed this very attractive girl, talking to a Sailor. She was looking at me and came over and said, "Hello." I introduced myself and Corporal Brooks, and she said her name was Thelma Carter, and said, "Would you like to dance?" I wasn't a very good dancer but I thought to myself, that dance floor is so crowded she will never know if I can dance or not, so we danced, and talked. I found out she was a secretary and worked at an insurance company and lived with her Dad and Mother there in Newport News. I asked her if I could take her home but she declined saying she had come with a couple of her girlfriends and must go home with them. She did however, give me her address and telephone number, saying to call her sometime. I called her Thursday and made arrangements to meet at her house Saturday night. This was the beginning of a long affair. Thelma and I were together constantly. Her Mother and Dad took a liking to me and I was welcome at their home anytime. In fact, they gave me a key to their house.

The next week our new company of recruits arrived. We were to train these men and have them ready for combat in 13 weeks. There were many things to learn to stay alive in such a short time, but we did an excellent job. My specialty was giving a lecture on the nomenclature of the 40MM anti aircraft gun. I wrote the script, put a lot of comedy in it, memorized it, and it wasn't long before I was giving the lecture to other companies at Fort Eustus. Also, they sent me to Fort Monroe to present it to a class of Officers. This was quite an honor and I was invited to Fort Monroe a number of times to give the lecture.

In our company of new recruits was a skinny young kid named Jack Buck. He was sharp, learned quickly and it wasn't long before they promoted him to the rank of Corporal and made him a member of the cadre. They assigned him to room with me and we became fast friends. He was interested in show business and we talked about careers after the war was over. Of course, I was destined to go back to show business, as I had known it, but little did either of us realize that Jack, one day would be Sports Director of Radio Station KMOX in St. Louis, the voice of the St. Louis Cardinals, Anchor of CBS sports and announcer for CBS football, and above all, elected to the Baseball Hall of Fame.

In early October, Jack and I went to the post Theatre to see the great move, Casablanca. I really enjoyed it and told Jack I wanted to see it again. We had just settled in our room when there was a knock at the door, it was 1st Sgt. Weaver. He said, "I have some news for you. Both of you are being shipped to Camp Stewart, Georgia along with 48 other men, including myself. Don't ask me why because I don't know." He continued, "I do know we will still be training men in an anti-aircraft outfit. We leave in three days." With that, he was out the door. Jack and I were both stunned. I had been at Fort Eustus from the time I entered the Army and I just never thought about going somewhere else. Jack said, "I believe it will be just a short time before we are shipped over seas." I agreed with him. I wondered how Thelma was going to take this news.

The next day I called her and we met at the main gate as I was restricted to the Post. I told Thelma about my transfer to Stewart. She was shocked and said, "Let's get married now." I told her that was impossible as I was restricted and was not allowed off the Post. She said, "Then I will come to Savannah next week and we will be married there." I tried to explain to

65

her that moving to a new outfit I would no doubt be restricted for a couple of weeks. But she was insistent saying she would see me in Savannah next week. I was in no mood to discuss the situation any further at that time, so I kissed her and went to the bus stop to catch the bus to the barracks. As the bus pulled away I once more looked at Thelma. She was a beautiful girl and at that moment I had mixed emotions. I thought about the good times we had in the past, I thought about the way she had treated me, always trying to do things she knew would please me. I knew I thought a lot of Thelma, but I also knew I was not getting married. My future was too uncertain. I didn't want to be married and then shipped over seas with the possibility of not coming back. And I knew it would only be a matter of weeks before I would be getting on a boat to the Pacific or European war.

When I walked in our room, Jack was on his bed and immediately jumped up and said, "Well, how did she take it?" "Not so good," I replied, "She wants to go ahead and get married." "Look Billy, your not foolish enough to get married now, are you?" "What do you mean foolish?" I said, "And anyway, what business is it of yours what I do?" With that statement I stormed out of the room and slammed the door. After walking around the barracks a couple of times, I was back in the room

apologizing to Jack.   "That's OK.   I
should have kept my two cents out of
it." Then he paused, smiled, and added,
"I still think you're nuts if you get
married now."   As bad as I hated to
admit it, I knew he was right.

Our move from Fort Eustus to Camp
Stewart   was   uneventful.   However,
instead of a private room like we had at
Eustus, we slept in a tent on a fold up
Army cot. No mess hall, we lined up at
a chow wagon and ate out of mess kits.
A far cry from all the comforts at Fort
Eustes.

Friday afternoon about 3:00 a voice
over the P.A. system said there was a
telephone call for me at the office.   I
knew it was Thelma before I picked up
the phone. She said she was at a hotel
in Savannah. One of her girlfriends had
come down with her. I told her I would
see her as soon as possible.   1st Sgt.
Weaver was still with us and it was easy
for Jack and I to get a four hour pass
from him.   We did, and headed for
Savannah. We had dinner at a very nice
restaurant and then went back to the
hotel. Thelma was still very determined
we were going to be married, and soon.
In fact, she told me she had found out
how and where to get a marriage license.
I told her I would try and get a weekend
pass and we would discuss it at that
time.

I   didn't   get   the   weekend   pass.
Instead   we   were   moved   to   Okefenokee

swamp on maneuvers. Everything happened so fast I didn't have time to call Thelma. This worried me as I knew there was no way for her to get in touch with me and I had no idea how long we would be on maneuvers.

I knew one thing, I couldn't wait for the maneuvers we were on to be over. I had heard about the Okefenokee swamp, but I never realized what a terrible place it was. Nothing but trees, quicksand, swamps, and snakes. The place was full of copperhead and cotton mouth snakes. Everyday, one to five soldiers were taken to the hospital for snake bite. I was scared to death of snakes (and still am) so I took an army mattress cover and made a hammock between two trees. That afternoon, we had an inspection by the staff officers and the Colonel ordered me to take it down. Later that night I put it back up as I knew the colonel would not be back out there at night. I overheard Jack talking to Cpl. Riley and he said, "I hope Choate stays in that hammock, when he sleeps with me he gets amorous." Riley replied, "Maybe he is thinking of that good looking gal of his, sitting in that hotel room in Savannah." Of course, this was all for my benefit, as they knew I could hear them.

I finally got to a phone and called Thelma. She was very upset that I had not called her. I told her she should go back to Newport News as I didn't know

68

when I could see her or when we would
get off the maneuvers. She agreed with
me as there was no use in her sitting in
Savannah unless we could be together
once in awhile. She said she would
catch the next bus and I was to call her
as soon as I could. As I hung up the
phone I had the feeling I might never
see Thelma again and I was very sad.

The next morning, a Sgt. pulled up
in a Jeep wanting to know where Choate
was. "Right here Sgt." He said, "Get
your things together, you are going back
to Stewart. They will pick you up right
after chow." Jack was standing with me
and after the Sgt. drove away he said,
"Wonder what this means?" "I don't know
for sure." I replied, "But I imagine I
am being shipped out of Stewart, and
this, no doubt, is the parting of the
ways for you and I."

Right after chow, the Jeep pulled
up, I gave Jack a hug and got in and we
took off. Jack and I had been together
over a year, we were very close and I
hated to leave him, but there was a
saying in the Army, every time you move
it gets worse, but you always find a new
buddy. I knew it would be hard to
replace Jack Buck.

When we got to Stewart, I reported
to personnel to get my orders. The Cpl.
who was filling my papers told me I was
to leave the next morning for Camp
Gorden, Georgia. There, I was to take
six weeks of Infantry training. He

didn't say, but he knew and I knew, after that six weeks I would be going over seas.

The six weeks at Gorden was nothing but misery. I thought I was in pretty good shape, physically, but I knew they were going to kill me before the six weeks were up. We were up at 5:00 and would run three miles before breakfast. If you were outside you had to be running. Every morning we ran to the rifle range for a couple of hours. Then back to the company for lunch. A couple of classes and then maybe a ten mile forced march with full pack. At 11:00 they would wake you to run the obstacle course. This was the routine every day, day after day. Finally the six weeks were up and we were shipped to Fort Meade, Maryland. We were told we would be going to the European Theatre of War. I wrote Thelma and told her I was being shipped overseas and I would keep in touch by mail.

I was hoping for a furlough so I could see the folks. Instead, I got a three day pass which was just enough time to go to Washington and see the sights. Two other soldiers, whose names I don't remember, went with me. When we arrived in Washington we rented a suite in one of the big hotels and then rented a cab and told the driver to show us around the Capital. We saw the White House, Congress in session, the Washington Monument, Smithonian

Institute and many other places of interest. I enjoyed the day immensely. However, that night I would just as soon forget. One of the soldiers and I went to dinner. The other one said he wasn't hungry and would wait for us in the room. When we came back to the room, we found him drunk and in a belligerent mood. We were on the 20th floor and there was a balcony off our room which was directly above the side walk. Before we knew what was happening, he took a bottle of whiskey, went to the balcony and dropped it to the sidewalk below. Luckily, it didn't hit anyone. Of course, the five minutes in house detectives were knocking on our door. After some pleading they decided not to arrest us but told us to pack our bags and get out, which I was happy to do. I certainly did not want an arrest on my records, when I had nothing to do with what happened. I was so disgusted I went to the bus station and caught a bus to Fort Meade. I blew a three day pass, but I didn't care, I was happy to be back on the base, and not in jail.

Four days later on January 1, 1945, we were sent to New York and boarded the Queen Elizabeth for the trip overseas. The war for me had finally begun. I will never forget the moment I laid eyes on the Queen Elizabeth. I couldn't believe anything that big could float. It was the largest and most modern passenger ship afloat. It was owned by

England when the war began and was converted into a troop ship. It was 963 feet long, that is longer than three football fields. It was said to be submarine proof on account of its speed, which was 32 knots. It changed course every minute, this, along with its speed, made it impossible for a submarine to zero in with torpedos. They had put as many as eight bunks in the luxurious state rooms. It carried five thousand troops and made the crossing in a little over four days. It had four swimming pools, four restaurants, two theatres and a ballroom. Of course, all of these were closed. There were two hundred waiters and one hundred and forty kitchen personnel. You would think with that many cooks, they could come up with a good meal once in awhile, but they couldn't. The Limey food was terrible. I lost weight during the time I was on the ship.

We landed at the Firth of Clyde in Scotland. A quick train trip through England, a treacherous ride across the English channel on an LST, and we were in France. We were in a staging area and one by one were being shipped to different outfits. I was assigned to G Company, 10th Infantry, 5th Division, with Gen. Patton's Third Army, somewhere in France.

When I joined the outfit they were in a holding position. Darkness had fallen and the company was beginning to turn in for the night. A Sergeant was sitting on his helmet next to a fox hole. I introduced myself and he said, "I am Sergeant Cottrell, are you one of the new replacements?" I replied, "I was." I took a liking to Sergeant Cottrell then and there. He had been with G company since they landed some months back and he was combat wise. He told me about his wife and little boy and how he couldn't wait till the war was over so he could be with them. The he said, "There are a few things you have to remember if you are going to survive this lousy war." He continued, "don't start feeling sorry for the Germans. Remember, they are the enemy, it's kill or be killed. Also, when you run, don't run in a straight line, zig zag. When you stop, take your shovel and start digging. You may not be in that position but just a matter of minutes. However, if Germans send in a mortar barrage, you need a place for cover. If you are in a forest and receiving incoming artillery, stand up beside a tree-----there will be more protection against the tree bursts standing than in a prone condition." He lit a cigarette and continued with his lesson on combat and staying alive. "When you are under a small arms fire, remember, a bullet doesn't sing, whiz or whistle. It snaps, just like someone snapping their fingers. So when you hear the snaps, you know the bullets are a couple of feet from you, get down. By the way, how old are you?" "Nineteen," I replied. "Well, I am thirty-two. I know that seems old to you, so you can call me Pop, everyone else does. Come on, let's get some sleep." When I layed down on that cold ground, many thoughts ran through my mind. I wondered if I would be able to face the fear and horror of combat, which I knew was to come shortly. I knew one thing, I was glad "Pop" was going to be with me.

A few days later, we were loaded onto trucks and traveled fifty or sixty miles. "This is it! This is it!" a voice inside me kept repeating over and over. Maybe it would be good to get may first day behind me. The trucks rumbled to a stop and we waited for the command to dismount. "Pop" who was sitting beside me said, "Scared, Choate?" "A little," I admitted. I took a long, slow drag on my cigarette. "We all are," he said, "We always are."

It had been raining but it stopped. Somewhere there was a moon that was hidden by the clouds as we collected our equipment and set out on the night march to "the front." It was a slow, fatiguing march under the burden of the mounting tension and equipment. We came to a patch of fir trees and were told to dig in. That night I was introduced to the German Nebelwerfer, a multi-barreled concussion bomb fired electrically, whose terrifying moaning shells gave them the GI nickname of "screaming meemies." They would bounce you around like a rubber ball.

I had now had my first taste of combat, but I had yet to see anybody killed, or even wounded. I knew, however, casualties would be high when we went into a full scale attack. Would I be paralyzingly afraid when this day came? Would I personally come out alive? Two days later I had my chance to find out.

We loaded on trucks and finally reached our destination, a giant forest. We had been five hours on the road in the cold and terrible driving conditions. The men jumped and half fell from the open trucks.

We hiked for some time along the highway. Finally, I heard the Captain yell, "This is it, fallout and dig in." I felt like crying. My feet felt like they were frozen, and the thought of spending the night in a frozen fox hole made me miserable.

I shared a hole with "Pop" and a boy from upstate New York named Kelly. I spread my sleeping bag over two inches of mud that had accumulated in the bottom of the hole. When I finally laid down, I put my overcoat over me, and with my helmet for a pillow, I tried to get some sleep. However, every few minutes I was awake shaking from the cold. I would get up, walk around, stamp my feet, and return to the hole to try once again to get some sleep. I don't know how long I had been asleep when I felt "Pop" punching me. He said, "Choate, would you like to go ice skating?" Then I realized water had seeped in our hole, frozen, and we were laying in ice about an inch thick. I had on three pairs of long handle underwear, a pair of wool pants and I was thankful the water had not soaked to my bare skin.

We got up and ate a K-ration as soon as it was light enough to make a fire from its cardboard container. Then we tried to get a little more protection by laying logs across our hole to protect against shell burst in the trees above us. We had just finished when I heard the Captain say, "OK, saddle up, let's move out." It never failed, you get everything set to stay awhile, and you heard, "Let's move out." I heard "Pop" say, "Damn."

The company lined up in columns on either side of the road. I noticed there were so many men in the company now whom I did not know. We had received over a hundred replacements in the last couple of days. It was difficult to tell by their faces who were the replacements and who were the veterans. There was the same anxiety on the faces of all of them.

We finally came to the edge of a woods and we could see the small village

76

we were to take. My Mother had taught me the 23rd Psalm and this was one of the many times I recited this scripture. The big guns from the rear suddenly opened up, and I heard the shells whistle over and crash into the town. There was no return fire and no movement or activity in the town. For one brief, exultant moment I thought the Germans had withdrawn from the town. But no, that was too much to hope for. That would be like asking for the war to end. Finally, the Germans let us know they were there by lobbing in some artillery and the order was given to move out. We started across the open field in a skirmish line. Little black puffs of powder appeared over the field. Every man hit the ground and rose again when the barrage lifted. The enemy was laying down a tremendous line of fire. They were firing mortars, 88's and shells were exploding everywhere. I noticed one young boy ahead of me did not rise after hitting the ground. I looked at him as I was running by. He was one of the new replacements and had just joined the company. I felt sick, but there was not time to stop and think about him. I kept running and suddenly I heard Snap, snap, snap. Immediately, I remembered "Pops" admonition about the small arms fire, and I hit the ground. As soon as the snapping quit, I was up and running again. I saw a hole about twenty-five feet in front of me and I made a bee line for it. I jumped in and jumped right on top of a dead German soldier. He must have taken a direct hit with an artillery shell as there was nothing left of his lower body. I took one look at him, with his eyes and mouth open and I knew I couldn't stay there with him, even though there was a good chance I might be killed if I left him-----I left-----after vomiting.

After about three hours of house to house fighting and many casualties, we finally secured the town. I went down to the CP and "Pop" was there. I was really happy to see him as I hadn't seen him since we left the woods that morning. I told him about my encounter with the German. He said, "Why didn't you stay in the hole with Jerry? He wouldn't hurt you." I said, "Go to hell."

That night the kitchen truck came in and we had a hot meal. I hadn't had anything to eat since morning and I was starved. It is funny how a good hot meal will make you feel better. Even though it was sometimes dangerous to them, our company cooks always tried to get us one hot meal a day. Those hot meals helped the morale.

"Pop" found us a house with a nice bed to stay in that night. We shaved and even took a bath. When I went to bed that night, I thought of all the things that had happened and what a terrible day it had been. I thought of

the German in the hole. I thought of
the young replacement who had been cut
down going across the field, and I
didn't even know his name. I thought of
the others who had been killed or
wounded that day. I said a prayer to
God thanking him for sparing me. Then,
exhausted, I fell asleep.

The next morning we ate K-rations
and heard the big guns bark to the rear
of us. Enemy shells whistled above the
town and crashed into the open fields
outside the town. Around 10:00 we moved
out to a woods about a half mile from
the town we were in. We had been there
just a few minutes when bullets began to
sing through the trees. That was enough
to tell us the Germans were not far
away. I heard our radio operator call
for artillery. The enemy had withdrawn
to the bottom of the draw and was
regrouping for an assault. The firing
stopped. A silence that was almost
deafening settled over the forest,
broken now and then by some soldier
firing a rifle. I lay in a slit trench
at the edge of the woods. It was so
cold I was shaking and my teeth were
chattering, but I was surprised at my
own calmness. I did not know what had
come over me to keep me so calm. I
probably would never experience a more
serious situation than I was in at that
moment. The Germans would assemble
behind the hill and then wave after wave
of fanatically screaming infantry would

storm across the fifty yards of open field toward us. Firing their weapons as they came and being met by volley after volley. German fell right and left. Our artillery zeroed in on them, and we could hear their screams of pain. But still they came! The open field was littered with their wounded and dead, but there seemed no way we could stop their attacks. "Pop" crawled up beside my hole. "Damn, but I'm glad to see you," I said, and I meant it too. I just felt safer when "Pop" was around. With all the combat he had been through, I just knew he had a charmed life, and he was indestructible. He said, "Get off your fat butt, we are moving out." I thought of going across that open field, facing the German fire, and that knot of fear rolled up in my stomach. "Pop" saw the fear on my face and said, "Don't worry, the Jerries have probably fell back and are running like hell." A few minutes later we were going across the field and over the hill, and sure enough, as "Pop" had said, the Germans had retreated. What a great feeling of relief!

The next day we moved on top of a mountain, or at least a big hill, to relieve another company. They had dug foxholes and things were set up for us. Lt. Singer came by and told me we were in a holding position and would probably be there two or three days. That was music to my ears. I was discussing this with Pop and he said, "Don't get your hopes too high. Come over here, I want to show you something." We walked to the edge of the hill. "Look down there. See those trenches and pill boxes? That's an underground network. You don't see anybody down there now but there are no doubt hundreds of Jerries underground. They know we are up here and they may decide to test us tonight. If they do, remember, stay in your hole and shoot anything that moves."

That afternoon the Lt. introduced me to a new replacement who had come in with about ten others. They always assigned the new boys to one of the veterans. His name was Harry Johns and he was from California. I could tell he was scared to death so I tried to relieve his fears the best I could. I told him the same things Pop had told me when I first joined the outfit. The more we talked, the calmer he became and I came to the conclusion, even though he was scared like the rest of us, he could be counted on when the chips were down and he was under fire. It wasn't too long until Harry was tested.

It must have been midnight or after when I awoke to the crack of small arms fire. Harry said, "What should we do Sgt.?" "You stay in this hole and shoot anything that moves." There was a lot of small arms fire but I couldn't tell where it was coming from and what or who they were shooting at. There was no

moon and the night was black. All of a
sudden this body came hurdling into the
foxhole and landed on top of me. It all
happened so fast I don't know what
really happened. There was a lot of
flailing arms and feet and then Jerry
took off. He was probably as scared as
we were. After a long silence, Harry
said, "Who was that?" "That was a
German soldier," I replied. "My God,
was it really?" My helmet was knocked
off in the scuffle and as I was feeling
around for it I realized the side of my
head was hurting and I was bleeding. I
could tell it wasn't serious and I
didn't want to yell for a medic until I
was sure the Jerries were gone. It
wasn't long until daylight, the Germans
were gone and everyone began to stir
around. I found a medic, he told me it
was just a scratch, put some sulfa on
it, a bandage and said I would be fine.

Harry was sticking to me like a
leech. I said, "Well Harry, how was
your first taste of combat?" He said,
"I had rather not talk about it." "Well
you did just fine." I thought the real
test for Harry will be how he holds up
under an artillery barrage. Just about
that time Pop walked up. "Well, I hear
you guys had a little tete-a-tete with a
German last night, is that right?"
"Yes, that's right Pop, he didn't stay
too long though. By the way Harry, did
you smell anything after that Jerry
left?" He said, "No, I didn't smell

anything." He looked at the ground then raised his eyes and looked at me and Pop and said, "Boy that Jerry sure must have been scared." Then I thought he was going to die laughing. Pop and I joined him.

Due to our rapid advance the Germans were forced to destroy much of their artillery. Eight tanks and many self-propelled guns were destroyed, and a large number of rifles, machine guns, and mortars were captured.

Intelligence reported the German soldiers morale was satisfactory in spite of the beating they were taking, their troops were in good and fairly secure houses in heated cellars. Hot food was brought to them regularly. Under these circumstances they were lulled into a false sense of security which made our surprise attack more effective. As our advances gained momentum and their positions were overrun, it became difficult for the Germans to move supplies to their front line soldiers. Also, many of their soldiers would just not fight in the cold weather.

I don't think there is any question but that we stood up better under the rigors of winter warfare than the Germans. I could never understand why more of us didn't catch colds, fighting in the snow, the ice and wind, and sleeping on ice in a cold foxhole. We learned to improvise. We learned the extra insulation provided by keeping our clothes loose. We never sacrificed a sound military position simply because a warm house was available in another spot. The Germans would select the warmest place first and then try to build their defense as best they could around them. As a result, they didn't stay in one place very long.

On February 7, we were given the job of crossing the Sauer river. To the river crossing veterans of the 10th Infantry Regiment, the Sauer was just one more river, but an early thaw had made the normally placid stream a river of treacherous current, and then there was the concrete pillboxes on the other side. Even with these obstacles, too much trouble was not anticipated. Approximately 150 yards back from the far shore of the river near the crossing site was an enemy pillbox. To the rear and up the hill were enemy tanks, with entrenched infantrymen, offering a grim menace to anyone daring to come their way.

Artillery fire that shook the earth for miles around opened up on the enemy positions. Company E moved down to the river bank to attempt the crossing in rubber boats. The initial effort to cross the river drew heavy fire from the enemy fortifications, which knocked out the boats before the troops could get ashore. A second attempt was made to cross, and this time all but two of the twelve boats were sunk, and only eight men succeeded in getting to the other side. Staff officers from Regiment visited the crossing site to inspect the proceedings. About this time, General Patton showed up. G Company was in support and we were dug in about two hundred yards, from the river, in a woods. A GI came running by saying, "General Patton is down at the river." Everyone got up to go and see him, but the Lt. stopped us. Later on I heard he was only there a few minutes and had come to see why we were not across the river. He was supposed to have said, "I want you across the river today. You are holding up the whole 3rd Army." I told Pop, "He must be a gutsy old bird to come down here and take a chance on those Jerries throwing that artillery." Which they did quite often. Anyway, I was sorry I missed him.

Company E again began to cross in the rubber boats. Opposition to the crossing renewed with shelling and machine gun fire, and the difficult terrain, and the swift current, aided the enemy. Even with these difficulties, within five minutes after crossing began, some of the Company had reached the other side. Shortly thereafter, the first wave of troops were on the other side and the next wave was on the way across. We followed them. All the Battalion was across the next morning. There were many casualties and the Germans fell back to a little town named Gonsdorf.

March 2nd, Company F was moving in the direction of Gonsdorf. As elements of the Company ascended the slope of a high hill, they were attacked by an estimated sixty enemy infantrymen supported by machine guns. After a short fire fight, enemy resistance collapsed and the leading platoons of F Company advanced to Gonsdorf and cleared the town, the enemy withdrawing to the high ground. By daylight, all resistance was wiped out in the river area.

Then the next morning, March 3rd, Company F was driven almost out of Gonsdorf by a savage counter-attack by approximately a hundred infantrymen supported by several tanks.

Gonsdorf was a small village of about fifteen houses surrounded by a high ridge of open terrain. The two platoons of riflemen and machine gunners of Company F fought tenaciously but tank fire was direct and twenty-five casualties were sustained in dead and wounded. Though eventually driven back to the edge of the town, their grasp on the village was never relinquished, and with supporting artillery fire, they beat off the attackers enabling us (G Company) to enter the town without a costly fight. We moved into Gonsdorf and relieved F Company. By this time, nothing but civilians occupied the town.

An old man and I presume his wife, came out of a house with their hands up. The woman was crying and he made me understand they were hungry. Here these two old people were, their house had been destroyed by artillery, they were crying and telling me they were hungry. I thought to myself, this is the reason I am over here fighting this lousy war and going through this misery. It is so my Mother and Father and grandfather and other relatives will not have to go through what these two old Germans are going through. I hated the German soldier and had no trouble killing him before he killed me. But, these two old people got next to me, so I took a K-ration and gave it to the women. She smiled through her tears, patted my cheek, and they both hobbled back to what was left of their house. Pop, who had been watching this scenario, came over and said, "Choate, you just can't get close to these people, and you can't let them get to you. Remember, these Germans are the enemy, all of them." I said, "Yes Sgt., I know, I know." He knew I was upset with him when I called him Sgt.

Sgt. Carter and I had an outpost with about twelve men on the edge of town. Just before dark, he and I went down to the CP to see if any orders came in, and to see if we were to stay in Gonsdorf for the night. I was hoping we would as the house we were in had a basement, and would make good cover if the Germans decided to throw artillery at us.

Sgt. Carter and I, along with two others, Cpl. Roberts and PFC Wells, were on our way back to the outpost when we heard the low whine of an artillery shell. We all broke in a dead run for the house. We were almost there when I saw the half track with the 88MM gun. He must have seen us as he stopped and swung the gun directly toward us. By this time, we were at the house and I dove through the door into the hall just as the shell hit the base of the house. I heard screams and someone saying, "I'm hit! I'm hit!" Then I realized I was hit, too. Blood was running down my arm, under my sleeve and my hand was bloody. I was terrified when I couldn't swallow and I knew I was hit in the neck. I put my hand to my neck and felt a small piece of shrapnel. Part of it was sticking out and I got a hold of the end and pulled it out. I could swallow and was relieved. My next thought was of Sgt. Carter and the other two men who were still outside the house and wounded, how bad I didn't know. I crawled to the door and could see all three were only a few feet from the house. I crawled out and got Sgt. Carter first. Then, I went back and got Brooks and Wells. Sgt. Carter was hit bad, also Brooks. However, Wells wasn't hit too bad. By this time, some of the others came up from the basement and we all went down to wait for the medics. They came and took us to the CP. By this time, it was dark and the Germans had quit firing the artillery, for which I was thankful. I asked one of the medics how Sgt. Carter and the others were and he said, "Fine." I knew he was lying. He took my coat off and cut the sleeve and I looked at my arm. There was a hole where the shrapnel went in, but it didn't look too bad to me. However, my neck, my arm, and my leg where another piece had hit me were hurting. "You are lucky Sgt. You have a million dollar wound," said the medic. He gave me a dose of sulfa tablets. "I'll wait and let them give you morphine at the evacuation aid station, unless it's paining you too much," he said. "You might have to do some walking before the night is over." Before he left, there had been a brief moment of exultation when he reminded me that now I could get a nice rest in the hospital, but I was sick with fear as I realized if the Germans would attack and run over us, I might never see an American hospital.

I dozed off and it must have been 0100 hours when I felt someone shaking me. "Up and at them, Choate," the medic who had taken care of me earlier said, "You are going to the hospital." I had never heard more welcome words. I felt a little groggy but I was ready to go.

They had Sgt. Carter on a stretcher over the hood of a jeep, and Brooks on one of the passenger sides. There were two other walking wounded. I asked the driver how far it was to the aid station. He said he thought is was about two miles. I knew I could make that, though I did feel a little weak. The driver had just started the jeep when "Pop" walked up. I said, "What are you doing here?" "I told the guard to wake me when you were ready to leave." He continued, "I want you to go back with those rear echelon bastards, have a good rest in the hospital, then get your butt back up here. This war is going to be over soon and I want you here to help me celebrate." With that, he gave me a hug and we were off. As I walked along side the jeep my thoughts were on Sgt. Cottrell, better known as "Pop". What a good soldier he was, what a great man he was. Then my thoughts turned to the fact I was getting off the line. I was getting away from the snow, mud, fear, horror, I would be sleeping between clean white sheets and having fried eggs, bacon and hot cakes (that were hot) for breakfast. Thinking about these things, my step became lively.

We finally arrived at the rear battalion aid station. A Lieutenant gave me a hypodermic of morphine, put me on a stretcher, and loaded me in an ambulance with Carter, Brooks and another casualty. We hadn't gone too far until the morphine began to take affect. My eyes closed, and with the swaying of the ambulance, I went into a sound sleep.

Our next stop was the division clearing station, a miniature hospital. I suddenly realized I was famished. It was now eight o'clock and I hadn't eaten for 12 hours. A medic said they were serving breakfast at the mess tent. He gave me and the other walking casualty mess kits and told us to go down and get in line. As we headed for the mess tent, he told me his name was Flenor and he was from Eastern Kentucky. He looked terrible, and I suppose I did too. He was wounded in the neck and his bandage needed changing as it was bloody. We hadn't bathed or shaved in days and I imagine we stunk to the high heavens. They were serving hot cakes and bacon and it wasn't long until we were the only ones in line. They took one look at us and decided they were not hungry.

Our next stop was a general hospital somewhere in France. They wheeled me in the operating room, and when I woke up I found shrapnel taped to my good arm. I suppose they thought I would want to keep it for a souvenir, which I didn't. They took me from the recovery room to the second floor to a room with about six beds. The soft mattress and clean white sheets were almost too good to be true. It was the first bed with sheets I had seen in

91

months.

A nurse came in and informed me I would get a shot every two hours. She said it was a wonderful new drug called penicillin. When she left the boy in the next bed said, "I don't care how wonderful it is, I don't like those shots every two hours." He introduced himself as Johnson, and said he was from Missouri. He was laying on his stomach and I asked him where he was hit, and he said, "Well you heard about the fella who got his ass shot off? Well, that's me, literally." When they came in to change his bandage, I saw what he meant. He had been hit by a shell that didn't explode and his rear end was ripped away. I almost threw up.

I learned that Carter and Brooks were being taken to the States. They had to take one of Sgt. Carter's legs. I was so sorry to hear about that. However, they would not have to face the fear and horror of combat again. Their war days were over. As for me, I knew it would only be a short time and I would be going back to the line. I tried not to think about it.

Thirty days later I was in a box car on my way back to the front. At least I was going back to my old outfit. When I found "G" company they were just across the border of Czechoslovakia. I was glad to see my old buddies, but I was especially happy to see "Pop" once again. Everyone was thinking the war would be over any day now and "Pop" said, "You got back just in time, Choate, to help me celebrate." He was right, three days later the news came down from the regiment. It was official! The war in Europe was over. We shook hands and patted one another on the back. "Pop" and I even did a little dance. There was no defining our joy. The next day was VE-day. May 8.

We were moved back to the German, Czech border. Refugees were streaming back into Germany and we were checking for SS troops. This is where I met Johnny Kopalay. He was a Hungarian who was staying in a school house with other refugees. Johnny could speak fluent English, was well educated, and we became very good friends. He and my mother started corresponding, and in 1947, my Dad and Mother brought Johnny to America. According to the law, they were responsible for him, and he had to live with them for two years, which he did. He then went to Northwestern and received a Doctor's degree in mathematics. He taught in several colleges, married a lovely girl and raised a nice family. So, my Mother and Dad, and America were good for Johnny Kopalay.

Our next stop was a tented city called Camp Lucky Strike. It was here that a momentous catastrophe happened that was to affect my life for months, and even for years to come.

That day, everyone was in a good mood. The sun was shining, it was a beautiful day, we knew it would only be a short time before we would be on a boat going back to America, and we were standing in line to get paid. I had no idea how dark it could become in just a few moments. No one knows what really happened. It was thought by some that a soldier, who was mad about something, kicked a shell that was laying in front of his tent. Anyway, it went off, killed him and two others close by. Everyone in the line hit the dirt and was slowly getting up, midst all the confusion there were screams for the medics. I saw there were two or three still on the ground, and I realized one was "Pop". I rushed to him. He was laying on his face and I rolled him over and immediately I knew something terrible was wrong. He mouth was open, his eyes were open, and I will never forget the look on his face. A medic shoved me aside and ripped "Pop's" shirt off. It was then I saw the hole in his chest with the blood trickling from it. The ambulance came and they were still working on him when they drove away, but I knew he was dead. I was completely torn up and could not stop crying. They took me to a first aid tent and the medics gave a shot which settled me down. It was impossible for me to sleep that night. My thoughts were on "Pop" and how much he loved life. How much he loved his wife and little boy, and how much he was looking forward to seeing them. Things are hard to figure sometimes. Here was a man who survived the snow, the freezing temperature, sleeping in a hole in the ground every night, facing the fear of death every day for eight months, only to be killed when the war was over by an accidental stray piece of shrapnel. After all these years I still ask the same thing I said that day, Why?

I finally got around to writing "Pop's" wife. I explained as best I could what happened, and how I loved him. I had a very nice letter with a picture of her and the little boy. Never heard from her again.

We left Le Harve, France, June 28, 1945 on a small ship and a far cry from the Queen Elizabeth. On July 19, 1945 we sailed into New York harbor amid the cheers of the American people and we saw the lady in the harbor with her torch. I thought of "Pop", and though I was full of joy and happiness, tears came to my eyes.

I was sent to Fort Benjamin Harrison in Indiana to begin my 30 day furlough prior to regrouping at Fort Campbell, Kentucky. The first furlough day was of immense importance. It was the dream that had kept men warm during the freezing vigils in foxholes. It was the prayer that kept men fighting against impossible odds. It was the greatest prize, individually, of the war. It was not a cheap prize. To make that day a reality, 7124 men of the 10th Regiment had become casualties.

The fighting record was brilliant. During the period July 14, 1944 to May 8, 1945 we had been in almost constant contact with the enemy. We had killed and wounded a staggering number of his men, captured 24,408 prisoners, and destroyed many of the best units in the German Army. We left America to face staggering odds with the promise: "We will." We returned saying, "We did!"

I caught a train to Flora, Illinois and then a bus to Wayne City. What a reunion we had! Grandpa Choate came up from Marion. Welby, Eva and Barbara Sue and little Judy, who was born while I was over seas, were there, and Mother fixed one of her usual outstanding dinners. What a great feeling it was to be home with my folks.

A couple of days later Grandpa decided he was to go back to Marion. I wanted to go to Cambria for a few days, so I took him in Dad's car. Gasoline was still rationed. However, Stanley Woods, who owned a service station in Wayne City, and was a good friend, gave me a number of extra stamps, so I didn't have to worry about running out of gasoline.

Dad and Mother still owned our old home place there in Cambria and I was staying there during my visit. As I was coming out of the house one afternoon, the church bells started ringing, guns were being fired off and it sounded like a 4th of July celebration. I said to myself, "I hope this means what I think it means." Simon Biggs, our next door neighbor came out of his house and was ready to fire a gun when I yelled, "Hey Simon, what's going on?" "Great news," he said, "the war in Japan is over." I let out a yell as Simon blasted away with his gun. I jumped in the car and drove down town. A big crowd had gathered and everyone was hugging one another and dancing in the street. No doubt about it, that was one of the happiest days of my life.

We had been told as soon as our furlough was over we were to report to Fort Campbell for amphibious training. We knew this training was to prepare us for an assault on the mainland of Japan. We were destined to be sent to help finish another was in another part of the world where another Army of American infantryman were fighting a dirty, miserable war. Plans were already scheduled for the invasion of Japan. The invasion would be costly. Military experts predicted that it would take another year, with 500,000 dead and 600,000 wounded Americans before Japan was defeated. To avoid American casualties, President Harry Truman decided to use the new weapon we had, the atomic bomb.

On August 6, 1945, the atomic bomb, named "Little Boy" exploded over Hiroshima, Japan, with force of 20,000 tons of TNT.

Three days later, on August 9, an even more powerful atomic bomb, named "Fat Man" exploded over Nagasaki, shooting steam, dust and ash 12 miles in the air.

Initial estimates listed 68,670 dead in Hiroshima and 37,507 in Nagasaki. But as hundreds upon hundreds of bodies were uncovered from the rubble of both cities, death counts were raised to 140,000 in Hiroshima and 70,000 in Nagasaki.

On August 15, 1945, Japan surrendered. The nuclear age had arrived and a miracle happened. The war was over.

I arrived in Wayne City the next day. The celebrating was still going on. Also, Dad had some good news. He had a telephone call from Jess Bisbee and he and Mary were coming up for a visit. About 2:00 p.m. the next day they drove into Wayne City and it was a joy to see them again. Jess told me of his plans for the coming road show season. He had ordered 1,500 new chairs from Acme. He was building a new stage and was painting all new scenery and was going to Chicago to order a 60 X 145 dramatic end tent complete with side wall, marquee and new poles, from O'Henry Tent Company. On account of the fire in 1942, everything would be new except the trucks. He wanted me to come down a few weeks before rehearsals to help him get things together. I could hardly wait.

I told Jess I expected to be discharged very soon. The war was over and the Government would be discharging service men fast and furious. I told him I would come to Memphis the last of February to get ready for the April opening. He and Mary left for Chicago saying they would stop on their way back.

After my furlough was up I reported to Fort Campbell, Kentucky. It was nice seeing my friends in the Company. For the first week we didn't do a thing except lay around the barracks and eat. I had a permanent pass, which meant I could leave the base anytime I was not on duty. So I spent a lot of time in Hopkinsville, Kentucky and Clarksville, Tennessee, the two closest towns to Fort Campbell, which was on the Kentucky, Tennessee line.

On Tuesday of the second week, I was called to the Company office and informed I had been awarded the Bronze Star for heroism. The medal was given in connection with the incident that happened in Gonsdorf when I was wounded. I was told there would be a post parade Friday afternoon and I would be awarded the medal at that time. I would also receive the Purple Heart. Others in the

99

Company would also receive medals.

Friday came and I was looking forward to the parade which was due to start at 2:00 p.m. This was the first time I had participated in a Division parade and it was quite a sight. There was approximately 18,000 men taking part. Two bands were combined. They didn't march but were stationed at the side of the reviewing stand. About 40 who were to receive medals were stationed and seated on the reviewing stand. So we had a good view of what was going on. When the parade was about half over our names were called individually and the medals were pinned on us. It was an impressive ceremony and something I will never forget. It took two hours for the Division to pass in review. It was a hot day and I understood there were a number who passed out, but I didn't see anyone.

We did very little during the next few weeks until discharge. The amphibious training we were to go through was called off. There was no need for this training now that the war was over.

Finally my name was called and I was sent to Camp Atterbury, Indiana where I received my discharge. I headed for Wayne City and decided to stay there and wait for the 1946 season. Also, I had started dating Vera Thomason, who I had met before I went over seas, and on account of her, I was content to stay in

Wayne City awhile.

One cold afternoon in October I had come from Denny Seabolts house. Denny had been in the Marines and we had become good friends. We had decided to catch the bus the next day for a trip to St. Louis. As I got out of the car, Les Lyle pulled up. It was the first time I had seen him since we trouped together on the Bisbee Show in 1942. He told me he and Bob Mclain had a promotion and were doing great financially. Bob would do a roping act and a blindfold drive sponsored by the merchants. The idea was to draw people to town. Les would book it under some club, sell the business places ads to be read during the day of the performance, and Bob would come in later and do the show. Les had $800.00 from the ads he sold in Wayne City. He was booking an average of five towns a week, so he and Bob were doing real well, money wise. Les and Bob were high powered promoters and cared little what the people thought of them after they left a town. I told Bob not to announce that he knew me. I knew people would be talking how they had been taken and I didn't want to be associated with them in any way. Thankfully, Bob didn't mention my name, or act like he knew me. On the afternoon performance Dad and I walked over there. They had a flat bed trailer parked on Main Street. At the designated time, Bob crawled up on the trailer, introduced himself, and went right into his roping act, which only lasted about three minutes, with no music. He asked for a couple of men from the audience to come up and they put the half dollars over his eyes and the blindfold on, and he was ready to do the blindfold drive. He asked Mr. King Chase, the local hardware man, if he would ride with him. He agreed that he would. Then he made an announcement and I couldn't believe what I was hearing...it went something like this..."Ladies and Gentlemen, you are about to witness the most dangerous feat ever attempted by man. I am going to drive my car completely blindfolded here on your Main Street. There have been eight men killed attempting to do what I am about to do." He took his handkerchief, wiped his brow, and continued, "Rest assured, I will be as careful and take all safety precautions however, I will not be responsible for any loss of property, limb or life, or any kind of accident." Then taking off his big cowboy hat he said, "Before undertaking such a dangerous feat, let us pray." And he prayed. Dad said, "Let's get out of here before God sends a bolt of lightning." We left. I understand he drove a couple of blocks, turned around, let Mr. Chase out of the car, and drove out of town. When he went by the crowd that had gathered, I understand he still had his blindfold

on, he was smiling and waved at the
people. They were dumbfounded and just
looked at one another. The performance
lasted about fifteen minutes. It was
five years later when I saw Bob and Les.

Vera and I started seeing more and
more of each other and it wasn't long
before we were together almost every
night. Also, it wasn't long until I
realized I was in love. At the time I
was 23 years old. I had always said I
wasn't going to marry until I was at
least 26 years old. However, Vera
changed my plans. She was on my mind
constantly and I didn't want to wait
three or four years to make her my wife.
So, one night she said "yes" to my
proposal. We set the wedding date for
June 2nd which was Brother Welby's
birthday. We decided I would go to
Memphis and join the Bisbee show and she
would come down for the wedding. By
that time, we would be in Kentucky
somewhere. My only problem was I didn't
know whether I could stand not seeing
her for that period of time.

PART VI
BISBEE'S COMEDIANS AFTER THE WAR

I left Wayne City for Memphis March 10th and rehearsals started the third week in March. It was great to get back to show business after a three year absence. I was also happy to see my good friends, Audra and Virginia Hardesty, Leo and Maxine Lacey, Ralph Blackwell and Boob Brasfield who would do the Toby and direct, now that Rod had gone to the Grand Ole Opry. Others on the show for the 1946 season were Mac and Maria Johnson, Cliff and Mable Malcomb, Sam and Lola Hudson, Lucille Stoddard and her daughter, June, Howard Johnson, Bob Fisher and the Mundee's, Connie and June, and Jess and Mary.

We moved to Lexington, Tennessee and set the outfit up on Friday before the Monday night opening. It was just beautiful. Everything was new. The tent was a 60 X 155 dramatic end with lots of fringe and color, 1,500 new chairs painted white with red tops, new stage and scenery and Jess had painted a new front curtain and street drop that brought raves from everyone who saw them. There is just something wonderful about the smell of new canvas, it's like the smell of a new car, it can't be duplicated.

We had a good cast and a good show and business was terrific. The doors didn't open until 7:00 however, people

104

were lining up at 6:00 it just seemed people were starved for live entertainment. We were packing them in every night.

Things went fairly smooth as we rolled through the established Tennessee towns. Lexington, Parsons, Linden, Hohenwald, Dickson, Waverly, Camden, Bruceton, McKenzie and finally jumping to Murray, Kentucky. Every town we played people seemed happy that Bisbee's Comedians were back on the road again. And I was happy to be in Kentucky. It would be only a couple of weeks and Vera and I would be married. I could hardly wait.

Monday afternoon on opening day in Murray, Mac Johnson and Jess got in a shouting match. Jess ended it by saying, "I have heard what a great dancer you are, but you couldn't prove it by me, I haven't seen you dance, in fact I haven't seen you do much of anything." It seemed Mac had been in Nebraska one winter and got caught in a flood. He got on top of his car and he wasn't rescued until late the next morning. It had turned cold during the night, getting down into the teens. By the time they got him to a hospital, his feet were frozen. In fact, he almost lost them. This was the reason he had to quit dancing. I had always heard what a great dancer Mac was, but like everyone else on the show, I had never seen him dance. That night as the orchestra was getting ready to go out Mac said to Bob Fisher, "Bob, I will be doing the dancing specialty after the second act. I have talked to Brasfield about it. Play me on with an eight bar introduction, I will make a short announcement then, I want a fast eight bar introduction to China Town and I do mean fast. Play three choruses and then just one chorus for the encore." Bob said, "Do you think you will get an encore?" "I know I will," Mac replied, as he walked away. Like everybody else on the show I couldn't wait for the second act to be over. Mac went out and gave a short talk about being caught in the flood and his feet being frozen. He also told the audience this was the first time in three years that he had tried to dance. He also said, "I might not be able to finish and if I can't, please bear with me. OK Bob hit it." Bob and the band played the introduction and I have never seen such great dancing. When he was through the applause and yells were deafening.

Mac came back on the stage and milked the audience with three more bows, nodded to Bob and finished with the encore chorus. When he came off the stage Jess was waiting for him and said, "Mac I owe you an apology I am sorry for what I said to you today. I will have to admit you are the greatest tap dancer I have ever seen." I thought to myself, Mac is a great dancer but Jess Bisbee is also a great man. He didn't have to apologize to Mac. Mac's feet were swollen, he could hardly get his shoes off. That is the last time he ever danced. He sure made his point on opening night in Murray, Kentucky when he laid the audience in the aisles with his dancing.

We moved from Murray to Benton and then Sunday morning June 2nd we pulled into Calvert City. I could hardly wait to go to Paducah. Charles Allen and Mary Doty, who were our good friends were bringing Vera to Paducah and would stand up with us at our wedding. They were engaged and had planned a September wedding and the plans were for Vera and I to stand up with them, which we did. As I didn't have a car I asked Mac Johnson to take me to Paducah. On the way, he asked me many questions, some I didn't like. He finally said, "This girl you are marrying, what about her ability? Can she act, sing, dance?" I said, "Look Mac, I am not marrying her for her ability or for what she can do. I am marrying her because I love her." "Well," he replied, "I suppose that is a good reason, but it looks like she is just going to be excess baggage." We were just coming into Paducah. "Mac I thought we were friends and you know I have come to your defense a couple of times but I don't care to hear anymore of your crap, so if you will stop and let me out, I will get a Taxi." He apologized, said he was just kidding and he was sorry. I accepted his apology and there was nothing more said about it. Years later he worked for me a couple of seasons after I took over the Bisbee show and we became the best of friends.

Charles, Mary and Vera were waiting for me in the lobby of the Irwin Cobb Hotel. We went to the First Christian Church and were married by Bro. John Parker. We spent our wedding night at the Irwin Cobb and the next day Leo and Maxine picked us up for the trip to Calvert City. We had a room at a boarding house, not a very good one with a Chick Sales which is an outdoor toilet. Vera didn't say anything but she must have been thinking, "I hope the rest of the season is not like this." One good thing, everyone on the show went out of their way to be nice to her.

That evening Jess handed me an envelope. In it was a congratulation card and a note from him and Mary informing us we were getting a raise. This was welcome and unexpected.

The next week we moved from Calvert City to Paducah. We were sponsored by the Paducah Police Department. My good friend Troy Clark was a Captain and later on a City Commissioner. He and his wife, Ruby, and their two daughters, Jackie and Marylyn, were more like family than friends. We spent many enjoyable hours in their home.

Jess would let us use his car to find a room, so Sunday afternoon we were driving around, when we saw a sign in the yard, Rooms For Rent. I parked the car and walked up on the porch where an elderly gentleman was sitting in a swing. I introduced myself and told him we wanted to rent a room for the week. He asked, "Are you married?" I replied, "Yes, we are." At this point he started telling me he had run this rooming house for thirty years. It was well run with a good reputation and he didn't allow any hanky panky so in keeping with that policy he said, "I must insist on seeing your marriage license before I can rent you a room." I immediately went to the car, got in a grip where I found our marriage license, returned to the porch and presented the license to him. He looked at it and said, "Well it looks OK so you can rent the room." We rented the room and before the week was over we became good friends with the old man and his wife. That was seven days after we were married and never again was I ever asked to show my marriage license. Leo Lacey always told the story about the actor who was asked for his marriage license which he produced and then he wanted the old man who ran the boarding house to produce his. He said, "Why boy, I have been married for over fifty years but I don't know where my license is." The actor replied, "I will not stay in a rooming house unless I am positive the proprietors are married and not just shacking up." With that, he got in his car and drove off leaving the old man standing on the porch with his mouth open and scratching his head.

1946 was a memorable year in more ways than one. The show was in Princeton, Kentucky. Monday evening just before the show started Jess came in the dressing room and told me he wanted Vera and me to come to his trailer as soon as the show was over. I told Vera and she said, "I wonder what this is all about!" I told her I had no idea. I didn't give a good performance that night. I couldn't keep my mind off what Jess and Mary would be wanting to talk to us at that time of night. As soon as the show was over and I got my makeup off we made a bee line for their trailer. Mary had made night lunch but I was not hungry. I knew Jess had not invited us over to have night lunch and I wanted him to end the suspense. Finally, he got around to saying, "Mary and I have been discussing this for about a week. We know you kids don't like staying in these flea bag hotels. We also know you have been wishing you had a trailer. Well, we have decided to loan you the money to buy one. We will let you have the money and you can pay us back any way you want to with no interest." I started to say something but Jess put up his hand and said, "Just a minute, I am not through. Now tomorrow morning you will leave here early and go to Evansville. Mary will go with you. We have called and there are a couple of dealers there that have some trailers on the lot. Maybe they have something you want. Here is another surprise for you. I have talked to Boob Brasfield and told him to break Vera in to a couple of parts. I am sure with his direction and everyone helping her she will do fine. Also, starting this week Vera will be receiving a full salary." By this time Vera was crying AND I felt like it. "What can I say Jess?" He said, "Nothing, get out of here and go to bed. Five o'clock is going to come early." We went to our room and I never slept a wink. Early the next morning we drove to Evansville and bought an 18 ft. trailer. It was small but we couldn't have been happier. It was like a fifty thousand dollar mansion to us. In 1948 we traded for a 26 ft. Elcar. Then in 1951 we bought a Liberty. A 32 ft. dream home on wheels. This was to be our home until 1966.

1947 was a great year. Vera opened with us but six weeks later I took her to Wayne City to await the arrival of our first baby. Tuesday afternoon, August 19th, I received a telephone call from Dad saying Vera had given birth to a boy and she and the baby were doing fine. The next morning Jimmie and Eddy Farrin and I headed for Mt. Vernon, Illinois. Vera was there in the Good

Samaritan Hospital. We got to the hospital around 10:00 a.m. and they informed me at the desk visiting hours started at 3:00 p.m. and I would have to wait until then to see my wife and baby. I explained I was with a show in Owensboro, Kentucky and if I waited until 3:00 I would not have time to get to Owensboro and do the show. This did not have any effect on her as she said, "Rules are rules." Jimmie and Eddy wanted to just barge in but I knew that was the last thing we needed to do. We would wind up in jail and never make the show. A janitor heard me talking to the nurse and motioned me outside. He told me there was a ledge outside of Vera's room that I could climb up on and see and talk to her through the window, which I did. Vera called her doctor, Dr. Jean Modert, and he came down and escorted me to Vera's room. Also, they brought our baby, whom we named Welby Charles and we had a wonderful time together for almost an hour. We made it back to Owensboro in plenty of time for the show. Everything was coming up roses. I had a healthy baby boy, Vera was fine and I was on cloud nine.

Vera and little Welby joined me while the show was in Hopkinsville, Kentucky. The next week we jumped to Union City, Tennessee to play fall Tennessee towns. Vera had plenty of help. All the girls on the show wanted to take care of the baby, especially

Maxine Lacey. There was one problem, every time the baby cried Maxine would say, "He needs an enema." I really believe the reason he cried so much was because he was worrying about the next enema he knew was coming.

Cherita, our pretty little girl was born on Saturday, August 18, 1950, while the show was playing Morgantown, Kentucky. I did the show that night and immediately after the show was over I headed for Illinois. It rained most of the way but I made good time. I spent Sunday, Sunday night with Vera and the baby at the hospital in Mt. Vernon. Monday morning I spent a couple of hours with Mother and Dad and Welby Charles. Then drove to Hartford, Kentucky where the show was. Vera and the kids joined me a few weeks later while the show was in Elkton, Kentucky.

Kuttawa, Kentucky was always good to Bisbee's Comedians and I looked forward to playing there. There was a swimming pool just outside of town which was fun and refreshing on hot summer days. Also, I looked forward to seeing and visiting with Mr. and Mrs. Martin. They had a big house on Main Street and the lot was directly behind their house. Vera and I roomed with them in 1946 and we became good friend. Miss Julie, as everyone called her, was a character. She wore a big brimmed straw hat and you knew exactly where she stood on any subject, especially politics. One time

113

when we were playing Kuttawa the primary
election was coming up and the campaign
for Governor was in full swing. A
gentleman from Clinton was running, if I
remember right, he was the Lt. Governor,
anyway Miss Julie was hot and heavy for
him. His name was Waterfield. One
morning Miss Julie and I were standing
on the side walk in front of her house
when all of a sudden she ran out in the
street and flagged a car down. She told
the driver, "Park that car Glenn, I want
to talk to you." Glenn parked his car
and reluctantly came over to where we
were. "Glenn, are you going to vote for
Harry Waterfield?" Looking at the
ground and not at Miss Julie, "Well I
don't know Miss Julie, I haven't made up
my mind as yet." She took his face in
her hand and turned it so he had to look
at her and said, "Let's see if I can
help you make up your mind." Then she
proceeded to lecture him on the virtues
of Harry Waterfield and how he would be
the best man to lead the great common
wealth of Kentucky for the next four
years. Finally, with a look of
exasperation on his face he said, "OK
Miss Julie, I'll vote for him." After
he drove away, I said, "Do you think he
will vote for Waterfield Miss Julie?"
"I don't know," she replied, "I may have
to give him another talking to before
election day." Politics in Kentucky is
wild and very interesting. It was then,
and it is today.

One other thing I remember about
Kuttawa. I believe it was the man who
owned the Cafe, he had a two legged goat
that walked on his front legs. He
brought it to the show one night and put
him on the stage where the audience
could see him walk on those two front
legs. It was one of those "Ripley,
Believe It or Not" things and very
unusual. However, after seeing it once
I didn't care about seeing it again. I
had too much sympathy for the goat.

The Kentucky State Penitentiary was
located at Eddyville which was a few
short miles from Kuttawa. It was built
on the road as you came into Eddyville.
It was a large imposing building with
long and wide steps leading to the front
door. It was landscaped with nice
shrubbery and of course the American
flag at the top of a high flag pole. As
you entered the atmosphere changed. It
just smelled different. You couldn't
put your finger on it, but you knew this
was a place you wouldn't want to stay in
very long. And some men were spending
the rest of their lives in this
building. Inside the prison walls there
were men from all walks of life. They
did have some great musicians and a fine
orchestra but live entertainment was
almost non-existent except when Bisbee's
Comedians came and entertained. This we
did every year for many years. We would
take the orchestra, Jess would do a
magic act, Boob Brasfield would do a

monologue, I would sing a couple of songs and we usually had a juggling act or a dog act that would work. We didn't take any of the women but no matter what we did the prisoners would eat it up. They were starved for live entertainment and we were the only live show they would see until we came back the next year.

For many years, the Warden at the prison was Jess "Buck" Buchanan. He was a giant of a man, both physically and mentally. He must have been 6 ft. 6 in. and I am sure he weighed over three hundred pounds. I loved to hear him tell the stories about things that happened in the prison, some funny, and some not so funny.

Once, Jess, Boob and myself were in his office visiting, just killing time as we were to give a performance in about 30 minutes. The door opened and in walked a nicely dressed man. Buck got up and said, "Fella's I want you to meet our new Chaplain. He just came here last week so he is still getting his feet wet." We all shook hands as Buck explained we were there to do a show. After sitting down the Chaplain started asking Jess all kinds of inquisitive questions and finally ending by asking, "Are you going to tell any dirty jokes in your program today?" Before Jess could answer Buck said, "Why are you asking all these silly questions, Chaplain?" I could see the

Chaplain was backing himself into a corner. "Warden, I just don't think the men here should be subjected to a lot of filthy jokes. There is enough cussing and dirty stories circulating among the prisoners now. They don't need more filth presented to them from a stage by a bunch of actors." Buck was up and out of his chair, around his desk and towering over the preacher. "Now look here Chaplain, these people present good clean entertainment, the show has a great reputation, not only in the towns they play in Kentucky but also the towns they go to in Tennessee. I have known Mr. Bisbee for many years. He is a fine gentleman and has not and would not allow anything questionable to be presented on his stage that would be a detriment to anyone. Now, I have one more thing to say to you and then I want you to get back to whatever duties you have. He walked around his desk, sat down in his big chair and continued by saying, "Every year for a number of years Mr. Bisbee has brought his troupe over to entertain the prisoners. This is the only professional entertainment they see and they look forward to them coming. Now, one other thing, we have thousands of prisoners in this prison. This might surprise you but it is true. We have five preachers and not one damn actor, you're excused Chaplain."

PART VII
THE CANVASMEN

The canvas crews were indispensable, they were the showmen who knew no applause. Bisbee's Comedians always carried a canvas crew of six men. In addition, the male actors helped set up the stage. I understand my Grandfather would not let one of the actors on the lot until the outfit was set up and ready to show. But like many things, over the years, that changed.

In 1940-41-42, Bisbee's Comedians carried a cook tent. Elrod "Red" Turner was the boss canvasman and his wife was the cook. The actors could have their meals, if they preferred for six dollars a week. 1942 was the last season for Bisbee to carry a cook tent.

There were some canvasmen who found a home with the Bisbee show. Roy Garrett was boss canvasman for nine years. Leonard Huston was with the show eleven years, Leland Hatchett ten years, and many others had a tenure of three to five years.

Roy Garrett was a character. He was with the Cole Brothers Circus, and was boss canvasman for W.I. Swain for many years before joining the Bisbee show. I loved to hear him tell his wild stories; I never knew if they were true or not, like the time the elephants stampeded on the Cole show and it cost twenty thousand dollars to replace what

they tore up. Or the time Mr. Swain
fired eight actors, after they were
thrown out of the hotel in Meridian,
Mississippi, for having a drunken party.
I asked Roy if they showed that night
and he said, "Why sure, Mr. Swain
carried extra's, just so he could fire
people."

Leonard Huston had polio when he
was a child and was crippled in his
right leg. He was a fine man but he
drank too much for his own good.
However, his drinking never interfered
with his work. One hot July afternoon,
the show was in Clinton, Kentucky. It
was one of these afternoons when you
knew the weather was going to turn wild
and Thor was going to rattle his chains.
It was quiet, and so humid and hot, that
you unconsciously walked around panting
with your tongue hanging out. About
three o'clock an ominous black cloud
appeared in the south western sky. The
boys were busy gying out the tent,
putting the grapevine up and driving
extra stakes, when Jess Bisbee came out
of his trailer and said, "Boys don't
worry about that cloud I will just call
on Allah." Then he raised his arms and
said, "Allah be praised, cloud go away."
Then laughing, he went back into his
trailer.

Ten minutes later the storm hit.
It was so fearfully strong the quarter
poles and the center poles started
jumping. Leonard and the rest of the

119

crew kept driving stakes and managed to keep the top in the air. When the wind died down, it started to rain, and poured down. It must have rained at least two inches. As it usually does in Kentucky, after a storm, the sun came out, and it was hot and humid once more. Leonard was wiping his face with a towel, when Jess came out of his trailer. In his southern drawl, he said, "Mr. Jess, I wish you wouldn't call on that Allah fella anymore, he like to have drowned us."

In 1953, Labor Day week end, we were making a jump from Hopkinsville, Kentucky to Union City, Tennessee. One of the canvasman, named Dawson, was pulling the working mens trailer with the sound truck. He went to sleep and turned over three times. He only received a few scratches. The truck was not damaged too much. However, the trailer was demolished. About eight weeks later, the show closed for the season and we pulled into Memphis for the winter. The winter quarters was a former garage that Bisbee had bought a number of years earlier. Cliff Malcomb, who was an excellent carpenter, immediately began building a new working mens trailer. When he finished it, people who didn't know, thought it was custom built in a factory. It was built on a tandem chassis 28 ft. long. It had six bunk beds, shower and chemical toilet. It was just beautiful until we

120

started to pull it out. It was at that
time that we realized it was too high to
go out the garage door. So, they tore
out the top of the door, let the air out
of the tires, and finally got it out.

In 1961, we opened the season in
Whitesville, Tennessee. I hired a boy
from Dyersburg. He was clean cut and
seemed like a very intelligent young
man. I decided to put him on the
curtains and running the switch board
and lights. I explained how important
his job would be, and he familiarized
himself with the switch board. The
front curtain and the street drop were
roll ups, and the bottom was a two by
one board. I told him to pull the
curtains up as fast as possible and,
when he let them down to turn loose of
them and let them fall. I gave him a
cue sheet, and we were ready for the
opening, or at least that is what I
thought. Everything was running
smoothly until Bert Dexter did his
speciality. Bert did a song and dance
and closed with a fast buck and wing.
When he finished he received a
tremendous round of applause. So, he
came back to milk the audience with
another bow. Of course my new boy on
the curtains didn't know this and let
the curtain go. Down it came and hit
poor Bert in the head as he was leaning
over to take his bow. Knocked him out
cold. When he regained consciousness,
he looked at me and said, "Where in the

hell did you get that idiot?" Later on, Bert would tell me the story and laugh about it, but it wasn't funny when it happened.

In 1946, a young man walked up on the lot in Murray, Kentucky wanting a job. That night we were making up and he came through the dressing room. I asked Ralph Blackwell, "Who in the world is that?" Ralph replied, "That is the new canvasman Jess hired, something else, isn't he?" And he certainly was. I have never seen a better built human being. He was six foot four, weighed 230 pounds, and was all muscle. He looked like Arnold Schwarzenegger, or keeping in that day and time, maybe Charles Atlas. However, it soon became apparent that he had very few brains and no common sense to go along with that magnificent body. The other canvasman named him Bombo. They discovered if they bragged on Bombo, he would do his work and their work also. He was so strong he would pick up a heavy wardrobe trunk, run and put it in the truck. For a concert opening, we did a Devil presentation. Several flash pans, loaded with black powder were placed around the stage. Then, when the devil made his entrance they were set off. There was a loud explosion and much smoke and it made a very impressive entrance for the devil. These flash pans had electric wires running to them and they were set off by a toggle switch off stage. Boob Brasfield would work two to three hours getting the pans and everything set for this opening. A sign above the toggle switch said, DO NOT TOUCH! No one was to get within five feet of that switch. On this particular night, during the second act of the play, the actors were in a very serious scene-----HERE COMES BOMBO. He couldn't read the sign, he looked at the switch and he couldn't resist the temptation, so he pushed the switch. All hell broke loose. Lucille Stoddard, the character woman fell over in a dead faint. When the explosion went off, half the audience left in a dead run fearing the worst. The other half sat in their seats too dumbfounded to move. Boob was confronting Bombo and crying, Why? Why? Why? Finally Bombo said, "I just wanted to see what it would do." The other canvasmen hated to see him go, but Bombo thought it was time for him to get over the fence into greener pastures, and to get far, far away from Boob Brasfield.

Wiley Gregory was with Bisbee's Comedians for three seasons. He was a good boy, a good worker and his second season, he was made stage manager. Sometimes canvasmen would get upset, thinking they did all the work and the actors received the most money. Wiley was no exception, he made his feelings known to me one day as we were discussing something else. I explained to him the actors had the talent and the ability to go out on a stage and give a performance and they deserved a larger salary. He said, "Well I think I could act." I said, "Fine, we will just find out." We were doing Neil Schaffner's What Mothers Don't Know. In the first act was a delivery boy bit part with one line. He enters and says "Package for Elota Watson" and exits. We rehearsed him and Wiley was ready to make his acting debut. That night the curtain went up and it was time for Wiley's big moment. We had put makeup on him but it didn't do much good. When he made his entrance he was white as a sheet, and he couldn't say a word. He just stood there with a wild look on his face, and had to be helped off the stage. Needless to say, that was the end of Wiley's acting career, and he said no more about it.

Others of the canvas crew that was with the show three seasons or more were: Calvin Smiley, Gordeon McGough, John Harris, Billy Joe, Blackie Alverson, Curtis Jackson, Sandy Evans, and Dawson Mencer. There were hundreds of other canvasmen who were on Bisbee's Comedians through the years, but I can't remember their names.

PART VIII
MAGICIANS WHO TROUPED ON BISBEE COMEDIANS

Jess Bisbee was known as Mahala, the Magician. After he retired in 1952 Bisbee's Comedians became a mecca for other magicians. A list of the ones that were on the show goes like this.....James Colley, Jimmie Weir, Willard the Wizard, George Rowe, Ken Griffin and Roberta, Bob Fisher, Bob LaThey, Alvi Maddocks, Dave Castle, Bill Martin, The O'Dowds, Charlie McDowell, Del Breeze and Mahala, and Everett Lawson.

But, before discussing the magicians I would like to go back and talk about a hypnotist that joined the Choate's Comedians in 1936. His name was Floyd Gilbert and his stage name was Gilbert, the Hypnotist. He was a great showman and before the week was over, he created a great amount of talk among the "towners". Gilbert even looked like what one would imagine a hypnotist should look like. He had long flowing, snow white hair, he was at least six feet two inches tall, he had a ruddy complexion and large piercing black eyes. He was a very intelligent person with a college degree and had written a number of books. He had a lot of nerve and I am sure he was the greatest of all stage hypnotists. His one fault I suppose, was that before he went on to

125

do his act, he would drink a bottle of wine. This never affected his work. He was a concert feature and before the week was over people were coming to the show to "see that fella that made people go to sleep and do crazy things."

He would conjure, cuss and threaten to make his subjects on the stage do what he wanted them to. Once, when Choate's Comedians was playing Elkville, Illinois, a young man who worked in the bank, bragged all week that Gilbert was a fake and he was going up on the stage Saturday night and prove that Gilbert could not hypnotize him. This caused a lot of talk and much betting took place on the out come. Saturday night came and the tent was packed. sure enough, the young man came on the stage when Gilbert called for volunteers. Gilbert made his opening speech and went right to work on the young man. He sat him in a chair, rubbed his neck and the young man fell out of the chair on to the stage floor, out like a light. Gilbert had a couple of people examine him and say he was asleep. Then he set him back in the chair, slapped his face hard a couple of times, and the young man was awake. Gilbert would not discuss it later and I don't know how he knocked the young man out. Later, others have told me he did it by touching nerves in his neck. Whether this is true or not, I do not know. I do know the young man was out asleep on the floor. After the

126

show closed, he went to California and was involved with a clinic that performed childbirth through hypnosis. Later, one of his patients died and as at that time it was against the law to use hypnosis medically, Gilbert was sent to prison for a few months. Gilbert was a great showman and I would have to place him along side Willard, the Wizard in that category.

In his time and day, Jess Bisbee had to be rated as one of the top magicians. In the nineteen forties, every home was not blessed with a television set. People in the small towns didn't get to see Blackstone or other well known magicians. They couldn't sit in their living rooms and watch David Copperfield on TV as they do today. So, when Jess Bisbee came out on his stage and did big allusions, people were amazed, fooled and fascinated. Jess did all the big things. The Glass Casket, The Barber Shop Switch, The Levitation, Sawing a Woman in Two.

For the 1948 season, Jess featured Sawing a Woman in Two With a Buzz Saw. They set it up in the winter quarters and it was so huge! The flat scenery and the ceiling piece had to come down to get it on the stage so it was used as a concert feature. Also, the motor was so large it wouldn't run on regular 110, so the light plant had to be fired up. I will never forget the first time Jess used it in Lexington, Tennessee. He thought the effect would be great if he put some liver where the blade would hit it. Lucille Farren was in the saw and when the blade hit the liver, it went all over her, all over the stage and out into the audience. Needless to say, that was the last time liver was put in the buzz saw. What Jess liked to do most was his Flower Act. He produced flowers from himself and around the stage. There was a trellis in the middle of the stage and it bloomed with flowers. When the act was over the stage was filled with beautiful flowers. He and Mary did an act I was very fond of. They called it Art of the World. This act was fast and moved quickly. Jess was a wonderful artist. He would do a beautiful scene with colored sand while Mary was doing a rag picture. Then he had a frame with white paper at least four feet by four feet with lights behind it on which he painted a beautiful girl. Then for a closer he painted The Statue of Liberty and the American Flag while the band was playing the Stars and Stripes Forever. These paintings were painted with water color. This act was so effective because it was done so fast. And of course, closing with the American flag didn't hurt. Jess had a peculiar voice, he knew this, so he never talked on the stage. The one time he did talk was a bit he did with Boob Brasfield. Boob would come out and ask Jess to teach him some magic. Jess would say, "OK, empty that bucket of water and blow out that candle." This was repeated over and over and each time the bucket would be full and the candle would relight. Jess wasn't fond of this act even though the audience howled at Boob's double takes as he kept pouring the water out of the bucket and blowing out the candle. Jess didn't like comedy in magic acts he did. He took his magic very seriously. He was the owner, he was the Star and he was the greatest Magician, or at least that is what the people of Kentucky and Tennessee thought. When the orchestra played his theme song, SONG OF THE ISLANDS, and he entered with his black tie, tails and floating cane, he would receive applause and many times a standing ovation. Absolutely no one was to stand in the wings when Jess was doing his act. Everybody was informed of this rule at the beginning of the season. He was from the old school and guarded his magic secrets. To illustrate that, Jess and Mary did what they called the Flight of Life. A couple of men from the audience would come up, put Mary in a sack, tie the sack, then put her in a box, pad lock the box and put a rope around it. Then Jess would pull a curtain around the box, say, "ONE, TWO, THREE, and Mary would be out and Jess would be in the box and in the sack. I worked on the Bisbee show many years and all that time

129

I never knew how they did the Flight of Life. In the spring of 1955, he and I were talking one day and I asked him to tell me how he and Mary did it. And he told me. Pretty simple after you know. But you will have to find out from somebody else.....I am not telling.

Del Breeze was the first magician on the Bisbee Show when Jess retired. When I first caught his act he was working a well known night club, The Silver Slipper, which was located just outside Memphis. He had a wonderful act and was a great manipulator. He used cards and balls and worked among the audience. He used some of Jess's magic. He and his wife Dolly were on the show one season.

Del and Dolly worked on the Cruise Ships out of Florida for many years and was one of the top flight acts on these boats. Magic had a great influence on Bisbee's Comedians and there are some great stories about the Magicians that made it happen.

Bob Fisher joined the show in 1946 as the piano player. He was also a magician, doing linking rings, billiard balls, whiskey glasses, etc. However, he only did this act the last season he was on the show. Bob was in a class by himself when it came to the piano. He was also an eccentric bachelor and an introvert. One time while the show was playing Henderson, Kentucky, Bob, for some unknown reason, went crazy, screamed at Mary Bisbee and cussed her. Mary made the ones who saw this incident promise they would not tell Jess, as she was afraid of what he might do to Bob. As far as I know, Jess never did know. However, the next season while the show was in rehearsals, Jess fired Bob. We were rehearsing the orchestra one night when Jess came in and told Bob, "I went up town today and bought this stock arrangement of Shout and Liza Trombone. Rehearse it and you can feature Audra Hardesty on the trombone. I will be here tomorrow night to hear it." And he left. Sure enough, the next night Jess walked in on the rehearsal and said, "Bob play Shout and Liza." Bob replied, "We are not playing that song." "Bob, I am only going to say this once. Either play the song I have asked you to play, or you are fired." Bob got up from the piano and said, "I'm fired," and walked out. I couldn't believe it. Here we were to open the next week and Jess had fired the piano player. However, the next afternoon Leon Block, a piano player who had been on the Bisbee Show before joined, and we opened on schedule.

The only other person I remember Jess firing was Jimmie Weir, another Magician. Jimmie and his wife, Jean, joined the Bisbee show for the 1954 season. They had been playing school assemblies and their Magic was tricks that could be carried in a couple of suit cases. However, what they did, they did well and they worked out well in some parts in the plays. We were showing Greenville, Kentucky when Jimmie came down with acute appendicitis. They operated on him at the local hospital and the doctor assured me he was going to be fine. However, he said it would be three to four weeks before he could work and rejoin the show. I talked it over with Audra Hardesty and we decided to pay them their salary for the time they were off. I had the boys set their trailer in a nice trailer park in Greenville so Jean could be near Jimmie. I told them what we had decided to do about their salary, told them to rejoin the show when Jimmie was able and not to worry. They were very happy with this arrangement. Two weeks later we were in Union City, Tennessee when Jimmie and Jean rejoined the show. As soon as I got the trucks and trailers parked, Vera and I were getting ready to leave for Memphis to see Jess and Mary on some business and to have dinner with them. We were just pulling off the lot when Jimmie flagged us down and told me he had signed up with a school bureau and would be leaving in two weeks. I told him Jess wasn't going to be happy when he heard this, especially after we paid him while he was off. He said, "I am sorry but you have only eight more weeks and this is a job which will last all winter." That afternoon I told Jess about Jimmie Weir leaving. He didn't say much, just, "Get in the car." We drove over to Leahy's trailer park where Jim and Rosalee Colley had their trailer parked while playing some dates with their Magic. They were old troupers, fine people and had been on Choate's Comedians when I was a kid. Jess asked them if they would like to finish out the season with Bisbee's Comedians and they said, "Sure we would." Jess told them the show was in Union City and to "join there tomorrow." When we got in the car, Jess told me he was coming up to Union City Monday afternoon, however, he wanted me to inform Jimmie, as soon as I got there, he was fired, which I did. He was very upset and the next day he and Jess had some hot words. I don't know what was said, but Jimmie and Jean pulled out of the lot. I never saw them again.

George Rowe was on the show two seasons. He didn't do magic because Ken Griffin did the feature magic act. George was a good boy and did an excellent job as our leading man.

Dave Castle and his wife, Maureen, were on Bisbee's Comedians a number of seasons. They were a very valuable team and Dave was an outstanding ventriloquist.

If I remember right, Ken and Roberta Griffin were on the show two or three seasons. They would play auditoriums in the winter and had their own truck to carry their illusions and props. Roberta did parts in plays, so they were a good team for a tent show.

Mike and Sandy O'Doud joined the show in 1965. They both worked out fine doing parts in the play and they had an outstanding mental act. Sandy was on the stage blindfolded while Mike was in the audience getting objects for her to identify. In Dyersburg, Tennessee we always set up on a lot next to the John Deere dealership which was owned by the Ozmont family. Tuesday morning, after the Monday night opening, I went over to visit. As soon as I walked in the door one of the Ozmont Brothers said, "I really enjoyed the show last night Billy and that girl who identified all those things blindfolded was outstanding. However, I will be there to night and I have a gold coin from Germany and she won't be able to identify it because she won't be able to read the words." Well, that night Sandy didn't read the words but she identified the coin by spelling the words on it. That made a believer out of Mr. Ozmont. He was flabbergasted.

Charlie McDowell did a couple of very good magic acts. He and his wife Vivian were on Bisbee's Comedians three seasons. They both did parts in the plays and she had a very fine singing voice. This, along with their fine appearance, made them very valuable on the show.

Everett Lawson was a clever magician. Later on, he was a maker of fine magic. He and his wife Jane were on the show a part of one season. The show was playing Smithland, Kentucky. They had a little girl named Toni. She was playing on a swing and fell, breaking her leg. They were not satisfied with the hospital, or the doctor in Paducah and decided to leave the show and take her to Chattanooga to their doctor. That fall the show was in Dyersburg, Tennessee. We had just moved from Union City. Alvie Maddocks had left the show to join an International Harvester show for the winter, and our ingenue had gotten drunk and was fired. Sunday night Vera and I were getting ready for bed when there was a knock on our trailer door. It was Everett and Jane. We talked for a while and they finally got around to saying they needed a job. I said, "Well, you've come to the right place." Then I told them about Alvie and the ingenue leaving. The next day we had a rehearsal and the show rolled right along with Jane taking the ingenue parts and Everett doing the magic. It was a lucky break for them and the show. Later on they were very successful on the Burlesque wheel, finally retiring to a farm south of Chattanooga where Everett made and sold magic.

In January of 1957 I had a letter from Bob LaThey. Pearle had passed on and he had remarried and was living in Greenwood Texas. For many years he had been playing schools with his magic act, and doing well financially. Bob's wife, Lona, had trouped on repertory shows and he said she was a fine piano player. Bob wanted to know if I could use them for the coming season. He said they wanted to troupe just one more season. I had already signed Gladys Bell so I didn't need a piano player. However, Bob had been like a Father to me when I was growing up on Choate's Comedians and even though I really didn't need them, I wrote them a letter saying, join us in April for rehearsals. They did and we had a memorable season because they were on the show. They both did parts and Bob did a couple of magic acts but what made them so valuable, Bob directed the shows. He had always been a good director and now that he was so happy to be back on a tent show, he threw himself into the job with gusto. One of the plays we did that year was Neil Schaffners The Old Grouch. Bob played the grouch and he was outstanding in the part.

It was January, we were in Wayne City and I was organizing the show for the 1962 season. Late one evening, I had a telephone call from Harry Willard, known professionally as Willard the Wizard. I had heard of Willard all my life. I knew he was truly one of the great magicians of all time. I also had

136

heard he was an alcoholic who stayed drunk all the time. Of course, he said he wanted to troupe with us the coming season and he would use his daughter as his assistant in his magic acts. He told me what kind of salary he expected and I told him I would call him the next week with a decision. I immediately got on the phone and called a few people that knew Willard. I called Lee Estis at Lexington, Kentucky, Robert Johnson in Texas and Dave Price at Nashville, Tennessee. They all told me the same thing. Willard was the greatest magician living, but he was also a drunk. However, they all agreed his drinking would not affect his ability on the stage. Even though I had second thoughts, the next week I called Willard. Our first conversation was about his drinking. He said, "Yes, I drink every day, however, when I step on the stage, I am the greatest magician in the world. Also, I will stay on the lot and I won't give you any trouble. I am not going to lie to you, I will be drunk when I do my act. I know you have seen many magicians, but I will present magic tricks that you have never seen and no one else knows how to do them except me." I said, "OK come on, our rehearsals are here in Wayne City and start the second week in April. I must tell you if your drinking causes problems or trouble, I will let you go without notice. Is that understood?"

"Yes, it is," he replied, "we will see you in April." I hung up the phone not knowing whether I had made the right decision or not. Well, at least I could say the greatest magician in the world had worked for me. I just hoped he would work out. One thing, Willard knew what tent show trouping was all about. He had never been on a repertory show but he and his father had a tent theatre for years in Texas presenting nothing but magic. My understanding was they had made a lot of money but Willard got in trouble with the government over taxes and lost most everything.

When Willard pulled into Wayne City in his house truck in April, I could hardly believe my eyes. Here was the greatest magician in the world, I was told, and he looked like a bum. He had on an old flannel shirt, a dirty pair of pants and an old faded hat. His two daughters, Francis and Rosemary, were with him and Rosemary's little boy. Both of the girls were nicely dressed and very attractive. In fact, Francis was a real beauty. She had been Miss Texas and had been in the Miss America Pageant. She didn't win but, as far as I was concerned, she should have. I thought to myself, Willard has one thing going for him, he has a beautiful daughter working as his assistant. I showed him where to park and a few minutes later there was a knock on my door. It was Willard. "Billy, where is

the closest place to get beer?" I told
him Wayne City was dry, but the American
Legion sold beer, however, you had to be
a member to get in. He said, "That's
fine, I have a card." I told Vera when
he left, "Well, he told me before he
joined he drank so I shouldn't be
surprised. He sure doesn't try to hide
it."

The two week rehearsals went
smooth. We had a good cast and good
show for the 1962 season. Boob and Neva
Brasfield had just finished on Red
Foley's <u>Ozark Jubilee</u> TV show at
Springfield, Missouri, playing the roles
of <u>Uncle Cyp and Aunt Sap Brasfield</u>.
Boob directed and he and Neva did a
specialty each night. They were also
featured in the show, <u>Sweet Hearts Again</u>
and both were stars in their parts. I
was looking forward to the 1962 season.

We opened in Wayne City to a packed
house. Willard worked after the second
act. I went out by the orchestra stage.
I couldn't wait to see him work. After
three or four minutes with Willard and
Francis on the stage, I came to the
conclusion that Willard was the greatest
showman I had ever seen. He was
magnificent. He even looked the part,
with his black tails, his white tie and
his long silver hair. I was just
thinking to myself how lucky I was to
have Willard on the show when I heard
him say, "Will you please get off the
stage." Then I heard another voice over

the music, which I knew to be Boob Brasfield's say, "I am the director. I don't have to get off the stage." To which Willard replied, "Either you get off the stage or I quit doing my act." Oh what a way to start the season and it was all my fault. Willard had told me to tell everyone to stay out of the wings while he was working and I had forgotten to do so. The next day, I told everyone including Boob and I apologized to Willard. This seemed to smooth things over but I always felt it would only take a spark and they would be at each other.

We played Wayne City and Cisne and then jumped to Morganfield, Kentucky and our regular Kentucky route. We had a good show and business was very good. Willard and Francis was wowing the audiences with their magic act, they were wowing me. Every night when they came on I would go out front and catch their act.

David Price, author of books on magicians, a friend of Willards, and owner of the Egyptian Hall Museum in Nashville, Tennessee which is full of magic memorabilia said, "Harry Willard's genius at performing magic is too elusive to point to one reason-----or two or three or more. It would probably be as difficult of explanation as determining how Wolfgang Mozart could write symphonies at age eight. However, there can be no doubt that Harry Willard was a veritable genius at performing magic.

Harry's greatest trick was "the transformation". He would be on the back lot in old shabby clothes, the flannel shirt and pants he joined in, along with his soiled hat. I have seen him so drunk that he had to be literally helped to a chair in the wings to await his entrance cue. But when his cue came and Willard stepped upon the stage and established eye contact with the audience, a transformation did, or at least seemed to, take place. He became a magician-----not a mere "conjurer" who performed tricks but a genuine magician whose magic was accomplished through magical powers. Willard, from the moment of entrance and continuing throughout his performance, radiated magnetism and personality.

Lee Estis, a magician and captain with the Kentucky State Police and a good friend of mine, came to visit while the show was in Owensboro. He brought two other gentlemen with him who were also magicians. They arrived in the afternoon and, of course, wanted to meet Willard. As we stood talking in the men's dressing room, Willard crawled out from under the stage. I introduced them and said, "Gentlemen, this is Harry Willard." I could tell Lee was flabbergasted. They talked for 15 or 20 minutes and finally Lee said, "Mr. Willard, I have heard so much about it,

141

I was wondering if I could see the pistol you use in shooting a bullet through the woman?" Willard said, "Sure." He went to his truck and came back with a beautiful case with a magnificent gun. He handed it to Lee and as he examined it I could see he was quite impressed. As Lee handed the gun back to Willard he asked, "Will it really shoot?" Willard said, "Hell yes, it will shoot," as he pointed the gun at Lee's feet and pulled the trigger. There was a loud explosion and dirt flew everywhere. For a minute, we all just stood there. Finally Lee said, "Well, fellas, I don't know about you but I have to go to the motel. We'll see you tonight, Billy," and they quickly left. I was mad and told Willard what a dangerous thing he had done and to never take that pistol out of the case again. He pulled his old hat down, laughed, and headed to his house car.

I think that Willard the Wizard can be classified as an illusionist. However, the one Willard trick associated with him as long as there are any magicians alive is a piece of small magic-----the thumb tie.

First, Willard would have volunteers come up from the audience and tie his thumbs with binders twine with the stage lights full up and in the glare of a spotlight. Willard would then pass his hands through a hoop and out again-----just enough to establish in the audience's mind what the trick was all about. Then he came down into the audience and passed his hands through the first center pole. Then at close range he would pass his thumbs through people's arms, canes, umbrellas, anything that anyone could suggest. With spectators on all sides he repeated and repeated it until everyone was satisfied. No one could detect a clue as to how it was accomplished. David Price said, "Some magicians think that they have seen the same trick performed by some other magician. They are mistaken."

No other magician in the history of magic has been able to accomplish with the thumb-tie what Harry Willard did. He jealously guarded the secret and no one living today can duplicate Willard's performance of that trick. Harry spoiled me with his thumb-tie. On the nights he did it, I was out front, amazed and baffled along with the rest of the audience.

We had hundreds of magicians visit the show the season Willard was on. They came from New York, Chicago, St. Louis and about 25 members of the magician club from Louisville came one night while the show was in Leitchfield, Kentucky. They were amazed at Willard's act. After the show, they took him up town for night lunch. He came over to join them and he had on a nice looking suit and tie. I complimented him on how

143

nice he looked.   He told me that was his
"joining suit".   I said, "Well, you sure
were not wearing it when you joined the
Bisbee show."   He just laughed as he
walked away.

Yes, sometimes Willard was a
problem but I am proud to say, "The
world's greatest magician, Willard the
Wizard, worked for me on Bisbee's
Comedians during the 1962 season."
Also, it was a great pleasure having his
two daughters, Francis and Rosemary, on
the show.

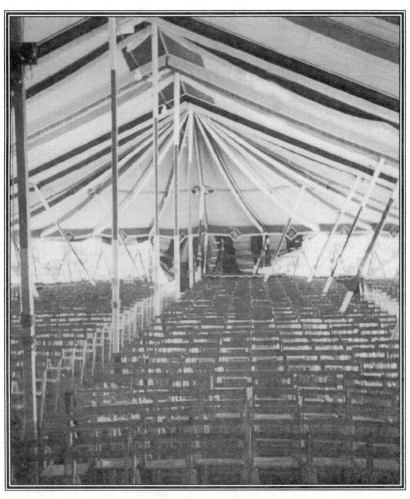

Inside the Bisbee's Comedians Tent

1954
Billy Choate, Vera Choate, Cherita Choate and Welby Choate
Owensboro, KY

Bisbee's Comedians Orchestra
(left to right) Toots Hodge, Otis Arnold, Les Lyle, Audra Hardesty,
Octavia Powell, Slim Osbourn, Billy Choate and Bob Fisher on piano.

Bisbee's Opening
(left to right) Billy Choate, Maxine Lacey, Vera Choate, Fern Espey,
Vivian Delmar, Mickey Lacey and Wendall Poe

Jess and Mary Bisbee

1888
Choate Brothers Show

Rod Brasfield

The Bisbee Girls
(left to right) Dean Tannis, Octavia Powell, Vivian McDowell, Ginny
Girard, Maxine Lacey and Vera Choate.

1936
Choate's Comedians
Shawneetown, Illinois

1964
Bisbee's Comedians
Dyersburg, TN

Billy "Toby" Choate

Bisbee's Comedians on the Lot
Obion, TN

Bisbee's Comedians Blown Down
Russelville, KY

1923
Choate's Comedians
Harrisburg, Illinois

Uncle Cyp and Aunt Sap Brasfield

PART IX
BAD LUCK

Most actors are superstitious. Yellow is considered a bad luck color; it is bad luck to whistle in the dressing rooms, to put a shoe on the makeup shelf or a hat on a hotel bed, or to use a Bible on stage. It is also bad luck to speak the last line of a play in rehearsal. But the greatest omen of all was a harmonica and the playing of the song, Home Sweet Home. That meant the show would close for sure.

One season, Dad hired Billy Bracken as a vaudeville feature. He billed himself as The Musical Bracken. There wasn't a musical instrument he couldn't play and couldn't play well. He was also one of the greatest of all ventriloquists. He did one act where he closed with a fast song playing a number of different instruments, including a harmonica, not on a holder, but just stuck in his mouth. He would stop the show with this act. However, the first night he did this act, Grandpa came backstage and told Dad he couldn't play that harmonica again. Dad finally persuaded Grandpa into letting Billy do his act with the harmonica. But on the night he played the harmonica, Grandpa and Grandma would leave the lot and go to the hotel. Everything bad that happened that season, Grandpa blamed on that damned harmonica.

145

Ben and Tot Wilkes owned and operated The Ben Wilkes Stock Company. The shows territory was southern and central Indiana but the shows winter quarters were at Albion, Illinois. Ben was eccentric, he was a practical joker and had the reputation of being able to out cuss a sailor. I have heard many wild stories about Ben, like the leading team from New York who joined the show in Albion for rehearsals. Ben met them at the train station, introduced himself, then said, "Folks, I already have your room reserved and will take you to it in my car." They loaded their bags and then Ben drove them out in the country to a dilapidated farm house that had not been lived in for years. He unloaded their grips, said he would pick them up the next morning for rehearsal, and drove off. After a couple of hours, he went back and picked them up still laughing. However, they didn't think his joke was funny and caught the next train back to New York.

One season, the show was playing Poseyville, Indiana. A little boy walked in the tent one afternoon playing a harmonica. Some of the actors proceeded to run him off the lot and had him out in the street when Ben drove up. He took in the situation, went out in the street, got the little boy by the hand and led him back inside the tent, set him in a chair and, to the dismay of the actors, told the little boy, "I just love to hear a harmonica. Do you happen to know <u>Home Sweet Home</u>?" He did and played it. That night a terrible storm hit the tent, blew it down and tore it up. I don't know if the harmonica was the cause of the disaster or not. But I bet you couldn't convince the actors that it wasn't.

PART X
POPCORN, SNOW CONES, AND CANDY

Concessions on the Bisbee Comedians was big business. Cliff Malcomb, who was with the show for years, was manager of concessions. He sold popcorn and snow cones. He received 50% of gross sales and he also did the advance work for the show. However, he didn't do any booking, he just saw that the paper was put up announcing the shows coming. Cliff and his wife, Mabel, had been with a number of well known Rep. shows, and had the reputation of being fine actors. But I never saw either one of them do a part, or step on the stage, and I trouped with them many years. Cliff was kidded about his popcorn being so salty. He was accused of putting more salt on than was called for, so they would buy more snow cones. Nevertheless, he made money for the show, and also himself.

The candy concession was owned by the show and was a big money maker. I remember Dad told the story that one season he gave Ray Zarlington and Christy Obrecht, who were on the #2 Choate's Comedians, each one third of the candy gross for taking care of it. He said it caused nothing but trouble and that was the only season that kind of arrangement was made with anyone, concerning the candy. Never was a percentage of candy receipts given to anyone on the Bisbee's Comedians.

At first, there were prizes in every box. Then later, the candy companies came up with something new. They provided an assortment of very nice prizes (kitchenware, dolls, hair brush sets, blankets) which could be displayed on the stage. In every tenth box, there was a coupon that identified a prize on the stage. The Bisbee's Comedians bought from Union Concession Company and later the Bob Hoffeller Candy Company, out of Chicago. Clarence Balleras, a very fine gentleman, was their salesman and he visited the show a couple of times each season. In Tennessee, during the cotton season, school was dismissed so the kids could pick cotton. Every kid had money and salesmen would only get to the fifth row and they would be sold out.

I suppose the candy pitch was about the same on all the tent shows. Here is a facsimile of the way Boob Brasfield did it on the Bisbee Show:

"Where in the world did all you people come from? We have a fine show in store for you tonight, but before the show starts I want to talk to you for just a minute, if you're not doing anything. I know many of you came tonight just so you could buy some of that good candy we sell. And can you believe it.....it's the same old price, just fifteen cents a box or two boxes for thirty cents. Now tonight every

149

cent taken in at this candy sale will go to the benefit of two orphans, Mr. and Mrs. Choate. Also, remember, this candy will not hurt you.....there isn't enough in a box to hurt anyone. And if you like to chew on something, this candy will last you all night. However, if you will look here on the stage you will see a lot of swell prizes. You'll notice there are dolls, pretty lamps, and beautiful blankets and lots of other nice prizes. Now every once in a while you find a coupon in a box. If you do get a coupon, bring it up to the stage and Maxine will give you what it calls for. Have the correct change and remember it is only fifteen cents a box."

It always amazed me the amount of candy that was sold on the Bisbee show.
Here is the way Bob LaThey pitched the candy on the Choate show:

"Good evening Ladies and Gentlemen. Welcome to Choate's Comedians. We have a fine show in store for you but before the show starts we are going to give you the opportunity to buy some of that good old candy we sell every year. Now this is good candy and also if you have a loose tooth or you are going to a dentist to have a tooth pulled, you can save a lot of money by buying some of this candy. Now, I must warn you when you chew this candy, you must chew it

fifty times, no more or no less. I'll
tell you why. In the stomach there are
cells that contain gastric juices. When
you take a bite of this candy right away
a message goes to the gastric juices in
the stomach saying, 'Candy coming.' The
stomach sends a message back to the
brain saying, 'Let her flop.' Now if
you don't chew that candy fifty times,
what is the result? All the gastric
juices run to the stomach at the same
time causing internal revolution, or
what is commonly known as stomachache.
Now, don't become alarmed, when the
candy arrives in the stomach, there are
no gastric juices to dissolve it. It
forms a large white lump-----that lump
finally dissolves into a fine white
powder. The white powder sifts all
through the system-----finally coming
out on the top of the head-----and this
is what is commonly known
as-----dandruff.

You will notice, we have a lot of
nice prizes on the stage. There is a
coupon in every five boxes. If you get
a coupon, bring it up to the stage and
the little lady will give you what it
calls for. The candy is only fifteen
cents a box. We are only allowed 10
minutes for the candy sale so get it
while you can. The boys will now pass
through you-----I mean among you with
the candy for sale-----only fifteen
cents a box.

PART XI
DON'T LAUGH

Many funny things happen on the stage. Any live show no matter how well rehearsed is threatened with the actor "blowing up" or forgetting their lines. In spite of hours of study, and direction, it is a live show and unforeseen circumstances are bound to happen.

Otis Arnold was doing a bit part and the script called for him to exit and go by the window. Boob Brasfield was directing and told Otis..."Now Otis, don't forget, you must go by the window." Otis made his exit that night and the audience heard him say..."Damn, I went the wrong way."

Maxine Lacey was doing the lead and her husband Leo, was doing the heavy. The script called for Maxine to shoot Leo at the climax of the second act. Leo made his move. Maxine pulled the gun and said, "Another step and I will shoot." Leo..."Why damn you." Maxine pulls the trigger but the blank gun did not fire... Leo kept coming... she pulled the trigger again... the gun still didn't fire so, Maxine drew back and hit Leo on the head with the gun. Down went Leo with blood streaming from the gash on his head. Down came the curtain. When Leo came to his senses, Maxine was kneeling beside him saying, "Oh honey, I didn't mean to hit you so

152

hard." Leo told her, "You are a good actress but, if you ever do that again, you are a dead actress."

In 1948, Bisbee's Comedians was doing Neil Schaffner's Toby Goes to Washington, one of the better plays that was written. Howard Johnson was doing the Senator. At the climax of the show he enters with his head bandaged. Someone has tried to kill him... "Senator, what about the papers?"....."They are in my briefcase, I managed to hang on to it somehow." But, he forgot the briefcase when he entered. It is imperative he have the briefcase. Everyone is looking at one another...about this time, Boob Brasfield, who is doing the Toby, enters. He doesn't say a word, just goes to Howard and hands him the briefcase and then exits. Two minutes later the audience had settled down enough that the actors could continue with the dialogue of the play.

For years Bisbee's Comedians always set up on the airport lot in Union City, Tennessee. For some reason, in 1947, we were on a lot uptown right next to the railroad tracks. We were opening with The Awakening of John Slater. At the climax of the first act, John is leaving to make his fortune in New York City. Everyone is crying as John tells the family good-bye. As he makes his exit, Illinois Central comes bolting through town, its whistle blasting away, and its

153

bells ringing madly. When the train
passed and everything was quiet, Doob
Brasfield, who was doing the Toby, said,
"What are you all crying for? John
ain't gone. Hell, the train was going
too fast for John to hop on it."

Sometimes the audience could be
"hoodwinked" into thinking that
something happened on the stage was an
accident. If the actors were good
enough in fooling the audience, this
usually resulted in a long and loud
belly laugh. This brings to mind,
Natalie Needs a Nightie, a farce written
by Neil Schaffner. Jess and Dot Sund
were on the Bisbee show and Jess did the
lead and I did the juvenile. In the
second act, my part called for me to
dress as a women. I went all out, high
heel shoes, a beautiful dress, a pretty
blond wig, and big round balloons for
boobs. During the action in the second
act, Jess would put his arms around me
and with a pin, puncture one of the
balloons. Of course, we would act as if
it were an accident. Sometimes, it
would deflate slowly, and at other
times, it would just pop. Whichever,
the audience would howl. We timed it
when the laugh would be four or five
minutes before we could continue.

Dr. Jere C. Mickel in his book
Footlights On the Prairie, published by
North Star Press of St. Cloud, Inc.,
talks about the J.B. Rotnour Players.
J.B. was noted for using worn-out, faded

154

scenery. All drops had been painted by some artist years before, and were so worn and faded by years of use that it was really difficult to tell what they really represented. The worst of the sets was the kitchen set. It was used on Saturday night, regardless of the bill they were doing. One season the company was using Jealousy as the Saturday night western.

The script called for a palatial ranch house. The fabulously wealthy cattleman was bringing his bride from the east. Up went the kitchen set. On one Saturday night it rained. The old tent leaked like a sieve. The Saturday night furniture consisted of a couple of wooden chairs, and a battered old kitchen table. Buckets and dish pans were placed under the leaks. The curtain went up on the first act and the leading team entered. Jewel Parsons, who was playing the bride, looked around at this poor old gray rag of a set streaked with trickles of water, with the tired old wooden chairs and table held together with wire, and with the rain splashing away in the dish pans and buckets she read her first line, "Oh, John! It's beautiful!"

Call Of The Woods by W.C. Herman is another play that caused another, almost lethal, on stage accident. Here is the scene as told by Jack Parsons.

...younger brother Willis, a mealy-mouth hypocrite, has for years

155

been stealing money from blind Mama's strongbox, and putting the blame on his older brother Dave. Willis, has got Hilda, the half breed hired girl, heavy with child. Hilda is bound and determined Willis is going to marry her. If not, she will tell on him about the money he has been stealing. He tells her she had better not talk if she knows what is good for her. But Hilda is stubborn.

So Willis picks up an ax handle and says, "Again I ask your silence." Hilda replies, "No." Willis: "Then you die," and he takes out after her with the ax handle. Hilda screams and runs around the center table with Willis in hot pursuit and she ducks into the bedroom off right, Willis and the ax handle right on her heels. A loud off stage whack is heard followed by a loud offstage scream. Another loud offstage whack is followed by a low moan. Willis then comes backing onto the stage with the bloody ax handle. He hears the others coming, attracted by the screams, and flings the handle away and runs off left.

One night everything was just going fine up to the point where Willis begins to chase Hilda. She ran away from him around the table and over to the bedroom door only to find it locked from offstage. In a fierce whisper she called offstage, "Open the door!" and madly took another turn around the

table. Willis would gain on her every
step in spite of anything he or she
could do. She ran back to the door and
shook it frantically, and whispered
again as loud as she dared, "Open the
door!" To keep from catching her,
Willis bumped himself into chairs and
stumbled over his own feet. At last, he
could do nothing else but catch up with
her. She was still shaking the door and
whispering desperate pleas to get the
damn thing open. Everybody back stage
must have been dead or asleep! Poor
Willis! There was nothing else he could
do but hit her over the head with the ax
handle. He must not have known how to
fake his blow for he knocked her out
cold. She had a lump on her head for
days.

When I was a young boy, Choate's
Comedians did The Vulture for a Friday
night feature. My dad played Brad
Burkhart, Chief of Detectives. In the
second act of this performance things
really got hectic. Dad has the line,
"If you want to know a way that you can
get that confession of your brothers and
still remain single and free, I'll tell
you." When he finished his line, his
upper plate flew out of his mouth, but
he caught his teeth before they hit the
floor. The audience became hysterical.
So did the actors on the stage. The
curtain had to be dropped. Finally
everybody got settled down, and the show
continued. This whole thing was very

funny to everyone but me, because I had never seen dad without his teeth and I was completely stunned.

One fall, after the tent season, mother and dad, Welby and Eva, Audra and Virginia Hardesty, and Ray and Berniece Zarlington and I, opened a Circle Stock with headquarters in Maben, Mississippi. Business was not good. However, we stayed there until the last of February, then headed back to Illinois to get ready for the tent season. We stopped in Adamsville, Tennessee and Ray went out and booked a couple of towns to play. He had booked Crump for Monday night. Monday, Audra and I went to Crump to put up the scenery in the school Ray had booked. When we got there Audra said, "Why in the world did Ray book us here? There's nothing here but a school house and it looks like it is about to fall down." About that time a man came out of the school house and said he was the principal. Audra introduced us and told him we were there to put up the scenery for the show and that we would see him that night at the show. He said, "No I won't be here. At night the boys get too rough so, I never come to the school at night. And by the way, whatever you take in moneywise, just keep it." He got in his car and left. Audra and I beat it back to Adamsville and told Dad and Ray what had happened. Audra suggested it was too dangerous to put on a show there, but

Ray said, "We might as well play it," and we did. There was only about 50 people in the audience when the show started and most of them were men and drunk. We were doing HOLY SINNERS. Audra and Virginia were doing the leads. They have a scene in the second act where she tells him (the doctor) she is quitting her job as his nurse. "No you can't," he says, "I won't let you." He then takes her in his arms and kisses her. She says, Oh! do it again." At that moment, one of the drunks down front says, as he is crawling up on the stage, "Let me do it for him baby." Audra knocked the drunk off the stage. Dad let the front curtain down and yelled, "Let's get out of here!" which we did. Luckily, there was a back door. We made our exit through it, jumped in our cars and was off like a flash to Adamsville. That's one time THE SHOW DIDN'T GO ON. However, we didn't give any money back. There wasn't time.

159

PART XII
STORMY WEATHER: BLOW DOWNS AND TEAR UPS

Earlier in the book I told about the disastrous fire that took place in Moscow, Tennessee. The outfit was completely destroyed in just a matter of minutes. Fire and storms were a hazard every tent show owner feared. The weather played a big part in determining whether the season was a financial success. If it stormed and rained early in the afternoon and ran the farmers out of the fields that usually meant a good crowd that night. However, if it stormed and rained at 5:30 or 6:00, just when folks were getting ready or thinking about going to the show, it usually meant a small house.

I remember one opening night in Livermore, Kentucky. A storm hit just before the doors were to open. No damage but, it thundered and the lighting was severe, knocking the lights out for ten or fifteen minutes. After the storm Jess Bisbee walked to the front of the tent. There were only twenty or twenty five people lined up waiting for the doors to open. A little old man walked up to Jess and said, "Nice little shower we had wasn't it?" Jess said, It sure as hell was." He had probably lost five or six hundred dollars and was in no mood to talk about "nice little showers."

I have always said, give us about

160

fifteen minutes to get ready for a storm and the tent would ride it as well as an ordinary house. We had two sets of stakes; one wood, and one set of iron. I have seen tree's blown down and the tent still standing after the storm was over. Of course, a few times the storms were too fierce and the canvas would rip from the ropes and sometimes go down.

What was really scary and caused a lot of worry was when a storm hit during the show with hundreds of people in the tent. During the 1950 season we were playing Morgantown, Kentucky. This was the week our daughter Cherita was born. It was Thursday, opening day and late that afternoon I went up to Fleenor's Cafe to eat. I had some of their delicious country ham, which they were famous for, and after I had dinner, I went to see my good friends A.C. and Opaline Hocker. I had met A.C. before the war when Bisbee's had played Morgantown during the 1941 and 1942 seasons when I was on the show. We had become very good friends. We discussed Vera and I told them the baby was due anytime. Finally, A.C. said, "The humidity is terrible. I hope it doesn't storm." "Well," I replied, "If it is going to storm I hope it does it and gets it over with before the show tonight." Opaline said, "It isn't going to storm." How wrong she was.

When I left Hocker's Insurance office it was so hot and humid that it was hard to breathe. By 6:30 people were lining up waiting for the doors to open. I walked in the dressing room and remarked to no one in particular, "Well, what do you think?" Boob Brasfield answered, "I think something has got to bust loose. It is just too hot." Boob had been in the repertoire business long enough to know when a storm was brewing. A tent showman could feel it in his bones. We knew a storm was coming, we just didn't know when it was going to hit.

As was usual every year in Morgantown, Kentucky on opening night the tent was packed and jammed with fifteen hundred men, women and children. Jess came back just before the orchestra went out and told Boob, I want everything that can be cut, cut. I want these people out of the tent before the storm hits." Boob said, "We can cut a couple of the specialties." "Do it and rush everything else." I walked out back and sure enough it was lightning in the southwest. Every time it flashed I could see ominous clouds. During the second act it hit. I was on the stage. At first, it was a gentle breeze, then a fierce wind. Looking over the foot lights I could see the tent bellowing and the quarter poles jumping. I could also see men hanging onto the quarter poles to keep them on the ground. The wind was terrible, the lightning was cracking all around and the thunder

162

roaring. And then the lights went out. The curtain had been dropped before the lights went out and everyone had cleared the stage. I was busy along with others in keeping the side poles up when all of a sudden it started to rain. The wind stopped blowing and the lights came on. There was tremendous applause from the audience and, I imagine, many prayers of thanks. Roy Garrett, the boss canvasman, came back with his raincoat and old rain hat and I asked him if there was any damage out front. He said, "Well, the marquee went down but I don't think it is hurt." He continued, "I'll tell you something, those men hanging onto those poles saved us. Did you see them? Another thing being new canvas sure didn't hurt. Did you know a big tree went down on the front edge of the lot? We sure are lucky," he said as he walked away. Boob yelled, "Places." The curtain went up and the show went on. It always does.

Years after, in Morgantown or Butler County, whenever Bisbee's Comedians was mentioned, the question would always be, "Were you there the night of the big storm?" The answer would probably be, "I sure was and scared to death."

In July of 1948 the show was playing Calhoun, Kentucky. The lot was on the bank of the Green river. My good friends, Dr. Harris of Owensboro and Dr. Washburn of Beaver Dam, and their wives came to visit and catch the show. Dr. Harris was on my grandfather's show when he was a very young man. They came over early so Vera and I decided to take them to Wilhites Cafe for supper. This was one of the finest eating establishment on our route. After supper we visited until show time and then went to the lot. We had a big crowd and during the first act it started to rain, not a storm, just a hard rain and it didn't stop. It was raining so hard people couldn't hear what was being said on the stage, so the curtain was dropped and an announcement was made the show would continue as soon as it stopped raining. The only problem it kept raining and raining harder. The working men came back and loaded the wardrobe trunks in the trucks and anything else that was on the ground. In a few short minutes water was running through the tent a foot deep. The men took off their shoes and socks and rolled up their pant legs, the ladies took off their shoes and stockings and prepared to stay and see the show come hell or high water. The orchestra was playing and Jess came back and told me to grab a microphone and go out and lead the audience in some songs, which I did. Everyone seemed to be having a good time when finally it stopped raining. Even though they were sitting with their feet in water and mud, we resumed the show and the audience enjoyed the rest of the evening.

The next day Jess thought about tearing down and moving to another lot for the rest of the engagement. But after considering the pros and cons, he decided to stay. Luckily, it didn't rain. There was no damage done but that was the last time Bisbee's Comedians used that lot. Oh yes, one of the songs the audience sang that night was "Down by the Riverside." Very appropriate.

November 1950. It was the closing week in Collierville, Tennessee. Thanksgiving day, Johnny and Connie Spaulding, Vera and I and the kids went into Memphis to have Thanksgiving dinner. When we got out of the car Johnny said, "I think I'll take my coat off. It is down right hot." It was hot, too hot. Even though we were in Memphis it was too warm for this time of the year. We had a delicious dinner and on the way back to Collierville we stopped to see Jess and Mary. They had just bought five acres and a lovely home at 5490 Poplar Avenue. We were going to stay there for the winter and help get the outfit ready for the 1951 season. Jess took me out back and showed me where I would park our trailer. As we were walking back to the house he said, "What do you think of this weather?" "I don't know, it sure is hot." A few clouds were already moving in from the northwest when Jess said, "It is hard to believe but I listened to the news at noon and the weather report says there is a possibility of snow tonight. Have you ever seen snow on a tent, Billy?" "No, I haven't," I replied. "I haven't either and I hope I never do."

When we pulled up on the lot a light rain was falling and the wind had shifted around to the Northwest. I noticed Roy Garrett had the boys starting the coke fires. We would sure need them tonight. I told Vera as we went in the trailer I didn't expect many people to come to the show. It being Thanksgiving day and the weather so bad and maybe getting worse.

When it came time for the doors to open at 7:00 the weather was really bad. The wind was blowing, it was raining with mixture of sleet but in spite of the weather there were a few people sitting in their cars and standing under the marquee waiting. I thought to myself, you crazy people.

There was only about 75 or 100 people in the audience and we were sitting around in the dressing room waiting to see if we were going to show or not. Jess finally came back and announced, "There's not many out there but they are a brave and loyal bunch of Bisbee fans to come out in weather like this. Let's give them a good show and we will cut the concert." In all my years in the tent show business I have seen some disastrous situations but I have never seen an audience given their money back. I asked Grandpa Choate one time, "Grandpa, why does the show have to go on?" "So we don't have to give the audience their money back." That's a very good reason THE SHOW MUST GO ON.

After the show was over I went to the trailer and had night lunch. After I had eaten I told Vera I was going over to the tent to see if I could give Roy and the boys some help. Jess and Mary were leaving to go home and Jess rolled the window down and said, "Well Billy, you and I have both seen a first, snow on a tent, see you tomorrow." And he drove off. By this time, there was at least three inches on the ground, and worse, three inches on the tent.

I went under the side wall and up to the front of the tent where Roy and the rest of the boys were gathered around the cook stove. "Have you ever had any experience with snow on a tent, Billy?" Roy said, as I walked up. "No I haven't, but as this is a one season tent, I don't think you will have to worry about the canvas. What I am afraid of, if it keeps snowing and the weight keeps building up, the poles are going to break and she is going to come down." Roy said, "What we need is more heat in here to melt the snow faster." About that time a policeman walked in. He said his brother had a sawmill at the edge of town and sold firewood and even though it's after midnight he would probably bring us in a load. That

167

sounded like a great idea and Roy told the cop to get the wood as soon as possible. Thirty minutes later the man pulled up with a truck load of wood. By this time the center poles were bending and I knew it wouldn't be too much longer and they would break and the tent would come down. The boys unloaded the wood and built little bon fires. It wasn't long until the heat from the wood fires was melting the snow and we could see the center poles straighten up. However, the smoke from the wood fires was making the tent black. In just a matter of minutes the beautiful tent with all it's beautiful fringe was black as the ace of spades. I said to Roy, "Do you think this can be washed off?" He said, "No way, I wonder what Jess is going to say?"

The next morning Jess came over, looked at the blackened tent and said, "Well, we will just have to order a new tent for next season." Then he turned to Roy and said, "Now Roy, I don't want you to worry about this. It is not your fault, you did what you thought was right, so forget about it. Now, get your boys and load the inside, the season is closed."

Jess ordered a new tent from O'Henry Tent and Awning in Chicago. He sold the old top to a carnival operator and we heard later he had a Fire Department in some town in Arkansas wash it and it turned out looking pretty good.

The second week of September, 1957, the show was playing Dyersburg, Tennessee. We set up on the Ozment lot at the East end of town on Route 104, the road to Trenton.

We were looking for a place somewhere in Tennessee to store the outfit and a place for winter quarters. Mary had sold the place on Poplar Avenue and had moved to a smaller place on courtland. We were looking for a garage with apartments upstairs that we could buy. We hadn't found what we were looking for. However, our good friends, Jr. and Evelyn Nicholson at Dyer had told us about a house with a big back lot and a small building that was for sale or lease in Dyer. Friday, we decided to go to Dyer and look the place over. It wasn't exactly what we were looking for. However, the house was nice, there was a top notch school for the kids and we had a number of friends in Dyer so we leased the place for six months with an option to buy. We drove back to Dyersburg looking forward to spending the winter in Dyer and feeling very happy.

Saturday afternoon about four o'clock, a terrible storm hit us. I thought any minute the tent was going down but the boys kept gying out (tightening the ropes) as soon as they loosened and driving the stakes as soon as they pulled and they kept in the air.

However, the wind was so strong it ripped the canvas to pieces. When it was over there were pieces of canvas just hanging from the ropes. About six-thirty everyone was backstage trying to take care of their wardrobe and get it dried out when Curtis Jackson said, "There is a big crowd out front, are we going to show?" I went to the front and I couldn't believe my eyes. There was at least two hundred people lined up at the ticket box. I ran to the back and told everybody to grab a rag and start drying off the seats. Boob and Neva were featured as "Uncle Syp and Aunt Sap" in "Sweethearts Again", our closing night show. They had been drawing good houses all season long, Dyersburg was no exception even though the weather was terrible and conditions miserable. When the curtain went up, the tent was packed and jammed. During the second act, it started to rain, just a light rain, but heavy enough to get the audience wet. Even the performers were getting wet. But no one left and we continued the show. We tore down in a steady slow rain and the next morning we moved to Halls, Tennessee. It had cleared off and was a beautiful day so the boys spread the tent out. The "Ditty Bag" (I don't know why it was called "Ditty Bag") that held the sewing paraphernalia, the twine, beeswax, needles and the palms, used to push the needles through the canvas was brought

170

out and everybody started sewing. We put it up Monday morning and it didn't look too bad. We had about seven weeks till the end of the season and some good towns. However, I knew the tent was in bad shape and it would be nothing but trouble. So, Monday night after the show I gave a two week notice. We jumped to Dyer the next week and closed the season there. We spent a very enjoyable winter in Dyer and opened there in the spring of 1958 with a new tent.

The first week of August in 1961, the show was in Russelville, Kentucky. The lot was at the east end of town between Route 68 and Route 431 behind A.C. Smith's Gulf Station. A.C. was an old trouper who had worked on the W.I. Swain show for many years when he was a young man. We had set up on his lot for years and he treated us just like family. I needed to make a booking trip to Tennessee and I figured Friday was a good day to do it. I left about four o'clock after instructing Vera to open the doors at 7:00 as I might be late but would make it in time for the show. I drove to Union City and had breakfast at the Airport Cafe. I made arrangements for the lot and then went to the city hall to see about the license and see if they had been raised. They hadn't, so, I told the clerk what dates we would be playing and was on my way. I booked Obion, Halls and Ripley and then headed

171

back to Russelville.   There was some
road   construction   on   Ky.   Route   94
between Fulton and Murray that really
slowed me down.   I looked at my watch as
I crossed the bridge over Kentucky Lake
going into Cadiz and realized I wouldn't
have time to stop and eat; I would just
have to grab something after I got to
Russelville.   As   I   pulled   into   the
business district, I noticed the clock
on the bank said 7:10 p.m.   Vera would
have   the   doors   open.   She   would   be
worried about me but I would have plenty
of time to grab a sandwich, get my
makeup on and be ready when the curtain
went up at 8:00 p.m.   As I neared the
lot, I saw Vera standing in front of the
service station with a number of other
people.   I pulled in the driveway and
said, "What is the matter, why haven't
you got the doors open?" Then I saw she
was crying. "Oh Billy, a storm blew our
tent down." I walked around to the side
of the station and I couldn't believe my
eyes.   Everything was in a mess.   Part
of the tent was on top of the chair
truck, the stage was down, chairs were
scattered, everything was in a terrible
mess.   I thought to myself, how in the
world am I ever going to get this outfit
back on the road?   I noticed there were
a number of town people helping clean up
the mess and I realized how fortunate we
were to have so many friends, not only
in Russelville, but in the many other
towns Bisbee's Comedians played.   Vera

172

was standing beside me and said, "It only hit about thirty or forty minutes ago. Did you run into a storm?" "No," I answered, "it has been beautiful all day." I noticed Cliff Malcomb walking toward us. He put an arm over my should as he said, "Now Billy, this is not as bad as it looks. The canvas is in good shape, just a few small tears, surprisingly the scenery is in good shape. The only real damage is the ropes, every one of them is broken. I can splice rope, so can Leo Lacey, Audra Hardesty and one of the canvasman says he is a rope splicer. So, get us new rope and give us one day and we will have this outfit up an ready to show." Cliff had no idea how he had raised my morale when it was at its lowest ebb. Early the next morning a truck was sent to Nashville to pick up a thousand feet of 1" rope and by 4:00 p.m. the new rope was spliced. We moved to Hopkinsville Sunday morning, set the outfit up and you couldn't tell we had been in a tornado. In fact, the office personnel at Hatch Show Print in Nashville where we purchased our billing paper, heard on the radio we had been hit by a tornado, so they drove up to see the damage and were surprised to see the tent up and with so little visible damage except the spliced ropes. We used this tent another season before replacing it.

PART XIII
THE BRASFIELD'S

Lawrence LaMar Brasfield was born March 1, 1898. His brother, Rod, was born August 21, 1910. They were both born at Smithville, Mississippi. They had a brother named Paul who had no inclination to go into the show business or appear on the stage. He remained in Mississippi and later became Sheriff of Monroe County. Their father's name was James Calvin and their mother's name was Nonnie. She was never on the stage but I am sure Lawrence (Hereafter, I'll refer to him as Boob) and Rod got their great talent and ability from their mother. She was a little lady with a southern drawl and a booming voice that could be heard for miles. She never met a stranger. If she met you once, the next time she saw you, she would say, "Honey, how ya all?" and then give you a big bear hug. She had a ferocious laugh. When she came to visit the show she had a special chair that was positioned in front of the stage on the front row. Before the curtain went up Boob would introduce her and she liked that. I heard her tell Boob one night as one of the boys was getting ready to escort her to her chair, "Don't forget to introduce me." The show would start and you could hear her infectious laugh above everyone in the audience. Boob said to me one night, after making an

174

exit, "Wouldn't it be great to have an audience of a 1,000 people like Mama?"

The show was playing Obion, Tennessee when Boob received word his mother had passed away. He asked me to drive him to Smithville and we arrived there early in the morning. Rod, Paul, the rest of the family and some neighbors were there and we went in the bedroom where Mrs. Brasfield lay. As I stood there with the grieving family who was most heart-stricken at the loss of this dear one, I thought of the many sorrows and heartaches she must have experienced, then I thought of all the laughter and happiness she brought to other people. Later Boob told me he was late getting to the funeral home on visitation night and there was a big crowd as Lonnie Brasfield was well known and respected all over the county. Boob said when he walked in the funeral home there was chatter and laughter. He said he was shocked and surprised. Then he went among the crowd saying hello and shaking people's hands and thanking them for coming and telling them how much he appreciated it and then, he said he realized why they were laughing. He said they were remembering their association with his mother. They were remembering funny stories she had told them and they were repeating these funny stories and pretty soon the room was full of laughter.

At the age of 14, the Mighty Haag

circus came through Smithville and Boob went with it as a canvasman. The next year he was doing blackface comedy with a horse and wagon show. Then before too long, he was traveling with a unit of the famed Red Path Chautauqua which featured William Jennings Bryan. Then for 10 years or so, he played in hit shows on Broadway and directed many of them on the road. In 1920, he was stage manager for Brock Pemberton's "Enter Madam" which had a two year run on Broadway. He left that to become stage manager for "Abie's Irish Rose" at the Republic Theatre on Broadway. After this he had a part in Pemberton's "Miss Lula Bett" which ran one year on Broadway and two on the road. Then he joined his first tent repertoire show, Cooke's Comedians in Alabama. This is where he met Neva. She had been a leading lady on the W.I. Swain show and they were married that summer.

I met Rod for the first time when I joined Bisbee's Comedians for the 1941 season. He and Elinor had been married a number of years. Elinor was from Hohenwald, Tennessee and they met while the show was playing there. They broke her into parts and she became a very good actress. She came from a very fine family. Her maiden name was Humphries and her brother and father were lawyers. If I remember right, her dad was judge of Lewis County for many years.

Elinor stayed in Hohenwald while

176

Rod and I joined Boob who had a show in the Gadsden theatre in Gadsden, Alabama. I really believe it was at this time that Rod started drinking heavily. It never affected his work but he had a bottle at all times within arms length.

We stayed with Boob until April and then joined Bisbee in Memphis for rehearsals. Rod continued drinking that summer and he and Elinor had problems which were not helped by his drinking. However, no matter how much alcohol he consumed he never missed a line. I have seen him when he could hardly stand up in the dressing room but when his cue came, he would hit that stage and the audience never suspected he had been drinking. Rod was a great comedian, like his brother Boob, his timing was perfect. He was a great Toby comedian on Bisbee's Comedians for years. Also, he could take his teeth out, put on a bald wig and he was a star in character comedy or G-string parts.

On account of the war, Bisbee's Comedians did not go on the road in 1943. It was at this time Rod joined WSM's Grand Ole Opry in Nashville, Tennessee. He became the best known male comic in the country music circle and drew hundreds of thousands to Rymer Auditorium. He was a comedy partner of Minnie Pearle for many years.

After the war, in the late forties and early fifties, Rod would work one night a week with the Bisbee show as a special added attraction. He was very popular at that time and was a great draw for us. We always packed the tent the night he worked with the show. Fordsville, Kentucky was a small town with a population of only 500 people. However, many a night we would put over 1,500 people in the tent. I had many friends in Fordsville. I considered Mr. Cooper and his son, who ran the Fordsville Bank, my good friends. I can't remember the exact year but we pulled into Fordsville, set up on the high school grounds and, as usual, we opened Monday night to a packed house. I announced that Rod Brasfield would be on our stage Friday night, knowing full well this would assure us of another packed house. Friday afternoon, Mr. Cooper came to the lot to see me. We visited for awhile and finally he said, "Billy, there is a rumor going around town saying that Rod Brasfield is not going to be here tonight." I said, "Why that is ridiculous, you don't think I would advertise he was going to be here if I knew he wasn't, do you?" "Of course not," he replied, "I just thought you should know what was going around town even if it is a rumor." "Well you just tell everyone to come on down and buy their tickets, Rod will be here. But if he doesn't show up, they will still see a good show." After he got in his car and left I stood there with many thoughts running through my mind.

Unless something drastic happened, Rod would be here to do the show. He always had. He was a trouper, he would never blow the show. Still I said a little prayer, please, don't let him miss this one. I went to see my good friend, Noble Midkiff. He and his wife were among our best friends. They had a boy and two girls and Welby Charles and Cherita practically lived at their house when we played Fordsville. I asked Noble if he had heard the rumor about Rod not showing up. He said, "Yes, I have. But if I were you I wouldn't let it worry me. Has Rod ever failed you before?" I answered, "No." "Well, he will be here. Another thing, Rod likes Fordsville and has many friends here I'll bet he is looking forward to seeing. Now, if I were you, I would just put it out of my head." As I drove back to the lot, I felt better after talking to Noble, but I sure would be happy when Rod drove up.

It was 6:45 and Vera came out of the trailer to open the box office. As I walked with her to the front of the tent she asked, "Wonder why Rod isn't here?" "I don't know, he is always here in the early afternoon on the nights he works with us. I hope something hasn't happened to him especially with all this talk about him not being here going around town." As always, Vera said, "Well don't worry about it."

The curtain went up on the first

act to a packed house and Rod still hadn't shown up. The second act was almost over and I was thinking about the announcement I was about to make. "Ladies and Gentlemen, we don't know what has happened but Rod Brasfield is not here. We fear he has had an accident. So if there is anyone here who came especially to see Rod, you can go to the front box office and your money will be gladly refunded." Luckily I didn't have to make that announcement. Rod came under the side wall just as the curtain came down on the second act. I was so happy to see him I grabbed him and hugged him. I said, "Tell me what happened later, right now you are on." I went out and happily introduced him, he grabbed his old oversized coat and old hat and went out and did the same routine he had been doing for years, and as always, the audience loved it.

It was a hot July day in 1958. The show was playing Morganfield, Kentucky. I had been visiting with my friend, Mr. Veatch, who owned the furniture store and had been a friend of my father years before, as I drove up on the lot. Rod was getting out of his car, a brand new Cadillac. After the usual pleasantries, I said, "That is a beautiful car, Rod. When did you get it?" "Just bought it this week," he replied, "There was nothing wrong with my Oldsmobile, I just wanted a new car. Another thing," he continued, "I have it financed with GMAC and I have their paid for death policy. The way I feel I doubt if I make one payment." I saw he was really serious. "Why Rod, you will out last me." Then he told me what I had suspected. "I went through a complete physical last week. The doctors tell me my heart is damaged beyond repair so, I don't have much time left. Jimmie is the beneficiary." (Jimmie is the boy he and Elinor adopted in 1947.) "So he will get the car if something happens to me." By the way, Billy, don't say anything to Boob about this. No use upsetting him."

Just a few weeks later in September while the show was playing Martin, Tennessee, Rod passed away with a massive heart attack. I understand he was at his home in Nashville. The phone rang, he got up to answer it and fell to the floor before he could reach the phone. I was so sorry I couldn't attend the funeral. I thought about closing the show for one night but I knew Rod wouldn't want me to do that. Rod was 48 years old and is buried in the Pearce Chapel Cemetery at Smithville, Mississippi where he was born.

Though they were brothers, there was a difference in the way Rod and Boob did their comedy on the stage. Rod was active, this is not to say Boob was inactive but Rod was always moving. He might even jump over a table and he talked faster than Boob. However, neither one of them could be surpassed

when it came to timing and double takes.
We did a show where the leading man
kisses the leading lady at the climax of
the second act. Boob enters the center
door, sees them, does a double take,
looks at them and then to the audience,
puts one arm over the other in his
favorite stance, and continues these
looks. The audience howls. He would
milk them for three or four minutes
before signaling for the curtain to come
down. I had witnessed this scene many
times but I always managed to get out
front or in the wings to see it over and
over again. I always laughed and when
the curtain came down, I always thought
to myself, "Billy Charles, you have just
witnessed a genius at work."

Timing can't be taught. It is not
a 1-2-3 thing. It is a natural ability.
Very few people are born with the God
given talent. Boob Brasfield was one of
them. We did a version of Trail of the
Lonesome Pine which I think was written
by Neil Scaffner. The following excerpt
is a fairly typical of a scene, to be
funny, depended upon the timing ability
of both actors:

TOBY: And cousin Fud and his four kids
were there.....
SUSIE: He's got five kids, ain't he?
TOBY: No, they's only four. Elviry is
one.....(counting
            on fingers) and his twins is
two.....Oliver is three

                    and the half witted one is four.
SUSIE: You said the twins is two.
TOBY: Well, the twins is two.
SUSIE: No, they ain't.   The twins is
three.
TOBY: All right then, the two twins is
three, Elviry is
                    four, Oliver is five and the
half witted one is six!
SUSIE: Toby Tolliver, you said the two
twins is three.
TOBY: That's what you said.
SUSIE: I did not.   Now listen, the
first twin is one, the
                    second twin is two.....
TOBY: Yeah, two and one is three.
SUSIE: Elviry is four.....
TOBY: Four and three is.....wait a
minute, Susie, you got
                    seven already and you ain't
counted Oliver ner the
                    half witted one yet.

          Boob was an alcoholic.   He hadn't
had a drink of whiskey or beer since
1945.   However, he was on terpinhydrate
and codeine.   This was a liquid which
was about 60 percent alcohol and was
used as a cough suppressant and could be
bought at a drug store without a
prescription.   There were times when he
took too much codeine and his speech
would become slurred.   Also, if he
didn't keep moving, when he set down he
would immediately go to sleep.
          We   were   playing   Greenville,

                    183

Kentucky. Boob had an appointment with a orthopedic surgeon in St. Louis. He wanted me to drive him. On the way back, I noticed Boob was hitting the codeine quite often. I stopped to get gasoline and asked him if he needed to use the rest room. He said, "No you go ahead. I don't need to go." I used the rest room, paid the attendant and got in the car. I looked at Boob, he was asleep but he had a funny look on his face. I tried to wake him up but could not arouse him. By this time, I was frightened and was thinking he might be having a heart attack. I grabbed him and started shaking him vigorously all the time talking to him. Finally, he opened his eyes and said, "Billy, what in the hell are you trying to do to me?" I explained I thought he was having some kind of attack and I was scared. He said, "Well, in the future if you want to wake me up, do it easy, pat me on the cheek and say, Boob, would you please wake up? I'll oblige you, and another thing, you better step on it. We don't want to be late for the show." With that said, he took a swig of codeine and was fast asleep once more.

Boob Brasfield had a heart of gold. I really believe he would have parted with his last dollar for someone in need. By the same token, he had a terrible temper and would cut people down unmercifully, even his best friends.

184

He also had the bad habit of taking
his feelings with him on the stage and
talking to the audience about whatever
had upset him. One night he was very
mad at me, I don't remember why, anyway
when he went out to make the
announcement he started talking about me
and making snide remarks, never
mentioning my name of course. However,
I knew who he was talking about. When
he came off the stage I confronted him.
He said, "Billy, I love you, I wasn't
talking about you." I told him if he
ever did it again I was coming out with
him and we would settle whatever was
bugging him before the audience. Never
again did he talk about me in his
announcements but that didn't stop him
from bringing up others he was upset
with. One night during his announcement
he went on and on about the many gossips
and backbiters there were on the show.
The audience thought it was funny but
Johnny Spaulding was very upset and when
Boob came off the stage they went round
and round. He threatened to give his
notice but stayed when Boob apologized
and said it would not happen again.
    In the fall of 1952, Boob decided
to put a show in the Arena Theatre at
Paducah, Kentucky. The Bisbee show
closed the second week in November and
we moved to Paducah for what we thought
was to be a nice winters engagement. It
turned out to be a disaster. We
rehearsed for about ten days and opened

185

the first week in December. Boob brought Rod in for the opening and we packed and jammed them for two shows the opening day. The next day, Vera and I had dinner with our good friends Roy and Ruby Clark. Roy was on the city commission and we had been good friends since 1946. Bisbee's Comedians played Paducah in 1946 under the auspices of the Police Department and at that time Roy was a Police Captain and this is how we met. We became friends and remained so throughout the years. After dinner we went out on the front porch. It was a beautiful December day. Roy remarked, "This is an unusual day for this time of the year. I am afraid it is a weather breeder. We are in for some bad weather." Little did I know how right he was.

We had another large crowd that night and between the first and second show Vera said I should go over to the trailer and light the stove. The wind was blowing and it had turned much colder, and had started snowing. The next morning there was eight inches of snow on the ground. It continued snowing off and on for the next five weeks and the temperature was in the teens and bitter cold. Business was terrible so Boob gave a notice and we closed the second week in January. Vera and I decided to go to Wayne City and await the 1953 tent season.

We had only been in Wayne City a

couple of weeks when I had a letter from Jess wanting me to come down and help get the outfit painted and ready to go for the coming season. We left Wayne City early one Sunday morning. The weather was good and we made good time and pulled into Memphis around 4:00 p.m. With the help of Cliff Malcomb, Leonard Houston and Calvin Smiley, we had the outfit painted and in tiptop shape for the opening in Lexington the second week of April.

Members of the show for the 1953 season were Boob Brasfield, Leo and Maxine Lacey, Mickey Lacey, Charlie and Vivian McDowell, Octavia Powell and Otis Arnold, Otto and Esther Imig, Neva Brasfield, Audra and Virginia Hardesty, Dick and Virginia Tannas, Marvin and Ginny Girard, Cliff and Mabel Malcomb, Carvelee Osbourn, Jess and Mary Bisbee, Vera and myself and a canvas crew of six.

Boob had been going to a doctor in Nashville. This doctor had given Boob an unlimited subscription for paraldehyde. As I understand it, this is a drug given for drug and alcohol abuse. Supposedly, it is given to calm a person down. It worked just the opposite on Boob. Of course, I don't know what else he was taking, but when he went on paraldehyde, he became very volatile, sometimes becoming violent. One night after the show, he broke all the men's hand mirrors, including mine.

187

However, the next morning Neva bought new mirrors to replace the ones he had broken.

We were showing Hopkinsville, Kentucky. Friday morning, I was coming out of the trailer when Neva drove up. "Billy, do you know if Jess is up? I must talk to him." "I am sure he is," I replied, "is there something wrong?" "Yes, there is something wrong, Bras is sick and won't be able to make the show tonight and it is all your fault." I couldn't believe what I was hearing. "My fault? Why is it my fault?" By this time, I am getting upset and her answer really provoked me. She said, "He says you have been talking about him to the other people on the show, telling them lies behind his back. He says he doesn't know whether he can finish the season with you on the show." I was dumbfounded and said, "Neva, you go back and tell Boob if he has anything to say about or to me, to get down here and say it to my face as I am not going to listen to anymore of this crap from you." With that I walked away. About ten minutes later, I was in the back of the tent when Jess came over. "Did Neva talk to you?" he asked. "She sure did." "Well, you know not to pay any attention to her. She says he can't make the show tonight so I am going to ask Otto Imig if he will do his part. Guess I had better call a rehearsal also." Otto Imig had been the featured comedian

playing the Toby parts on the Kennedy
Stock Co. in Ohio for many years. The
Kennedy show had closed and Otto and his
wife, Ester, had joined the Bisbee show
to do general business and character
parts. Otto did the Toby part Friday
and Saturday nights and did a bang up
job. Sunday we moved to Union City,
Tennessee. We set the outfit up Monday
morning and that afternoon I was in the
dressing room when Boob walked in. Jess
had told me he was in town and would
work that night. After the usual
pleasantries, he said, "Billy, I think I
owe you an apology. You know me well
enough to know I sometimes say things
that later I am sorry for. I hope you
will accept my apology?" I got up out
of the chair I was sitting in and said,
"Boob, there is something I need to say.
From now on if you have something to say
to me, don't send Neva to say it. Is
that understood?" "Yes, it is," he
replied. "Then let's shake hands."
Which we did. We had many more
disagreements over the years. Boob
thrived on trouble. If there wasn't
some trouble around, he would make some.

PART XIV
OWNER, MANAGER BISBEE COMEDIANS

At the end of the hectic 1953 season, we moved into winter quarters at Memphis and immediately started getting the outfit ready for the next season. We had been in Memphis about a month when one afternoon Jess said, "Billy, I want you and Vera to come to the house tonight. No particular time, just come when you are ready." I told Vera while we were eating supper I had no idea what Jess wanted. However, I knew it was something important as he wanted both of us to be there.

At 7:30 we walked in the house and went to the living room where Jess and Mary were. We talked a few minutes and I could tell they were both in a good mood. I felt a little easier. Being in this festive mood, what they had to tell us couldn't be all that bad. Mary fixed some coffee and served us some cake. Finally Jess said, "Well, we have a surprise for you and we think you are going to like the proposition we have for you. Billy, you are going to be the manager of the show for the coming season. You will be in complete charge. Now, it is a great responsibility but I know you can handle it. We will both "take a draw" until the opening expense is paid for. Then, we will split the net 50-50. I will put up the money for the opening. We need a new truck and

there are many other details to be
worked out. What do you think of the
proposition?" "Well, I am almost
speechless. I don't know what to say or
how to thank you." Mary spoke up and
said, "Well, we made our mind up last
summer we were going to turn the
management of the show over to you."
"Yes, and sometime in the future," Jess
added, "we want you two to take over the
ownership, outfit, name and all." He
also told us Boob would not be coming
back and he had hired and signed Dick
Ellis who had been doing the Toby parts
on Tilton's Comedians in Iowa. We had
heard that Dick was a very clever
comedian and what we had heard was true.
His wife, Lee, was also a fine actress.

We talked and discussed things that
should and could be done to improve the
overall operation of the show for the
coming season. It must have been about
1:00 when we decided to call it a night.
Vera and I left for home and we were
both on cloud nine. Maybe a little
higher than that. I went to bed but I
couldn't sleep. I lay there thinking of
the great responsibility that would be
on my shoulders. Besides the worry of
tearing down, moving and setting up a
tent theatre that seated 1,500 people
and moved on six semi trucks, there was
the weather and storms that was always a
worry. Then there were 30 people,
actors, actresses, and canvasmen that
were together practically 24 hours a

191

day, and some way, these temperamental people had to be kept happy. Otherwise, they would be at each others throat. Tent show people were very loyal to the show they were on but they would fight among themselves at the drop of a hat.

We opened in the spring at Lexington with a fine cast, including Leo and Maxine Lacey, Mickey Lacey, Dick and Lee Ellis, Otis Arnold and Octavia Powell, Gene and Audra Bradley, Leon Block, Jimmie and Jean Weir, Audra and Virginia Hardesty, Bud and Pattie Imig, and the Kriel family which consisted of Mom and Dad and three kids. The kids were very clever and were the feature vaudeville act. There was Dick, Jeannie, and Patricia. They did a number of outstanding acts including tumbling, balancing, juggling and they had an outstanding dog act. A number of years later, Dick married Judy Richards who was the ingenue. She was a very cute girl and later became a well known writer and author and has had a number of books published.

Jess and Mary came to Lexington to catch the opening. The show went over very well and I thought Dick Ellis did a bang up job. After the show, Jess and Mary came over to the trailer. While Vera was fixing night lunch, I said, "Well, what do you think?" "You have a good show," he replied, "however, I think Dick Ellis would get more out of his Toby part if he would slow down. He talks too fast." I told Jess I thought he was going to do a good job but we couldn't change his style of working and we didn't want him trying to imitate Boob Brasfield, even if he could. As Jess and Mary left, Jess said, "I may have a talk with Ellis tomorrow." I said to myself, I hope he doesn't, but I knew he would.

1955 was a memorable year for a number of reasons. After the 1954 season closed, I immediately started organizing and signing people for the 1955 season. Every three years we painted all the equipment, trucks, chairs, stage, blues, and poles. We dipped the chairs in large vats, then hung them by hooks on rods placed between scissor jacks. This method was fast but it still took a lot of time and work to finish 1,500 chairs. They were painted white with a red top. So, they were run through the process two times. Finally, the second week in March, the outfit was repaired, painted and ready to hit the road. We took a trip to Illinois to see our folks and was back in Memphis for rehearsals the first week in April. We had put together another fine cast, including Dick and Lee Ellis, The McDowells, Leo and Maxine Lacey and Mickey, Audra and Virginia Hardesty, Bob Fisher, Dick Lewis, Wendel Poe, The Girards, The Kriel family and Neil Suddard. Neil had been on the show back in 1947 and 1948. At that time, he had a unicycle act, a juggling act and played trumpet in the orchestra. He was a very clever and talented young man. He was also blessed with stage presence and a great personality. With that certain magnetism and smile, he had the audience in the palm of his hand, from the time he made his entrance to his exit. This is an attribute that cannot be bought, nor can it be taught. It is a God given talent that very few people are lucky enough to process. Of all the actors and actresses I worked with, only a few had this ability. Octavia Powell, Maxine Lacey, Vivian McDowell, Berniece Zarlington, Harry Willard, Boob Brasfield and my mother, Mae Choate, would have to be put into this category.

One sunny Sunday afternoon Jess and I were sitting on the patio discussing the coming season when Neil Suddard drove in on the concrete drive. He had an enclosed two wheel trailer on the back of his car with a sign on the side, in script, which said, NEIL SUDDARD ORGANIST. After the usual pleasantries, he told us he had been playing the organ for three years, playing all kinds of dates, churches, fairs, night clubs, etc. He said he would like to troupe on the Bisbee show one more season and asked if we could use him. I said, "What about your unicycle? Do you still do that act?" He replied with a smile and said, "Oh no Billy, I don't do any of my old acts. The only thing I will

194

do is play the organ. I will do three
numbers a night with an encore." He
told us the salary he would have to
have, which was a little high, I
thought. Jess got out of his chair and
said, "Neil when you were on the show
before you did some clever acts and
worked out fine. But I don't know about
this proposition. In the first place, I
can't see an organ on a tent show, and
in the second place, you are asking for
too much money." Neil brought out his
wallet, took out a card, gave it to Jess
and said, "Well, think it over.
Whatever you decide give me a ring. I
will be at this number all day
tomorrow." Neil got in his car and
drove off. Jess said, "Well, what do
you think?" "I think," I replied, "we
should hire him and I haven't heard him
play the organ." Jess said, "OK, call
him in the morning. We can always give
him a two weeks notice if he doesn't
work out."

We opened the season at Lexington
the second week in April. We moved in
there on Sunday morning and went to
church with our good friends, Henry and
LaVerne Davenport. We had known Henry
and LaVerne since 1946. Henry was a
Bisbee fan and had been even before I
joined the show.

O'Henry Tent and Awning of Chicago
had built us a new tent and the new
tent, side wall, marquee, and proscenium
was at the depot waiting to be picked up

195

Monday morning. I could hardly wait to
see the outfit. At 8:00 a.m. the new
60X155 dramatic end was raised in the
air, the marquee put up, the stage,
chairs and blues set and as Jess and I
stood by the reserve seat ticket box and
surveyed what was before us, Jess said,
"There may have been bigger tent shows
in the past but none as pretty as this
one." At that moment they dropped the
new front curtain Jess had painted. It
was magnificent! We didn't realize it
at the time, but this front curtain
would be the last Jess would paint.

Monday night we opened the doors at
7:00 and at 10 minutes till 8:00 we had
a full house. I could hardly wait for
Neil to do his specialty. We had built
him a small stage for his organ which
was at the left of the stage and in
front of the proscenium. It had two
spotlights and a large mirror so the
audience could see Neil no matter where
they were sitting. The show was going
over great and after the second act I
introduced Neil. The spotlights came
on, he came out in his tuxedo looking
like a million dollars. He sat down and
played three numbers. The audience went
wild. He tried to beg off but the
people would have none of it and he had
to do an encore, just like he said he
would.

After the last curtain came down I
got my makeup off, checked a few things
and headed for the trailer. Vera, Jess

196

and Mary were already there and of course we started critiquing the show. Finally I said, "Well Jess I don't think we were wrong in hiring Neil Suddard, he went over like a house afire." "Yeah," Jess replied, "it's that damn personality he has." Mary said, "It's God given." As I was pouring another cup of coffee, I said, "I wish God had laid some of it on me."

In every town we played, Neil captivated the audience. The old women loved him, the young girls loved him and the men thought he was great.

Jess developed heart trouble. He had three or four attacks. His doctor had ordered him to quit smoking but he was still having his cigarettes but not in front of Mary. When he lit a cigarette, Mary was nowhere in sight. One hot sunny spring day we had been lettering the trucks and Jess suggested we go in the guest house, cool off and have a coke. Which we did. I went to the bathroom and when I came out Jess was slouched in the settee. I took one look at him and knew immediately he had suffered a heart attack. As he was putting a nitro glycerin tablet under his tongue, he said, "Now Billy, don't get excited. I am going to be OK." "I'll call the ambulance." "No you won't, he said. "Then I will call Mary." "No, just get me a glass of water." I got him some water and said, "Please Jess, let me call the ambulance." "No, I am fine," and with that, he got up and went to the door, turned around and said, "Now Billy, I don't want you to say one word about this to Mary, do you understand?" I shook my head, yes. As he went out the door, I wondered how many heart attacks he went through when no one was around.

The show moved through its spring Tennessee towns and then into Kentucky. We got a break in the weather and business was good. Also, there was not too much trouble. For this I was thankful.

The second week in June we played Benton the first part of the week and then Thursday we jumped to LaCenter and opened there Thursday night. Friday morning I went to Paducah to pick up some things. When I arrived back and as I was going in the trailer, Curtis Jackson handed me a note that had a number I was supposed to call as soon as possible. I recognized the number as Jess and Mary's and I immediately knew something had happened as Jess never called me. I jumped in the car and hurried to the telephone office which was located in a home. I went in and a little lady sat at the single switch board. I gave her the number and she motioned me to a wall phone. She put me through and George Jeanught, Mary's brother, was on the line telling me Jess had passed away the night before at 11:00 p.m. with a heart attack. The

funeral was to be Sunday at 3:00 p.m.
He told me of other arrangements and
continued by saying, "Billy, I
understand you and Jess had discussed
this possibility and he had told you
what he wanted you to do, so you just
carry out his wishes and we will see you
Sunday."

I knew the operator had heard our
conversation and as I was leaving I told
her I would appreciate it if she would
not say anything about Jess passing
away. She replied, "Mr. Choate, you
can't keep something like this a secret.
Mr. Bisbee was too well known." She was
right. The wire services had already
picked it up and the local radio
stations were broadcasting the news at
that moment.

As I drove back to the lot many
memories flooded my mind. Some good and
some bad. Jess had been so good to me,
Vera and the kids and though he hadn't
been with the show a couple of years, I
wondered if Bisbee's Comedians could
continue without his guidance. I knew
he wanted the show to continue but I
knew it would be a problem not being
able to go to him for advice. One thing
I knew for sure, I was certainly going
to miss him.

When I arrived at the lot I called
a meeting for 2:00. When everyone was
assembled I told them of Jess's passing
and that the funeral would be at Memphis
at 3:00 p.m. I told them the show would

continue not closing even for one night. Everyone was very sad and I wondered if it would effect the performance that night. It didn't, however, it did effect our business. We had a small house and Saturday night was worse.

Early Sunday morning we moved to Clinton and as soon as everything was set on the lot we left for Memphis. Jess had a nice service and was buried in Memorial Cemetery on Poplar Avenue, just a few blocks from the Bisbee winter quarters.

Jess's death was hard on Mary. I tried to get her to go back with us and stay with the show a few days but she didn't want to. Her brother and his wife, George and Myrtle, lived in Memphis and would be there to see about her. I was thankful for that.

Monday morning after the outfit was set up, Vera and I met our good friends, Dr. Jackson and his wife, Marie, for lunch. They had been in Clinton for many years. Later they moved to Lexington and he was the doctor for the University of Kentucky basketball team.

The rest of the 1955 season was uneventful. After Jess passed away, it just seemed everyone pulled together to make the show run smooth. So we rolled along with no major problems and closed the season in Collierville. Once again, we moved into Memphis winter quarters and immediately started getting the outfit ready for the next season.

All through the years Jess had
never carried insurance, liability or
otherwise. The show had only been sued
one time. That was in Russelville when
the canvasmen got in a fight with the
two drunks during the show and a
pregnant woman was injured. However,
when I took over the show in 1956 times
had changed. It seemed like every time
you turned around, someone was getting
sued. I figured I had better get
liability insurance before some disaster
hit the show and wiped us out. There
was an agent in Florida who insured
outdoor amusements. His name was Lenz
and the company he represented was
Lloyds of London. I contacted Mr. Lenz
and when we hit the road in 1956 we had
liability insurance. The cost was high
but I felt better knowing we were
covered if something did happen. We
closed the 1956 season in Collierville,
Tennessee. We moved into winter
quarters at Memphis and tucked
everything away for the winter. I was
thankful we had gone through the season
without any serious accidents. I was
thinking I could sure use the money I
had paid out for the insurance. It
amounted to quite a sum of money as the
premium was high and they also took a
percentage of the gross. But I was
happy that nothing serious had happened.

A few days later, Vera, the kids
and I were getting ready to leave on a
trip to Illinois when the phone rang.

201

It was an insurance adjuster informing me Bisbee's Comedians was being sued by a woman in Collierville who claimed she had tripped on a rope causing her to fall and hurt herself. He said, "Now Mr. Choate, don't worry about this, our lawyer will take care of everything." I told him we were leaving for Illinois and would be gone for a week. He said, "That is all right, I am sure it will take weeks before this is settled. If we need you, we will get in touch. Here is my phone number, you might check with me when you get back from Illinois." We spent a week in Illinois with our folks and as soon as we got back to Memphis I called the adjuster. He had no news for me. Time went on and with the help of two boys and Cliff Malcomb, we proceeded to paint and repair the outfit for the coming season.

I had completely forgotten about the suit, when one afternoon in January the adjuster came out to the house. We talked for awhile and finally he said, "Well Mr. Choate, the lawyer had decided to settle with the woman. Her lawyer has agreed to a $4,000.00 settlement and not go to court. We could beat her in court, but this is the easy way out. If we went to court it would be years before it was settled. Of course as you know," he continued, "there was a $600.00 deductible and I would like to get your check today, if that is possible?" That was another thing I had forgotten about, the $600.00 deductible. It hurt writing the check but I was wise in taking out the insurance as it would have cost me much more without it.

The next season we were playing Linden, Tennessee. The second act was just over and I was getting ready to introduce the specialties when a gentleman asked if he could talk to me. I came down off the stage and he said, "My little boy just got hurt. A chair he was sitting on folded and he hurt his hand." I told him how sorry I was and he asked, "Do you have insurance?" "No," I told him, "however, you take your son to the hospital and I will pay the bill." "Well," he said, "if you don't have insurance I think I will just wait and see how he is in the morning, me and the wife want to see the rest of the show." And he turned and walked away. I vowed right then, no matter what happened, I would not admit to having insurance. I was thinking of that $600.00 deductible.

Princeton, Kentucky was one of our better towns. If we got a break in the weather we always did well financially. In most of the towns we played we changed lots quite often. Usually, a new building forced us to a new location. But not Princeton, Bisbee's Comedians set on the same lot for 42 straight years. In later years, it was owned by Francis Dawson and had been in her family for years. Her father owned a drug store in Princeton and if I remember correctly, they called him Deacon Dawson. Directly in front of and across the street was a grocery store owned by J.W. Quinn. He had six pretty girls. My kids played with his girls and our families became very close friends. If I needed a favor in Princeton I could always count on J.W. to help me.

It was a beautiful July night in Princeton. As usual on opening night the natives were lined up buying tickets for the show. I was walking to the front of the tent to tell the boy running the P.A. and playing the records to turn the volume down as it was too loud when I noticed a couple getting out of a new Ford. When she shut the door she fell. Her husband went around the car and helped her to her feet. They talked awhile then she got back in the car and he came over on the lot, went to the ticket box and asked where he could find the manager. I was standing just outside the marquee. He came over and said, "My wife just fell." I said, "Yes, I know she did, I saw her fall." Then he inquired if I had insurance. I told him I did not carry insurance. I could tell my answer shocked him. "How in the hell can you run a business like this and not have liability insurance?" I told him it cost so much I just couldn't afford it. He turned and went back to his car. I watched him and

204

thought to myself my story was not going to work this time as I really believed he was going to sue. However, after talking to his wife for a few minutes, they both got out of the car, bought their tickets and went to the show. I never saw them or heard from them again.

It was always a pleasure to play Eddyville, Kentucky. I had many friends in Eddyville. Mr. and Mrs. Bill Henninger, L.B. Fuqua and Frank Tanner were among the many I was privileged to call my friends. At that time, Frank Tanner was the mayor. He was a fine gentleman who owned a clothing store. We became friends and he proved his friendship by helping me in many ways after I became owner of Bisbee's Comedians.

One year we pulled into Eddyville for a three day engagement. The campaign for governor was in full swing, and as usual, things were getting hot and heavy. Things always picked up at election time in Kentucky. I remember once we were showing Morgantown. Back at that time, Saturday was the big shopping day. Everybody came to town on Saturday. It was also the custom for the politicians to set up their public address systems on the courthouse lawn and make their political speeches. On this particular Saturday in Morgantown, there were four politicians and one itinerant preacher with the volume on their PA systems turned on high. No one could be heard but that didn't stop them from talking. I had just come out of Fleenor's Restaurant and was making my way through the crowded sidewalk to the courthouse lawn as I wanted to hear some of the political oratory. All of a sudden I heard this yelling and screaming and I could see a fight was in progress and many men were involved. Soon, it seemed the whole courthouse lawn was full of flying fists. The police came and broke up the fights and took some to jail and others to the doctors. I heard one old man standing behind me say, "I wish the cops wouldn't break these fights up, I like to watch them. Also it's a good way to get rid of politicians." I was wondering what had become of the preacher when I noticed him going down the street in his old car with a sign on the back which said, "Jesus Saves." I am sure Jesus took care of the preacher but I imagine his running feet also had a great deal to do with him getting away from the fracas.

The afternoon of our opening night in Eddyville I went to Tanner's Store to see Frank, have a visit with him and take him his passes for the show. He waited on a customer and after he left Frank said, "Billy I don't want to impose upon you but as you know Happy Chandler is running for governor and he will be here Saturday afternoon for a rally. It was planned for the courthouse lawn. Some of the boys and I were thinking, if you would let us have it here in your tent, it would be better for all concerned," he continued, "you have the stage, the chairs, the sound system, in fact everything we need. Of course, we would be more than willing to pay you for the use of your tent theatre, what do you say?" "Frank, I need to do something to repay you for all the help you have given me in the past, of course you can use the tent theatre and I will not charge you one cent." He seemed real happy and said, "That is great, we will get it advertised." We shook hands and as I left I had a warm feeling because I was able to help my old friend. When I got back to the lot Vera was sitting under the awning of our trailer. She asked, "Did you see Mr. Tanner?" I explained to her that Happy Chandler would use the tent Saturday afternoon for a Democrat rally. She said, "Do you think some people might get upset if Happy Chandler holds a political rally in Bisbee's Comedians tent? You know how radical politics are here in Kentucky." "To tell you the truth, I hadn't thought about that." The next morning I drove to the post office to get some stamps. As I was getting out of my car a gentleman approached me and said, "My family and I have been going to Bisbee's for years, but I want to tell you if Happy Chandler holds a rally in your

207

tent Saturday, I'll never attend another one of your shows." He didn't wait for my answer, he just turned and walked away. I wondered how many other people felt the same way he did. I knew I had to talk to Frank and fast. As I walked in his store he was standing behind the counter and I was relieved to see he had no customers and we were alone. I told him what had happened at the post office. He was very sympathetic and said under the circumstances he thought they should have the rally at the courthouse as planned. Even though I had given him my word, and I would stick by that word, I was very relieved Frank had made the decision. Frank was not upset and as I left the store I vowed I would never again get mixed up in politics again.

At that time Kentucky had a 5% tax on all amusements. My good friend, L.B. Fuqua, who owned the theatre, suggested we go to the rally and talk to Chandler and see if this tax could be take off the books. I told L.B. what had happened and I didn't want to attend the rally. He understood and said he would talk to him, which he did. Later on the tax was rescinded. Whether L.B. talking to Chandler had anything to do with it, I don't know. I like to think it did.

Greenville, the county seat of Muhlenburg county Kentucky was one of our better towns financially. I have a picture taken in Greenville at 5:30 p.m.

and in the picture are 200 people lined
up to buy tickets and the box office
didn't open until 7:00 and the show
didn't start until 8:00. The lot was on
a hill behind a beautiful big two story
house about three blocks from the square
and business district. It was owned by
Mr. Martin. He was an eccentric old man
but he was also a gentleman. We set up
on his lot for over twenty-five years
and he always treated us fair and
square. However, he charged us for the
lot rent and there was an extra charge
for every house trailer that parked on
the lot. No other town we played, did
we have this type of arrangement. It
griped me but it was too good a location
to quibble about. Mr. Martin was always
waiting for us when we pulled onto the
lot and he seemed to get great joy out
of collecting the rent and getting his
passes to the show. We called the lot
<u>Martin's Hill</u> and I always looked
forward to seeing the old gentleman.
Another reason I always looked forward
to playing Greenfield was seeing my old
friend Bill McSpeeding. Bill owned the
theatre and every year he would run a
special matinee for members of the
Bisbee show. He even treated us to free
popcorn. None of the other theatre
owners on our route treated us so
royally. Most of them were fighting us
tooth and toe nail, cutting prices, etc.
for when Bisbee's Comedians came to town
it killed the movie theatre business.

Bill and I were talking once and he told me, "No doubt about it, when the Bisbee's Comedians come to town my business goes to pot. But competition is the spice of life. There is something going on here in Greenville every night of the year, 365 nights, so I don't worry about the Bisbee show playing here once a year for three nights." Bill was a real friend of Bisbee's Comedians and never missed a performance.

I don't remember the year but one Saturday night we tore the outfit down, loaded it on the six semi trucks and the next morning at daylight we moved to Greenville to our next show date which was Calhoun the county seat of Mclean County. We left Greenville on state route 181 to Sacramento, Rumsey then across the bridge over the Green River into Calhoun.

As you come off the bridge there are two sharp curves and then a curve to the left in front of Wilhites Cafe and you are on the main street. I always led the convoy and as we came off the bridge I checked to see if all the trucks were closed up. They were, and we preceded on to the lot. I remarked to Vera what a lovely day it was. There wasn't a cloud in the sky and that early in the morning temperature was not too high. It was just a pleasant morning and I was looking forward to a leisurely Sunday afternoon and evening.

As we made the curve in front of
Wilhites and headed down the main street
I noticed two men running across the
street to the courthouse, which was on
the right side of the street. Even
before I asked Vera the question, I knew
what her answer would be, but I asked it
anyway. "Those two men that just ran
across the street, did they have guns in
their hands?" "They sure did," she
answered. About that time we heard gun
shots. I pushed the accelerator to the
floor board and I was hoping the drivers
in the trucks were doing the same thing.
We made it to the lot safe and sound and
everyone piled out of their vehicles
with the same question, "What the hell
was that shooting about?"

Later, we heard a prisoner had
escaped and managed to get a gun. After
a few shots being fired, he was
surrounded and gave himself up to the
sheriff and his deputies. Monday night
in my announcement I joked about
Bisbee's Comedians being welcomed to
Calhoun by gun fire. It got a laugh but
it sure wasn't funny when those bullets
were flying around us. Luckily no one
was hit.

We always moved from Hartford to
Leitchfield going to Beaver Dam and then
picking up US 62 which went through
Caneyville and always seemed to me it
took forever to make this move and it is
only about 35 miles. The lot for the
show was up town a few seasons, then a

couple of years we set up at the fairgrounds. However, most of the time we set up on the ball diamond. A few of my good friends in Leitchfield were the Duvalls. They owned a clothing store on the square and then there was Mr. Cubbage and his son, who were lawyers. Mr. Cubbage had been a Bisbee fan for years. In fact, Jess Bisbee had given Mr. Cubbage a lifetime pass to the show. He carried it in his wallet and never failed to show it to me when we would meet.

Our advance man, Paul Caulpert was from Memphis. He was a very distinguished looking man, well dressed and his wife was very attractive. He did a good job of routing and billing the show and they were an asset to Bisbee's Comedians.

One afternoon as Vera and I were getting ready to go to the restaurant I had a message to call Paul at a number in Leitchfield. I knew something was wrong as Paul never called me. I had told him if he ran into a problem, to take care of it the best he knew how. So, the first thing I said when he answered the phone was "What's wrong?" He informed me the city council had raised the city license to $100.00 a day. In past years we had paid $20.00 a day. He also said the City Clerk had told him there was no way the ordinance could be changed. "What do you want me to do?" he asked. I told him I would meet him the next morning at 10:00 and we would decide what to do.

The next morning over coffee, Paul and I discussed what we could do. We decided first to see the mayor. We went to his house, rang the doorbell and the mayor came to the door. We introduced ourselves and he invited us to come in and be seated in his living room. I explained why we were there and as he was filling his pipe he said, "Mr. Choate, I know Bisbee's Comedians has been coming to Leitchfield for many years. The show has a wonderful reputation and many people look forward to your coming, but the city council voted unanimously to raise the license and there is not a thing I can do about it." We thanked the mayor and as we were walking to the car I said to Paul, "Let's go and see Mr. Cubbage." His office was on the second floor, we went up the stairs and went into the offices which he shared with his son. We shook hands and after being seated we talked about past years and the good relationship and friendship he had with Bisbee's Comedians, with Jess and myself. Finally, he asked, "When is the show coming to Leitchfield?" Then I told him about the city council raising the prohibitive license. I told him about our visit to the mayor and then I said, "Now, Mr. Cubbage, I have come to you. We don't want to take Leitchfield off our route but we just cannot pay a

$100.00 a day license. Do you have any ideas?" After a long silence, he finally said, "Put a big ad in the paper saying Bisbee's Comedians are coming but this will be your last appearance in Leitchfield on account of the high license imposed by the mayor and city council. If there is enough negative feedback to them, they may repeal the license back to what it was. If not, you may have to pay the license and be assured of a full house every night, or just cancel and not play Leitchfield. I hope you don't have to do that." He was right. A couple of weeks later, I had a call saying the license in Leitchfield would be the same as it always had been for Bisbee's Comedians, $20.00 a day.

In many of our towns we had to fight the city administrations raising the license. The one big reason for doing this, so they said, was because we took so much money out of town. I countered this argument by answering, "Sure we take some money out of the town but we always leave some here. We have thirty people on the show and they spend money for groceries, clothing, restaurants, gasoline, etc. Another thing, there is not a business here that doesn't depend on out of town goods. Even the bread that is sold comes from some other town where it is baked and trucked here. So, all of the money taken in by your local merchants does not stay here." This was a good argument against a raise in license but in some towns it didn't phase the city fathers, they raised the license and had no qualms about doing so.

In the late forties, we played Hopkinsville, Kentucky and we had an uptown lot in a small park. The show did a bang up business and it was about this time I met Dink Embry. Dink was an announcer on radio station WHOP. We hit it off and became fast friends down through the years.

One night after the show was over, Dink said, "Billy why don't you go to the station with me in the morning. We can talk and at the same time plug Bisbee's. I have quite a few regular listeners so it would be some good publicity for the show and you might have some fun and enjoy it." "Sounds great to me." "OK," he replied, "I'll pick you up at 4:30, we will have breakfast and then go on out to the station." I thought I had misunderstood him, "What time did you say?" "4:30, that isn't too early for you is it?" "Oh no." I didn't tell him I never got up until 10:00 or 10:30 and anyway, Jess would reimburse me so it was worth the extra money even if I did have to get up in the middle of the night. Dink picked me up at the allotted time and we had breakfast at a little cafe uptown that I believe was called Ferrells. We had breakfast and then opened the station and went on the air at 6:00 a.m. Later

Dink would tell the story and say I went to sleep right in the middle of the program. I didn't but will admit getting up at 4:00 a.m. is not my cup of tea.

A number of years later while we were playing Hopkinsville and I had taken over operation of the show, Boob asked me if I would be interested in having Brenda Lee work with us one night. He and Neva had worked with her while doing Uncle Cyp and Aunt Sap on Red Foleys Ozark Jubalee TV Show at Springfield, Missouri. He knew her mother and manager and said, "Billy I think I could get her for a Sunday night, if you are interested?" "Of course I am interested, unless she wants too much money." Boob replied, "I'll see what I can do." He contacted them and they agreed to have Brenda perform with us the following Sunday night in Hopkinsville at what I thought was a reasonable price. We seldom played on Sunday night but when we did it was all gravy. All the people on the show were on a seven day contract so there was very little expense. This is why I could bring a star like Brenda Lee in to work with us on a Sunday. Some of the Northern shows played every Sunday night and Neil Shaffner told me Sunday was his best night of the week. Not so in the Bisbee territory. In fact, there were many towns that had blue laws and the show was not permitted on Sunday. Also,

Grandpa Choate never played on Sunday and always said, "Whatever you make on Sunday, you will lose on Monday." For some reason it seemed to work out that way. But I was looking forward to showing this Sunday night because I had dollar signs in my eyes and visions of making a lot of money. Brenda was hot. She had a couple of hit records and had recently been on a number of top rated TV shows including The Steve Allen Show. There was no way we could help but pack them in. We did a good business in Hopkinsville without Brenda and with her there was no doubt in my mind we would turn them away. All I had to do was get the word out and this I did. We went all out on an advertising blitz.

At that time, Jimmie Wilkins was working for the Kentucky New Era which was the daily newspaper. Jimmie worked up some readers and displayed ads that were very good. We also ran a number of commercials on both radio stations and we had 8X10 pictures of Brenda, around two hundred of them. I had a caption printed which glued to the bottom of the picture telling about her appearance with Bisbee's Comedians Sunday night. We put these on the juke boxes and in the stores around town. We had done a good job with the publicity and I could hardly wait till Sunday night. Saturday afternoon I went by to see Paige Ooton, my good friend who ran the shoe shop. I asked him for his reaction to the show

217

Sunday night. He said, "Billy I don't think you will have enough seats to take care of the crowd." I knew he couldn't guarantee that but it was good to hear his opinion.

It must have been around 3:00 p.m. when Brenda, her mother, manager and four musicians they brought from Nashville to back up Brenda, pulled up on the fairgrounds where we were set up. After introductions we went to the motel where Boob and Neva were staying, picked them up and went to a restaurant for dinner. After dinner and a nice visit they followed Vera and me back to the lot. Brenda and the band went up on the stage and tried out our sound system. We had an excellent system and they were satisfied with it. Everything was set for that turn away crowd we were all expecting.

The doors opened at 7:00. At 10 minutes to 7:00, I walked around to the front of the tent and there were just a few people lined up to get tickets. When the curtain went up at 8:00 there was just a little over 200 people in the audience. It was a beautiful night, I had spent a good deal of money on advertising and we had been playing to big crowds all week. I just could not understand why there wasn't a full house. The show went over great. Brenda laid them in the aisle. It was just a shame we had such a small crowd.

After the show was over Brenda's

mother and manager came to me and she said, "Billy we know you have taken a beating financially so we have decided not to hold you to our agreement. You pay us for the musicians we have and we will forget about the rest, is that satisfactory?" "Well yes, but Vera is over in the trailer now getting you the money I agreed to pay you." She turned to go and said, "If you don't mind I will go to your trailer and settle with Vera." Which she did. After the hugs and good byes, they left for Nashville. As they drove off, I told Boob what they did about the money. He said, "That was mighty nice of them, wasn't it?" "I'll say it was, it saved me a bunch of money and I appreciate them."

We opened the 1958 season in Dyer, Tennessee and we had our usual two week rehearsal there. I had ordered a new tent from Anchor Supply Co. and Sandy Evans and I went to Evansville to pick it up. We set it up Wednesday and opened Thursday night for three days. As usual the outfit just looked beautiful and with the smell of new canvas, a good show, which I knew we had, I was looking forward to the new season. Among the personnel that season were Floyed Ditto, Marv and Ginny Girard, Wally and Nan Marks, The Espey's, the regulars including Boob and Neva, Leo Lacey, Otis Arnold, Audra and Virginia Hardesty and others.

It started raining Thursday

afternoon and didn't let up until Sunday
afternoon. By Saturday the lot was a
quagmire. The lot was so muddy that
just walking was difficult. Needless to
say, the weather hurt our business. We
tore down Saturday night and I hated to
let that beautiful new tent down in the
mud but it had to be done. I made
arrangements for a wrecker to be at the
lot early Sunday morning as I knew we
would have trouble getting the trucks
and trailers off the lot. And did we
ever, the chair truck sunk to its axles
and it took two wreckers to get it off
the lot. What a way to start the
season. We got everything off the lot
and made the jump to Lexington,
Tennessee.

We played our Tennessee towns and
jumped into Kentucky. Even though we
had a very good cast and show, business
was far from being good. However,
things were running smooth until we hit
Owensboro then a catastrophe occurred.
I didn't realize it at the time but what
happened that day was to change my life
and the operation of Bisbee's Comedians
from then on.

I had been talking and visiting
with my good friend Cliff Goodall. As I
drove up on the lot Neva Brasfield
pulled up and parked beside me. She got
out of the car and said, "Billy I have
bad news. Boob is in the hospital. He
is very sick and I doubt if he will be
able to make the show tonight." Vera

220

came out of the trailer and I told her
what had happened and that I was going
to the hospital. As I drove down 9th
Street to the hospital I was thinking
what I would do if Boob was unable to do
the show. As I walked in his room he
was asleep, immediately he woke up as I
neared his bed. As I looked at him I
knew he would not be able to do the show
that night or for many nights to come.
"How are you doing, Boob?" He said,
"Not too good. I may be back in a few
days but there is no way I can do a show
tonight." Before I could say anything
he continued, "I know you can't afford
to close for a few days so my red wig is
in the top drawer of my trunk and my
wardrobe will fit you. You do the
Toby's until I can get on my feet. I
know you can do them." As I left I told
Boob I would figure out something. As I
was getting in the car I realized I had
very little time to do whatever I was
going to do. It was 3:00 in the
afternoon and the doors opened at 7:00.
As soon as I got back to the lot I went
directly to Audra Hardesty's trailer to
get his advice. He had heard about Boob
and I asked, "What should I do, Audra?"
"Well," he said, "you don't have many
choices. You have thirty people to
think about. You can't afford to close
the show and pay these people waiting on
Boob Brasfield to return. He might be
gone a week, a month or he may never be
back. I would suggest you start doing

221

the Toby's. I know you can do them and this is a good time to start." I told him Boob had suggested the same thing. "Well, do it! And you better make up your mind. It is getting late."

I had done a lot of light comedy but had never had on a red wig or done a Toby part. However, I had been raised and worked with some great Toby comedians, including Ray Zarlington, my brother Welby, Rod Brasfield, and Boob Brasfield. I was still leery of stepping out and doing a Toby on such short notice. I talked to Vera and decided to do it. There wasn't much else I could do. I immediately called a rehearsal. We were doing "The Girl Next Door." I had worked in this bill many times so all I needed was a position rehearsal for the Toby scenes. After the rehearsal, I jumped in the car, drove out on a country road to study. At that time, I had a quick study and thirty minutes later I knew the part.

We opened the doors and had a good house. As I walked in the dressing room, I think every one was a little apprehensive about me doing the Toby part. However, they all let me know they were behind me a hundred percent and were there to help me anyway they could. I set at the makeup table and put on a very conservative Toby makeup. I put on a flesh as a base, some red on the cheeks, on the nose and lips, white over the eyes and then a black eye

222

pencil used to make dots to look like freckles and a black vertical line over my eye lids. I powdered my face good and picked up the Steins spirit gum bottle and spread it liberally on my side burns to hold the red wig on. As I put the wig on and held it in place for the spirit gum to dry, I remembered the story I had heard Boob tell many times about the wig. It was given to him by Mr. Cooke when he was a young man on Cooke's Comedians in Alabama. This was the first time Boob had done a Toby part. It wasn't a new wig at that time and Boob didn't know how old the wig was. I have figured and it must be over 75 years old. I wore it for 12 years and still have it and it is in pretty good shape. I have often thought how interesting it would be if that old wig could talk and could relate stories, the heartbreak, the happiness, the laughter and joy it helped to bring to so many people.

Before the curtain went up Floyed Ditto made an announcement explaining Boob was in the hospital and wouldn't be able to perform and I was taking his place. While Floyed was making the announcement everyone was coming to me with good luck, break a leg, etc. I had no idea how the audience was going to take me but I sure appreciated the people on the show because I knew they were all rooting for me. The orchestra played the curtain music, the house

223

lights went off, the curtain went up and I said a little prayer. My first scene was a disaster. I did get a fair laugh on my exit gag but I was worried. I was standing in the wings looking at my part when Marv Girard came up and said, "You are doing OK. They are a little shocked by that announcement about Boob being in the hospital. Believe me, you will have them before the second act is over." Marv turned and left before I could say thanks. I sure appreciated his encouragement and he was right, I did have them laughing and with me during the second act. When the curtain came down on the last act I was completely exhausted but was pumped up when everyone started slapping me on the back and congratulating me. As I was taking my makeup off I knew I would be doing this Toby character many times in the future.

The next day, I went to the hospital to see Boob. He was much better and the doctor told him he expected to discharge him in a couple of days. We discussed the show and I told him I had decided to do the Toby parts, he would do characters and we would feature him and Neva one night in the characters of Uncle Cyp and Aunt Sap in the play "Sweethearts Again." Boob seemed happy and satisfied with my decision. In fact, he said, "I think this is a wise move you are making. I am just too old to do the Toby's and

224

will feel more relaxed and at ease doing the characters and Uncle Cyp." I left Boob telling him to get well and back to the show as soon as possible. As I was driving back to the lot I was thinking of the many things I had to do, the most important was to learn the Toby parts. I grabbed the scripts and headed for a country road. I didn't know it at the time but I would be doing this Toby character for the next 12 years and I would become to love him.

Grandpa Choate lived happily and comfortably until 1952 when he began to slowly decline. He moved to Wayne City and rented an apartment in what was at one time the hotel across the street from Dad's theatre. He stayed about six months, but he constantly thought he was too far from "home." So in order to satisfy him, Dad and Uncle Ed made arrangements to move him to Marion. But after living in Marion for about eight months, he got restless and decided to move back to Wayne City.

Once Grandpa passed his ninetieth birthday, his eyesight began to weaken and his energy began to sag. He lost some of the rambunctiousness of his personality and his interest in everyday affairs. The only thing he insisted upon was going to the "show" (as he called Dad's theatre) every evening. His eyesight was too dim to watch the movies and his hearing was too weak to listen, but each evening Dad helped him across the street and sat him in a chair in the lobby by the popcorn machine. There he sat quietly all evening until everyone had come and gone, then Dad and Mom helped him home. It is difficult to speculate about why Grandpa insisted on this, but one can only suspect that the smell of popcorn and the bustle of people crowding into a theatre, unlocked, in a far off corner of his mind, memories of his own show days----memories of Peg Leg Jones dancing around a walking cane, of wagons mired in the mud, of audiences watching breathlessly the death scene of Little Mary Morgan in "Ten Nights in a Barroom" or of blow downs, fires and catastrophes he had been through with his tent show. Perhaps the hours Grandpa spent sitting silently with his hands folded on his cane in the lobby of Dad's theatre were not as interminable to him as some might have thought.

Grandpa was well taken care of during his last years, and even regarded locally as something of a hero out of the past. It was not until 1957, shortly after his 94th birthday, that he died peacefully in his sleep. We were showing Morganfield, Kentucky when I received the call saying Grandpa had passed away. The funeral was to be at Marion, Illinois at 10:30 a.m. I made arrangements to be there. There was a big crowd at the funeral home when I arrived and many friends and relatives I had not seen in years. Clyde Simmonds preached and Grandpa would have been pleased as he held Clyde in high esteem. Grandpa was buried in the Webb Cemetery at Tunnel Hill, Illinois.

On my way back to Morganfield, my memory wandered back and I thought of the good times we had and the lessons I learned from him. I remembered all the exciting stories he told. Grandpa was an inexhaustible storyteller and I never tired of listening to him. However, there were times when he retold some of his favorite ones, I suspected he added parts I hadn't heard before. When he was finished with a story he would always ask me, "What do you think of that Billy Charles?" "That was great Grandpa." Then he would take a big draw on his pipe, blow the smoke out and smile.

In 1961 significant changes in Bisbee's Comedians took place. I had hired a character actress through the Benn Theatrical Agency in Chicago. We were to start rehearsals Monday and on Friday I received a telegram stating she was sick and unable to fulfill her contract. I didn't know what I was going to do on such short notice. Finally, I went to Mother and asked her to go back on the road and do the character parts. Dad's theatre business, after making good money for sixteen years, had begun to slack off. By 1960, he was only open three nights a

227

week, and closing for the summer presented no problem. The problem was that Mother was seventy-one years old and had not been on a stage in twenty years. My doubts, however, were not primarily about her capabilities, her mind was sharp and she still had a quick study. I wondered about her desires. She seemed perfectly happy as she was, and returning to a full line of parts meant hard work and a strenuous schedule. But, I had miscalculated about Mother's attitude. She was as anxious as a school girl to go back on the road. She was fifty-one years older than she had been when she first joined the Choate show, but she was in excellent health and looked considerably younger than her years. She jumped into rehearsals at once, learned her parts, and when the show opened she was eager and ready to hit the road. Dad, in the meantime, had leased a theatre, bought a trailer, hooked it on the back of his car and, when the time came, set out for another season on a tent show.

Members of the cast were Dick Lewis and his new wife, Honie. He had met her in Germany when he was there with the Army band. She was a good looking girl and did a couple of parts and did them well. Also, Dick Kriel, Bert Dexter, Ralph Blackwell, Leon Block, Judy Richards, and a country singer Art Buchanan. Dick Kriel and Judy Richards were married at the end of the season.

228

Mom and Dad got along exceptionally well that summer. Mother was able to perform six nights a week without difficulty, and Dad helped me take care of the daily details in running a show. In fact, Dad's capacity on the show was much like Grandpa's had been during the last years of the Choate show.

Circumstances worked out so well in 1961 that I decided to keep Mother doing the character parts for the 1962 season. But in 1963, even though Mother was healthy and strong, I was reluctant to allow her to continue doing a full line of parts. She was seventy-three by this time and I was fearful that sooner or later doing a long part every night would become burdensome for her. So, Mother didn't do any parts during the 1963 season, but she and Dad continued to travel with the show as they had the two previous seasons----Dad selling tickets and handling other daily details, Mother supervising the concessions and filling in when necessary on the stage.

We had a very good show in 1963. We featured Boob and Neva as Uncle Cyp and Aunt Sap and also Harry Willard and his daughters. His stage name was Willard the Wizard. I have discussed Willard in another chapter, but one incident concerning Willard needs mentioning.

We were playing Dawson Springs, Kentucky. The lot was behind the Dawson

Springs Hotel. A beautiful old hotel that featured hot baths, steam rooms and a masseur. They also had a fine restaurant and I still remember their delicious vegetable soup.

After we tore down Saturday night and the trucks were loaded I was in the trailer eating my night lunch. There was a knock and when I went to the door a policeman was there and said, "Toby, we have one of your men in jail. He is drunk and was causing a disturbance up on main street." He continued, "The judge is at the jail now. You can come over and pay his fine if your care to, if not, we will have to keep him in jail till Monday morning." I told him I would be over. I paid the fine and told them to keep him in jail until morning. I went to bed but I didn't sleep a wink. The next morning at 6:00 a.m. I was in the working men's trailer getting them up to make the jump to Owensboro. As I was heading back to my trailer I saw Willard coming across the lot. I followed him to his trailer, knocked, and Francis came to the door. I said, "Francis I hate to do this on account of you girls but your Dad has caused me nothing but trouble and worry and I can't take anymore. Here is a two week salary. I am sorry." She didn't say anything and I turned and walked away. Vera was upset and all the way to Owensboro berated me for letting them go. She was concerned about the girls.

So was I but I just felt I couldn't take any more of Willard the Wizard even if he was the greatest magician in the world.

As we pulled on the lot I was looking forward to our showing Owensboro. We would play there two weeks and it would be nice not having to tear down and move. Also, I had many friends I was looking forward to seeing. A good friend, Mr. Rice and his family, was on the lot to greet us. Then there was Karl and Erma Burton, Doc and Nell Hendricks and Cliff and Cappy Goodall. Cliff picked up the phone and said, "Just a minute." "It's long distance and for you." And he handed me the phone. It was Dad, "I am still here in Dawson Springs and so is Willard and the girls. Now Billy, you just can't leave them sitting here. I know Willard has caused you a lot of grief but you must think about the girls. Your Mother is really upset about this and will be more so if you don't take them back." "OK Dad, tell them to come on over. Of course, this is not going to change Willard. Nothing is going to stop Willard from drinking and causing me trouble. Maybe I can weather it the rest of the season, I just don't know." Dad said, "I'll go tell them, and believe me Billy, you are doing the right thing."

Tuesday morning at 5:00 a.m. I came out of a sound sleep and heard this

231

yelling, "The tent is on fire!" At
first I thought I was dreaming, then I
realized this was no dream. I jumped
up, put on my pants and shoes and ran
out. At the same time the working men
and everyone on the show was out of
their trailers. Willard was still
jumping up and down yelling, "The tent
is on fire!" I told him to shut up.
There was no fire in the tent. What he
was seeing was smoke from some tires
someone was burning on a lot two blocks
from the tent. In his drunken stupor,
he thought the black smoke was coming
out of the tent. As I got into bed I
told Vera, "We have fourteen more weeks
and the season will be over. Maybe I
can last until then."

There were many boarding houses in
the towns Bisbee's Comedians played.
Houses that rented rooms and served
family type meals. "Pitch till you
win," we called them. Similar to the
"Bed and Breakfast" houses. One of the
finest of these eating establishments
was in Smithland, Kentucky and was owned
by Mrs. Hale and her husband. It was
called simply, Mrs. Hales, and was known
far and wide. People drove for miles to
eat Mrs. Hales delicious food. I first
met Mrs. Hale in 1941. Jess Bisbee had
been telling me what great food Mrs.
Hale served. Sunday morning we pulled
into Smithland and set the outfit up on
the school lot. At that time, Mrs.
Hales place was downtown on the main

232

street.   At noon, along with other
people on the show, we headed for Mrs.
Hales.   What I had heard was true, the
food was outstanding, and so much of it.
Chicken, roast pork, roast beef, ham and
all kinds of fresh vegetables.   Besides
the great food, Mrs. Hale employed one
of the prettiest girls in Livingston
County.   At that time, I certainly
wasn't allergic to girls, especially one
so beautiful.   So when she went to the
table to get another pot of coffee I
went over an asked her if I could take
her home after the show Monday night.
She said, "Probably," then added, "What
are you doing tonight?"   I said,
"Nothing."   "Would you like to go to
church with me tonight?   I have a car
and can pick you up."   I couldn't
believe what I was hearing.   This good
looking girl with those beautiful blue
eyes, pretty blond hair and a figure any
girl would have been proud of, was
asking me to go to church with her.   I
said, "That would be great."   I didn't
even ask her what church she went to.
"OK," she replied, "I'll pick you up at
6:30."   I had been looking forward to
eating some of Mrs. Hales homemade pies,
but I was too excited for dessert.   We
were together Sunday night and Monday
and Tuesday nights.   But like many young
and frivolous romances it was just a
fling.   And I never saw her again.
Through the years, Mr. and Mrs. Hale and
I became good friends and she would kid

233

me about trying to steal her waitress.

One of the more amusing episodes to occur on the Bisbee show took place in Smithland the summer after Boob and Neva had been on Red Foley's TV show, "Ozark Jubilee" at Springfield, Missouri. It was opening night and the tent was packed. There wasn't an empty seat and the SRO sign was hung out. However, a heckler was in the audience and boisterously booed Boob from the time the curtain went up. Naturally we tried to ignore the disturbance, but the heckler was persistent in keeping it up. Finally, I made the decision and told two of the canvasmen to escort the troublemaker out the door. But just as they prepared to take action, the fellow himself rose from his seat and walked down the isle to the stage. It was a few moments before the cast and audience knew what was happening, for the man approaching the stage was an old friend of Boob's and a well know entertainer himself....Red Foley. Needless to say, the crowd, which had earlier been unhappy at the disturbance, was delighted at the turn of events. Before the evening was over, as one might imagine, Red sang a number of his songs and when he was through the audience gave him a standing ovation.

The 1963 season was a good year financially and we had an outstanding cast, which included Boob and Neva Brasfield, Dave and Maureen Castle, Ken

234

and Roberta Griffin, George Rowe, Flo
and Shannon Darling, Audra and Virginia
Hardesty, Sybil Batts, Mother and Dad,
and the Baranek's who had a high class
outstanding dog act and had been on the
Ed Sullivan show. Also, Mississippi
Slim Osbourne who worked with Elvis
Presley.

1965 was not a good year. It just
seemed like every time we opened the
doors it was pouring rain or a storm was
coming up. Also, it was an unusually
hot and humid summer. By 1965, every
home was air conditioned and it was hard
to pull people away from a cool living
room to sit in a tent where the
temperature might reach 90 degrees or
more. As I look back on those years, I
have come to the conclusion we didn't
compete with television, air
conditioning was our greatest
competitor. Business didn't drop off
all at once, of course, in fact the tent
continued to be filled to capacity in
some towns in spite of the weather, but
there were beginning to be periodic
spells of slow business here and there.
Also, the nut (expense) just
skyrocketed. The three L's, License,
Lot and Lights all went up. Salaries
also jumped. The result was the show
grossed about what it had in previous
years, but the net profit was way down.
In fact, it was the lowest net profit
the show had ever experienced.

Even though 1965 was not a good

year I started making plans in January 1966 to open Bisbee's Comedians in the spring and play the regular established territory the show had been playing for 42 years. The trucks, chairs and other equipment had been painted in the spring of 1965 so there was not too much to be done to the outfit. The tent had been used two seasons and was in good shape. It wouldn't take much money to get the show on the road and I was looking forward to the coming season.

The last of February I had the cast pretty well set. Boob's health was not good but he had called and said he and Neva wanted to troupe one more season, and I was glad to have them. I was making plans for a booking trip to Tennessee when a call came from a gentleman in Louisville, Kentucky who said he was the Vice President of Park Mammouth Resort, which was located just a few miles from Mammouth Cave National Park. He wanted to know if I would be interested in setting the show in there for the summer. Before I could answer he continued by saying, "Now Mr. Choate, I know there are many details to be worked out before you could make a decision on this. We also, have many questions. Tell you what, why don't you and your wife come down and spend a couple of days at the resort. We will pay all your expenses. You can look the place over, you and your wife can spend a couple of leisurely days and maybe we can come up with something that will benefit us both. What do you say?" I replied, "That sounds fine. What about coming this weekend?" "Great! Just go to the desk. Your reservation will be waiting for you and I am looking forward to meeting you." When I hung up I told Vera about our coming weekend and they wanted the show down there for the summer. She said, "Well it would be nice to set up and not have to move every three days but I am wondering about business. Could we make any money?" I said, "Well, we'll go down there, look it over, and maybe have an idea what the business will do. At least we will have a nice weekend at their expense."

That night, as I lay in bed, I wondered what kind of proposition these people would offer me. I remembered a few years back when I had a call from Mac Johnson who was in Springfield, Missouri. He had talked to the owners of Silver Dollar City, a resort that had just opened, and they were interested in me bringing the show in there for an extended run. At Mac's insistence I made a trip down there and we had not talked to them 10 minutes until I realized we could never come to any kind of terms. They just wanted too much. I wondered what the people in Kentucky had in mind. I wouldn't have long to wait to find out.

Vera and I left Friday morning for

Kentucky. We went through Morgantown and visited with our good friends, A.C. and Opaline Hocker. The resort was located just off 31W between Bowling Green and Cave City and just about a mile from Park City. There was a big grade sign next to the highway and a winding black-top road that led you up to the motel and resort which was located on top of a mountain. After getting settled, we decided to look the place over. They had a miniature train that was just leaving the station so we got on it. The first stop was at a gift shop that was called the Dome House. It was located over a small cave and was operated by Tom and Patricia Moran. They were lovely people and they, their kids, our kids and Vera and I became fast friends. We continued our ride on the train and went by the golf course, riding stable and back to the motel where there were tennis courts, and an in-door swimming pool.

That evening we had dinner at the motel. The dining room was beautiful. It was built in a round shape with solid windows and a clear view that let you see for miles. The sun was just setting as we sat down and it was a sight to behold.

We had just finished eating when a gentleman came to our table and introduced himself as the manager. His name was Liman Demondrum. He had been a US Marshal and had retired and took the

238

position of running the resort. Mr. Demondrum was a big man, well over six foot and I am sure over two hundred pounds. He said, "Now Mr. Choate the owners will be here tomorrow night and at that time they will have a proposition for you to consider. I hope everything works out and you can bring your show in here for the summer. I think it would be good for all concerned and I know the show would be an asset to the resort." With that said, he told us if we needed anything to let him know and he said goodnight and left.

The next day we met with the owners and they offered me, which at the time, I thought was a good proposition. They were to furnish the lot and lights, there was no license. I was to furnish the outfit and show. The show was to take the first two thousand gross then we were to split 50-50. Also, we were to retain and control all concessions. There was thousands of people visiting Mammouth Cave everyday and this is where we were going to draw from. We decided to open the first week in June and close Labor Day week as that was the end of the tourist season.

I contracted a local trucker, Bill Mcrill to pull the trailers to the resort as there was no use in buying license when we were only going to make one jump.

We were to leave Sunday morning however, Saturday night I received a call from Ken Griffin that was disturbing. He said, "Did you know you cannot advertise at Mammouth Cave?" I replied, "No, I didn't." "It is a national park and advertising of any kind is prohibited." "The owners of the resort are influential in Kentucky, maybe they can square it." "I doubt if they would have any influence with the Department of the Interior of the US Government." I knew he was probably right. I told him it was too late to back out of the agreement and we were leaving and would see him tomorrow afternoon. He and Roberta had rented a house in Park City. He told me where it was and said, "Come by as soon as you get here."

We pulled into the resort Sunday afternoon about 2:00. The trucks were already there on the lot. As soon as I got our trailer set up I went to the motel and Mr. Demondrum and one of the owners and I went to Mammouth Cave to see about the advertising. We met with the manager in his office. He was very nice to us but informed us what I already knew. There could be no advertising of any kind in the park. They were not even allowed to hang a calendar with advertising on it. On the way back, I said, "Well fella's we will go ahead and open the show, but unless we figure some way to reach those thousands of people in the park, we will never make it." My morale was at a low ebb.

We did two shows and rehearsed in a banquet room at the motel. The shows we did were "The Return of John Slater" and "Sweethearts Again" which featured Boob and Neva as Uncle Cyp and Aunt Sap. I contacted Joe Creason and he gave us a great story, along with pictures, in the magazine section of the Sunday Louisville Courior Journal. We opened Monday night to a full house but I knew these people were from towns we played and Bisbee fans. I ran newspaper ads and spots on the radio at the stations in Glasgow and also Bowling Green but after the first week business just went down to nothing. We were lucky if we had a hundred people.

Vera was pregnant and the baby was due the last of September. We decided to keep the show open and close Labor Day week. That would put us back in Wayne City a few weeks before the due date and Vera could be under the care of her doctor, Dr. Modert, who had delivered Welby Charles and Cherita. Also, that would fulfill my commitment to the resort and the people on the show. I knew we could not make any money, but I thought we could at least break even.

One night after the show was over Boob asked me if I would drive him over to Glasgow as he needed to see a doctor. So, the next morning I picked him and Neva up and drove to a clinic where a doctor Mr. Demondrum had recommended had his office. We made three more trips to the doctor and on the third trip he asked me to come in his office. He was sitting behind a desk and motioned for me to sit down. He was looking at some papers and without looking up he said, "I understand Mr. Brasfield and his wife work for you on a show over at Park Mammouth Resort." I answered, "That is right." Laying the papers aside he continued, "Well Mr. Choate I hate to tell you this but Mr. Brasfield has cancer and it has spread to most of his organs. He doesn't have too much time left so I am going to suggest he go to his home in Texas as soon as possible. I am going in now and talk to them. I wanted to let you know his condition before I told him. Would you like to be there when I talk to them?" I told him I thought it might be best if I just waited for them in the waiting room, which I did. When they came out Neva was crying but nothing was said until we got in the car. They got in the back seat. We had gone a couple of blocks and finally Boob said, "The doctor said he told you. I don't think we can give a two week notice Bill. We will work a couple of nights. That will give you time to switch parts and have a couple of rehearsals. Then we'd better head for Texas as that doctor says I don't have too much time left." It took me a few moments to get my emotions under

242

control. Finally, I said, "Don't worry about the show. Maybe you'd better get packed and leave in the morning." Boob replied, "No, a couple of days is not going to hurt me and won't make a difference." Then he started reminiscing, remembering funny things that had happened, like the time Booger Lewis hid a pint of whiskey in the ceiling fan above the stage at the Gadston theatre and during the show someone turned the fan on and when the bottle broke it spread whiskey all over the stage. The place smelled like a still for weeks. He then told the story about Rod. He was 12 years old and he came to visit Boob and Neva. At the time they were on the Mickey Obrion Stock Co. and were showing Troy, Tennessee. One night just as the show was over Rod came backstage and asked Boob where Mr. Rube was. Boob said, "I don't know any Mr. Rube, what are you talking about?" Rod said, "Well there are two fella's beating up Mr. Obrion in front of the tent and he is yelling HEY RUBE and just between me and you Boob, he wants that Mr. Rube pretty bad." For years Rod was called RUBE BRASFIELD. Even though our hearts were heavy and tears were in our eyes, Boob kept Neva and I laughing as we drove back to Park City. As we pulled up in front of their apartment Boob said, "Billy did you ever stop and think how fortunate we have been. Most of our lives you and I have

243

been making people happy, we have entertained them, made them cry and made them laugh. As actors, we had this God given talent and we were lucky to be able to use it so other people could benefit from the ability God gave us. I just hope God takes that into account when we stand before him." I helped them up the steps to the front door and as I turned to go, Boob said, "See you tonight Bill."

I drove to the motel and made a few calls to people I knew would be concerned about Boob and his illness. I then went to the trailer where I broke the news to Vera.

That evening Boob came down early to put on his makeup. When I walked into the dressing room he was sitting just outside the tent in his favorite canvas directors chair. I grabbed a chair and joined him asking, "How you feeling Boob?" "Just fine," he replied. We continued talking and soon Vera walked by on her way to the front to open the doors. Boob said, "Well Bill, it won't be too long until you will be a Father again. I told Neva I was going to ask you this....as you know my name is Lawrence LaMar. I know that is not a terrific outstanding name, but I was wondering if that baby is a boy, would you name him after me?" Not hesitating, I said, "If the baby is a boy we will name him after you and Bob LaThey and call him LaMar LaThey." "That sounds

244

like a winner to me," he replied. Then after a long pause, he said, "Thanks."

The curtain went up and I knew Boob would be depressed and suffering a lot of pain but the audience never knew it. He gave a magnificent performance. We were doing Sweethearts Again, a show which featured Boob and Neva in their characters, "Uncle Cyp and Aunt Sap" and there is no doubt they both were stars in this show. All through the play they are fighting and arguing with each other. This is how one scene played out:

AUNT SAP: I wish you would shut your mouth.
UNCLE CYP: Don't talk to me like that. This is my house, my furniture, my ground and I won't have you talking to me that way and in that tone of voice.
AUNT SAP: There you go again saying my house, my furniture, my ground. Why don't you say our house, our furniture, our ground....What are you doing now?
UNCLE CYP: I am pulling up our pants.

I had worked with Boob and Neva for over 25 years and I do not believe they had given a better performance than they gave that night. I joined Boob at the Gadston Theatre in Gasden, Alabama in

245

the winter of 1941. Rod Brasfield and I joined after the Bisbee show closed. We had a room at the Leak Hotel for three dollars a week. Back then you could get a plate lunch for thirty cents. Sounds unbelievable, but you could also get a hamburger with everything on it for a nickel. My salary was twenty-seven dollars a week, which was very good as WPA workers were only receiving forty dollars a month.

As I stood in the wings watching these two great performers, I thought of all the good times we had together and also the bad times we had gone through. Leon Block said, "They are really letting it all hang out tonight" on his way to the piano to play the curtain music. There weren't too many people in the audience, but what were there were eating the show up. Boob and Neva were giving the performance of their lives. They were not thinking of cancer or sickness or the long trip to Texas the next day. All they could hear was the applause and laughter from the crowd and it was enough to make them forget everything except the glow the applause and laughter were giving them. After the show everybody was congratulating Boob and Neva on their fine performance. I said to him, "Well Boob, of the thousands of shows we have done together, I believe tonight was the best of your long career." He quit wiping the grease paint from his face, looked at me and said, "I knew this was to be my last one and I wanted to put out a little extra effort." Then he paused and with a smile he added, "Even if I do say so, that was one damn good show."

Early the next morning I helped them load and when the last suitcase was put in the trunk Boob said, "Bill, you know I love beer and I haven't had one in twenty-three years. Somewhere in Arkansas we are going to stop and I am going to get a six pack. It won't hurt me now and I might as well enjoy something I am very fond of." I hugged them both and as they drove off he said, "Don't forget to name that boy LaMar. Hell you might as well name it LaMar if it is a girl."

I watched the car until it was out of sight. I knew I would never see either of them again and my eyes were full of tears.

The next week I received a call from Welby telling me Dad had been stricken with a massive heart attack. He was rushed to the Fairfield Memorial Hospital and, after a few days of improvements and setbacks, he died peacefully. Boob passed away September 9, 1966 and Neva died March 1, 1980.

We closed the show for good at Park Mammouth Resort, Labor Day week, 1966. Boob's death and Dad's passing seemed to represent the end of an era. The Choate family had been involved in the tent show business from it's beginning in the late nineteenth century until it's end in the mid-twentieth. It seemed oddly appropriate, therefore, that Boob and Dad's passing and the closing of Bisbee's Comedians occurred almost exactly at the same time.

At the Jefferson Memorial Hospital in Mt. Vernon, Illinois on September 26, 1966 at 11:00 a.m., Vera gave birth to a beautiful baby boy. He weighed 7 1/2 pounds and we named him LaMar LaThey Choate.

got friends?
Real Stories of Real Fairbanks Friends

Printed in the United States of America

Table of Contents

"Friendship is born at the moment when one person says to another, 'What! You too? I thought I was the only one.'" – C. S. Lewis

acknowledgements

I would like to thank Jeff Wall for his vision for this book and Brian Bennett for his hard work in making it a reality. And to the people of Friends Community, thank you for your boldness and vulnerability in sharing your personal stories.

This book would not have been published without the amazing efforts of our Project Manager and editor, Marla Lindstrom Benroth. Her untiring resolve pushed this project forward and turned it into a stunning victory. Thank you for your great fortitude and diligence. Deep thanks to our incredible Editor in Chief, Michelle Cuthrell, and Executive Editor, Nicole Phinney Lowell, for all the amazing work they do. I would also like to thank our invaluable proofreader, Melody Davis, for the focus and energy she has put into perfecting our words.

Lastly, I want to extend our gratitude to the creative and very talented Ann Clayton, who designed the cover for *Got Friends? Real Stories of Real Fairbanks Friends.*

Daren Lindley
President and CEO
Good Catch Publishing

introduction

Despite the fact that Fairbanks is a tight-knit community of less than 100,000 who depend on each other, sometimes for their very survival, we still know amazingly little about the personal lives of the people we come into contact with.

We nod, we wave, we might even open a door for the person we see with an armful of groceries; yet, we often cannot say that we are truly more than acquaintances — that we are *friends.*

Do we share our own stories of struggle? Do we talk to one another about how we react and survive in the midst of untimely deaths and destructive addictions of loved ones, the heartache of broken relationships and divorce, the agony of devastating physical illness? Or do we feel isolated and suffer with the pain alone?

This book contains the stories of several brave and, by their own admission, grateful ones whose lives have been saved by God's boundless grace. They have known your pain. They have been afflicted by your sicknesses. Their lives have been forever changed by the loss of things dear.

These are real people. These are your friends, your neighbors, your co-workers. As you read the following pages, you will no doubt find yourself saying, "I thought I was the only one!" But you aren't.

got friends?

There are friends nearby, waiting to walk with you through your deepest struggles — and share your greatest joys!

Many blessings,

Pastor Jeff Wall
Friends Community Church
Fairbanks, Alaska

an edge to the answer
The Story of Bill
Written by Richard Drebert

A finely crafted hunting blade slices flesh in a single stroke and holds its edge even after striking bone time and again.

My knives are forged of the finest Damascus steel, and I sculpt each one according to personal taste: balance, heft and the haft designed of antler, steel or wood stock. My knives have skinned moose and caribou, filleted salmon and whittled walking sticks from Homer to Nome.

When I was a young man, I apprenticed with no artisan to learn my trade; self-taught, I trained in an emotional furnace called Phoenix. At a junkyard I foraged rusty files, saw blades or steel leaf springs to create my weapons, and I served a diverse clientele — desperate junkies and dope dealers — whom I manipulated to feed my vices.

I was the Teflon Man; the one you never read about in the newspapers, the drug pusher who dodged the steel jaws of law enforcement, and I guarded my perceived calling with the passion of a meth addict — which I was.

Today I'm severed from miserable addictions as deftly as a scalpel cuts away gangrene to save a limb. Now I serve my community as a craftsman, a family man working in a time-honored Alaskan tradition, and I am humbled by mercy so wrenching to my heart that tears come when I tell my strange story.

Fairbanks is my home, where God deposited me to heal and carve out undeserved fulfillment among friends and loved ones, but I still recall the bitter taste of wasted years …

❧❧❧

My father was always The Sheriff to me.

After his military career, Dad took up law enforcement and prided himself in never having to discharge his .44 while apprehending a criminal. Later in life he worked as a photography professor at an Arizona college, but long after his death he loomed as the gun-toting Texas lawman riding shotgun on my guilty conscience.

Dad was a sizable man with an exacting sense of right and wrong. If his errant cud of tobacco splattered a parked car as he passed, Dad chased down a freeway exit and returned to the "scene of the crime" to make things right. And he never shrank from confrontation. A biker once scratched his car while parking. The biker tried to deliver "explicit" physical grief upon Dad, and I watched my father tie him into a painful greasy pretzel. When Dad let him up, he sped away on his Harley.

Mom affirmed my Dad's strict code of conduct in a house brimming with eight strong-willed children, two of whom were adopted. Dad and Mom never argued in our presence, and I know that they yearned to pass on moral values in a structured, loving environment. In our tiny house each day they systematically worked through the chaos of school lunches, baths, homework, table manners and finished up with bedtime prayers. Often the 10 of us attended a little Baptist church down the street where preacher Hansen endorsed Dad's firm principles.

Yet the "force" in my father's ethics failed to hold me on a path of decency. Dad fired deafening volleys on how NOT to live, but I never understood the *reason* to live right. Our parents watched helplessly as their values were crushed under the heel of temptations. I drifted from their moral custody the first week I climbed the steps at Isaac Junior High, a predominately Hispanic school.

"Hey, got any money?"

"Some."

"I can get you cigarettes. And how 'bout some weed? Give it up …"

My new friend Joe could have turned me upside down and shaken the dough out of me, anyway, so I dug out my lunch money, and he crumpled it into a chest pocket with his smokes. Joe was as good as his word, and soon we were smoking reefers together in a vacant field.

I needed someone to teach me survival skills before I graduated to the corrupt Phoenix streets, and at Isaac my untested youthfulness filled dry riverbeds with perverted passions. I hated dodging bullies, and Joe (who had failed academics a couple years) was as big as a school bus compared to most of us. He was respected for his street smarts, and in junior high, I hitched my wagon to his lifestyle — and learned. Joe thrived on risk, like stealing booze, smoking weed, ditching school. I faked notes to teachers in the writing style of my mom to spend more time with Radar, with his big ears, Sonny, flabby and rotund, and Little Mickey, a goofy kid who attached himself to me as I did to Joe. This rounded out our group of potheads, and I scraped through junior high leaving little academic impression.

By the time I was 15, I had discovered my gift for networking, and my people skills hit a new level when I attended West High School.

Joe had been supplying me with weed to sell to friends, but I searched out a new source — and a hungry market extending past high school borders. My client base suddenly included adults to whom I traded weed for a new poison: black beauties (speed). My new friends could order "medicinal" amphetamines from overseas companies that advertised in magazines, and weed became my currency to acquire them.

When my lucrative black beauty enterprise dwindled, due to a flood of other punk dope dealers, I searched for a more potent lure to expand my territory. It seemed that the more exotic the drug I peddled, the simpler it was to mix with the "easy" girls at West, and my craving for sex kept pace with a growing appetite for staying high.

At around 17, I'd been ditching school without regret for months, and I finally dropped out. Dad and Mom demanded that I find a job, and I worked as a busboy for a month or two, then flat out lied to Dad about how I paid my bills while I lived at home.

Why didn't everybody deal dope? I could get high on my own product, and I had girls hanging on me wherever I went. No boss hassled me, and best of all I got *respect.* Dad just didn't get it.

I was still living with Mom and Dad when an event shot me to the top of the drug-dealing ladder in my hometown, without touching a single rung. In the dim lights of a Circle K convenience store a scrawny white kid doubled over while two Latinos pounded and kicked the stuffing out of him. I jammed the brakes on my '73 LTD and jumped out, fists flying, into the fray. Between the kid and me, we fought our way back to my car. We exchanged names as my slicks laid rubber trails.

"Where you wanna go?"

The kid was grinning and *cocky* — considering he'd just escaped waking in a gutter, face down.

"My dad'll pay you for this, man. Take the next left."

I followed his lead through neighborhoods, expecting a 10-buck "thank you" from a grateful daddy, until he pointed.

I sidled up to a driveway. "Pull up here."

"Shshsh**… you sure …?"

Chrome glinted from a score or more of Indians, Harleys and Triumph choppers grazing in an un-mowed front yard, like slavish warhorses. A hard-rock drummer pounded through the windows of a two-story house, and I suddenly remembered to shut my mouth when the kid slammed the door to my LTD. He reveled in my angst and trotted through the maze of motorcycles; I didn't shut down my engine, in case he bumped one of the Harleys …

"It's okay. Come on."

My people were junkies and minor felons — not killers and outlaws. My hands seemed glued to my steering wheel for a moment as The Sheriff hollered in my head to *"Peel out!"* But I cut my engine.

Gingerly, I followed the kid through the steel lawn ornaments to the concrete porch, and my new friend opened a door that set me on a fast track to ruin.

Big Hoss' son strolled into the biker's sanctuary like he owned the place, me slinking behind him, hands in pockets, eyes stinging from crack and marijuana fumes. Bikers — nodding "high" with their servile chicks — slouched on couches or stretched like sated hounds on the dirty living room carpet. Topping off my wonderment: a glass coffee table where anthills of cocaine melted away. Bikers snorted the white powder with colorful Dixie straws.

I truly stood in a Phoenix den of iniquity — *invited.*

"Dad, this is Bill …"

A great tattooed hulk in a greasy t-shirt and turquoise-studded necklace and wristbands stood at the kitchen table; he whirled to his son's voice, and I felt like the old biker scooped out my soul to weigh its value. He listened to the tale of how I stood up for his boy, then Big Hoss ran his meaty fingers through gray stringy hair. Our eyes met as he nodded approval — a contract between us being wordlessly drawn. All that remained to seal the vile bond was my unwitting mark.

Bikers clomped into the kitchen from a fenced motorcycle "graveyard" near an alley behind the house. They unburdened a parked Chevy Impala and stacked cocaine bricks on the kitchen table.

"Ever do coke?" Hoss asked me.

I nudged the "cool" Bill to answer — the tough guy respected on my own turf — but he had tiptoed out of the building. I took a deep breath.

"No. But I know what it is," I said carefully.

Big Hoss picked up a butcher knife and hacked off a slab from a cocaine brick. He weighed it, wrapped it in a piece of brown paper and handed the "gift" to me, his upper lip forming an unconscious curl.

"This is worth 2,500 bucks. Cut it up and package it, and it's worth six grand." He jerked a greasy thumb at a pan full of packaged white powder. "Those sell for 25 bucks apiece."

Who'd pay $25 for a few flyspecks of coke?

Big Hoss read my mind. "This is direct from Cuban nationals. Pure. The best you can get. Everybody wants it."

He grabbed up a straw, crushed out a line of cocaine atop the corner of the table and sniffed hard, shutting his red watery eyes in painful ecstasy. Then he handed me a straw. I mimicked my newfound mentor — in effect scrawling my signature in the white powder. My whole head went numb; I hoped it would wear off before I drove home.

I did what Big Hoss told me. In my room, with Mom and The Sheriff sleeping a couple doors away, I packaged my treasure and plotted a strategy.

In a week I had more customers than I could handle, adding coke to my drug smorgasbord for the Phoenix suburbs. I bought pagers to keep connected to buyers 24/7, and my clients *loved* me.

One day I walked into my parents' home to find my bedroom door gaping open and the lock twisted out of the jam. Dad had smashed in and rifled my room until he found 25 kilos (25,000 grams) of cocaine in a "secret" compartment.

"I should send your sorry a** to jail."

Dad glanced at Mom and then at the telephone. *I had to act quick.*

"Dad. Listen. Please! It's not mine! I had to hide this stuff for some guys — or I'm dead. You know what happens. I … I owe a lot of money."

I embellished my story as I stuffed the cocaine and a few clothes in suitcases.

"Get the h*** out, and don't come back."

I glanced at Mom, crying, and left my home for good — not so sure that I had suckered The Sheriff at all.

Not all my customers had cash, but a good .45 semi-auto or sex with a wife or girlfriend was as good as gold to me, if you were desperate enough for a fix or hit. I littered my descent into depravity with personal conquests, manipulating each soul who crossed my path. Discovering a person's weaknesses fed my lust — and getting them dependent on me for drugs evoked a misshapen emotional gratification in my mind.

Somehow I fooled my drug-sotted brain that I was a benevolent provider for these addicts, while my own addiction overwhelmed me like fungus on a tenement toilet. Big Hoss had read me right; I was an enterprising young man, hungry to score big in my (likely) short career. Piece by piece cocaine nicked slices off my wits; I was a "user," and the drama of the Phoenix nightlife occupied every waking moment.

Big Hoss became my primary supplier and his bikers my allies. Hoss trusted me to haul high-dollar loads of cocaine from Rialto, California, to Phoenix (he paid five grand and a kilo of cocaine for my delivery by bread truck), and everyone knew his bikers had my back.

One night a player named Rob took me behind the curtain and taught me how to cook up cocaine and make crack. Rob and I converted the white powder to "rocks" that could be smoked or injected, and in days I was hooked on my own sh**. Later I chucked Rob to cook my own product for selling. Powerful and potent, my crack, made from the finest Peruvian flake, turned me into a celebrity dealer in Phoenix, and I felt invincible. I never wanted to come off my high … and when I did come down, I cringed like a beaten child, drapes drawn for days, hating myself, until I climbed the crack mountain again.

During drug deals, sometimes my sixth-sense paranoia clanged an alarm if my drug buyers seemed hinky, suspicious. This paranoia often rescued me from serious prison time, although I frequented the downtown lockup for petty stuff, like minor possession and driving infractions. Jail turned out to be a great place to network with the hard-timers who got to know me as a solid dope supplier — an honest crook.

I clung to an egocentric code of ethics forged in a conscience where my parents' values harangued me. I took a twisted pride in my ability to create the best process for crack, and I liberally shared my product with my own siblings who often stayed with me. I taught them how to be crack addicts, too.

I found a ready currency when cash was scarce on the streets: firearms of all kinds. Most cherished were semiautomatic rifles and pistols traded to me for weed, coke or crack. And like my drugs, I took pride in the guns I sold, cleaned and honed to an individual's particular grip. Gangs on both sides of the border knew my weaponry and reputation.

By the time I was 20, a squad of vices held me dead center in their crosshairs (as well as Phoenix law enforcement, I discovered later). Each depressing morning I shaved the face of a crack head, and I despised him. No longer did a youthful entrepreneur stare back from the bathroom mirror, but a haggard man who failed to keep his clientele supplied and organized anymore. I pleaded for relief to any Power that would listen and decided to cut myself free from the web of drugs that held me fast — somehow.

But what about Hoss?

A cadre of armed men welcomed me into a condo that Big Hoss secured as a "traveling" drug processing center.

"Hoss around?" I asked.

A stocky man still high from some favorite poison nodded, and I entered a large room where Hoss sat with a woman. She rose from the couch and left the room, sizing me up through smeared mascara and bloodshot eyes. Hoss grinned at his star franchisee and pointed to a chair.

"I can't do this anymore."

I tossed a satchel of money and jewelry and a suitcase chock full of guns onto the impression the woman had left on the sofa. I tried to explain that I was losing myself in crack addiction, and I thanked Hoss for everything, but seconds into my narrative my "friend's" face clouded like a desert storm — in disbelief, then rage. At one time I might have grabbed a loaded piece from the suitcase or at least tried to escape from Hoss' fury (it was rumored that he had murdered his own wife), but I just didn't care anymore.

Hoss snatched up a baseball bat within reach and took a step toward me. I closed my eyes, pondering my pathetic end: *brains discharged all over tables and lamps.*

But the blow never came.

I opened my eyes as Hoss' low deep voice oozed through my consciousness: "I want every grain of coke you've got. You owe me." His red face nodded toward my luggage, and he sneered. "And everything you've stashed for a rainy day. All of it!"

He pointed the bat an inch from my chin, and I

watched the polar bear tattoo on his forearm claw to life. "We ain't friends, got it? Don't look at me or use my name for nothin', and never come to my house again!"

❧❧❧

College boy.

At the time, enrolling in college seemed the best way to "rediscover myself," and Dad and Mom watched my contortions from criminal to student with hopeful anticipation. At college I hit the books determined to play the role of regular guy — while my addiction to crack hounded me without mercy.

I even found a steady girlfriend and moved in with her, hoping to form a relationship that might last, but I turned Trish into an addict before we had our first baby. I needed more money than my house-painting job supplied, and my days were filled with scheming and trying to resurrect my drug connections. I called myself a "weekend warrior," partying like the hundreds of middle-class dope buyers that I had serviced over the years, but in reality, I smoked every bit of crack I could afford the minute it was in my hand.

One day, Trish's wealthy grandparents dropped by our studio apartment with an unexpected proposition.

"If you marry our granddaughter, you can quit your painting job, and we'll give you an allowance to live on."

The elderly couple clearly hated me, but I didn't care. My luck seemed to be changing …

I married Trish, and our baby was born a few months later.

I put my free time to work immediately reviving my old drug contacts, borrowing enough money to acquire cocaine or weed and selling it in small batches to other addicts. And if my money sources couldn't loan me funds (even with the lure of a hefty return), I found other ways to find cash.

Robbery. Break-ins. Holdups. All in communities outside of Phoenix. I usually hid a fake mustache and glasses under my car seat.

A connection across the U.S.-Mexico border supplied prime marijuana for guns, and I obliged him, but fearful of doing a stretch of hard time, I never dealt in large quantities of dope as I had with Big Hoss.

Trish and I had a boy and two girls by the time we divorced. Her affair caught me off guard, and I dived deeper into my old drug culture, which only fed my depression. One night I met up with my old partner Rob at a bar, and he offered me a piece of his action.

"I know you're the go-to guy for guns, and I can set you up with my people. You interested? I'm cooking meth now, too, and might cut you in."

But what Rob really needed was a babysitter. I pumped him for everything he knew about cooking meth while running errands, acquiring coke for him or selling product. Rob's habit ruled him, and I moonlighted as his nanny, on scene to wrap him in ice and blankets when he overdosed on cocaine. Before I left Rob in the lurch months later, I reeked of a meth addiction, too.

In my early 20s now, I threw my creative abilities into producing my own special brand of methamphetamine to peddle through a growing network of addicts and pushers. I learned to make it cheaper than my competition (extracting components from fertilizers and gopher poison), and the profits poured in.

I moved my operation from house to house, losing myself in my own addiction and existing in a deep paranoia. I packed a 9mm semiautomatic in a chest holster, a .32 caliber handgun in my belt and a .25 caliber pistol in an ankle holster. I let everyone know I was packing.

If I despised myself when I was a young addict, now I *abhorred* this man who seduced and manipulated his friends, family and enemies alike. On his deathbed, The Sheriff, with disappointment in his old eyes, had summarized who I was: *Nothing but a drug-dealing punk.*

I lived on borrowed time — which was confirmed by a high school girl I knew from West. She now sported a shiny Phoenix police officer's badge.

"I don't want to see you go to prison, so get yourself straightened out. When we catch a druggie, we tell him to snitch on three dealers, and we'll drop the charges. Then we put the dealers on a watch list until they make a mistake. You've been on the list for a long time, Bill. Someone turned you in, and it's just a matter of time till we nail you."

In fact, I had been on this list since my days with Big Hoss.

ॐॐॐ

In my years dealing death on the streets of Phoenix, I lived a Jekyll and Hyde existence, often showing a distorted, self-serving kindness toward many who were down on their luck. Cathy's disability check went straight into her meth pipe like clockwork. I delivered drugs to her ramshackle apartment, where she lived with her two toddlers, and I often filled her fridge with food when I saw the kids eating crumbled crackers and milk or bread with sugar topping for breakfast. She thanked me as she lit up, and later I heard that she traded the food to someone for more meth. I was so blind! I never considered my role in destroying the lives of this family. In the seedy street life I lived in, often my attempt at kindness mutilated lives, rather than healed them.

A young man I met named Sam tended bar part time, and I offered him a lucrative opportunity he could barely resist — to set up drug deals among his patrons. Meg, his wife, was a sweet girl and worked as a nurse, and when they found out she was pregnant, I flashed wads of cash around Sam, who resisted the temptation to cross the line courageously. Sometimes I took them to dinner and brought up the idea, like it was a legitimate business Sam was made for.

Sam finally accepted my offer when the baby was born.

I had dropped off baby gifts, and my sales pitch included how "low risk" the plan was. All he needed to do was find someone he could trust to sell the drugs that I supplied and take his profit. He asked for half a gram for someone he knew, and I gave him the first one for free.

Sam's friend Paul came to their home and brought another potential dealer with him. Paul asked Sam to "front" the dope to him (give him the product and trust him to pay later). He begged and pleaded, but Sam turned him down flat. Paul waited for Sam to turn his back to get drinks and suddenly leaped off the couch and stabbed him multiple times. Meg tried to run upstairs to protect the baby, but he caught her and stabbed her to death.

Paul stole my half-gram and left.

The man whom Paul had invited to Sam and Meg's house reported what he saw to police two hours later. The surviving baby girl is in her 20s today.

What could I say to this woman if I found her? I feel that I have her mother and father's blood on my hands.

రారారా

One evening in my red Corvette, I proved that I could outrun the Phoenix Highway Patrol before they nailed me for possession of methamphetamine. Into the wind at 160 miles per hour, I tossed a personal baggie of crystals, and suddenly the patrol cars in my rearview mirror seemed to evaporate. I pulled into a Smalley's convenience store and waited, then lit up a smoke to enjoy my coup, leaning against the front fender — and that's when I heard the blades of a patrol chopper. Cops streamed into the parking lot, and I assumed the position as I had dozens of times before, wondering if this time my luck had run aground. Had they discovered the meth lab and linked it to me? I spent a few days in jail for driving violations, then drove away from the lockup in my Corvette, ignoring the fact that Arizona police had jerked my driver's license.

When the authorities *did* raid my mobile meth lab, it took months for them to gather evidence to charge me with possession of methamphetamine and equipment, possession of records concerning the distribution of methamphetamine and manufacture of the same. I sat in jail for more than 18 months waiting for a trial that never came. Jail had a peculiar effect on my mind. Dead sober I couldn't run away from guilt, and I prayed for mercy — how could I survive a decade of prison time?

To expect God to help a liar and manipulator like me seemed downright perverted, but I begged him for deliverance, anyway, knowing he could see through me like a clear-bubble crack pipe. Arizona finally kicked me loose, and I immediately forgot about talking to God at all, though he would remind me in the weeks to come.

At the Sahara Casino, my sixth-sense alarm was ringing as I walked out the ornate double doors. I had been in negotiations to sell a substantial amount of meth, but never carried but a few personal crystals to toss in a drink or smoke with a pipe. As I drove back toward town,

I glanced in my rearview mirror and sure enough! A single highway patrol car tailed me. I congratulated myself for smelling a rat and drove far enough to swallow the incriminating evidence and toss the baggie. Where the meth baggie ended up worried me, but it was too late.

"What's the problem, officer?" I asked with mock sincerity, my throat burning.

"Sir, your license plate light is out …"

I didn't pray then — but I should have. Another patrol car pulled alongside, and a thorough search began, trunk, seats, engine compartment …

Several felonies still floated above my head like an anvil. If old evidence relating to my meth lab had gelled, my head would decorate the office of some Arizona prosecutor. I climbed into the back seat of the patrol car, worrying that my time had come.

❧❧❧

Twenty-one.

I had time to count the surly convicts the first time they visited my tent with the gorilla named Chaos.

I was a pretty low-escape risk inmate, housed in what we called "Tent City." The state had no more facilities to hold men waiting for trial, so here I sat, feeling naked without a piece or a blade, although I had scavenged a piece of tile and shaped and sharpened it for protection. I "prayed" that I'd never have to kill anyone, along with other prayers like: "Lord, if you get me out of here, I promise to quit meth …" and "God, I beg you not to let me get a long sentence …"

As I listened to Chaos informing me of my new prison occupation, I realized my mistake: I had disrespected the "Keister Bunny," a man guarded by gangs because of his role in smuggling dope and cigarettes. In fact, I had beaten him near senseless for pushing me and getting in my face.

In my dimly lit tent, Chaos was matter-of-fact. "You're gonna work this yard for us, now. You stow our smokes and dope or we're coming back to nail you."

I came apart inside: rage, fear, indignation, hatred — all of it poured out of my mouth in cursing torrents. The gorilla listened stoically and then left with his entourage.

"Bring it! Bring it, a**h***!" I screamed after him. I brandished a rock sock and fingered the shank hidden in my pants.

Then, weak in the knees, I sank onto my bunk.

Maybe I could take Chaos if I cut him before he got those big paws around my throat.

It was the first time in my life that I wished I was *behind* bars.

A couple nights later (I hadn't slept well since their first visit), Chaos appeared at my tent with his cohorts gathering around him. I blasted smack at him and challenged him at the get-go: "Let's do it, man! I'll take you first!" The shank magically appeared in my hand, and a few of the men stepped back a little. "Not so brave now, huh?"

But Chaos didn't flinch. He smiled smugly. "It ain't

like that. It's gonna be ALL of us." And with that, the score of men descended like locusts on a leaf of lettuce. I woke in the infirmary, footprints imbedded in my skin from stomps and ribs shattered. One arm dangled in a cast, and I had to pry open my swollen eyes to see past the swelling. A video camera recorded the backs of several men and not one frame of my beat down. When the prison officials questioned me, all I said was, "I fell out of my bunk," and the whole yard knew that I was solid. I limped around days later, a hero for taking on the gorilla and 20 other men.

And the Keister Bunny kept his foul job.

I spent about a year and three months in Tent City, until one day someone from the prosecutor's office offered me a deal: "Three years' probation, and you get out in two days."

"What's the catch?" I asked, figuring it was too good to be true.

"We're overcrowded. You do your drug rehab without one "dirty" (drug-related infraction) and you're home free. But one screw-up and your presumptive sentence kicks in."

"And that is …?"

"Eight years, Mr. Handel."

"Ah."

I took the deal, and when I got out, I immediately celebrated with friends by getting high. Weekly drug testing? I aced every one with tricks no one should an edge to the answer

advertise. After my mandatory visits to Parole Officer
Bayless' office, he sensed that I was skirting his rules, and
as with a thousand parolees before me, the justice system
simply waited; patience always trumped deception.

For months I was a one-man house-painting fiend,
smoking meth all day and crashing at my mom's house to
recover and go at both endeavors again and again. It broke
my mother's heart to watch my inevitable fall, and I finally
scraped the bottom of the fertilizer barrel the day troopers
led me out of Mom's house in handcuffs. This was it. I
faced eight years of grueling incarceration. And all because
of stupid mistakes: Driving without a license and keeping
a meth pipe on my person.

God! God, help me! Was my prayer sincere this time?
Even I couldn't tell. I sat in the patrol car, empty of
emotions and *scared* to death of my looming presumptive
sentence.

For three months at Tent City, I waited for a hearing,
my guts churning like I'd ingested broken glass. I feared
living behind bars; morning and night, I begged God for
mercy. But I had lied to God so many times before. How
could I expect his help now? And yet, I had nowhere else
to turn. An attorney finally looked into my case and
petitioned the court for a hearing — a day God has never
let me forget.

I stood before the judge as he pored over a long list of
pending charges and my latest parole violations. Finally he
addressed Mr. Bayless, who rose from his seat with a smile

in his eyes. "Sir, you have filed these violations with the court three days *after* Mr. William Handel's parole term ended. Are you aware of this?"

"Yes, Your Honor. I'm buried in cases. I know I'm a little late, but ..."

"Well, I have no choice but to set Mr. Handel free. You screwed *up*, Mr. Bayless ..."

❧ ❧ ❧

After this close shave with an ugly, long prison term, I reined in my meth distribution and serviced a select few customers to feed my own habit. Keeping out of prison was my goal, though the lure of producing the best product in Arizona still yanked at my ego. I knew I would fall into the deep old ruts again, without a drastic change akin to a heart transplant. All around me dealers I knew were getting busted, and I wondered if I had made "the list" again yet.

My younger brother, Brad, had finished up a five-year stretch in a Montana penitentiary and lived in the Far North now. Years ago he had shocked my poor meth-ridden constitution when he told me, "Bill, I'm walking with God now. And I'm working with the chaplain here at the prison. Men fear me, not because I'm the baddest, but because I have the power of God with me."

I had humored him and handed the phone back to my mom.

Today, as I talked to my little brother, even with 3,000

miles of phone line between us, I sensed a peace in him that drew me to ask for help.

"I'm afraid I'm getting ready to start cooking up a meth business again, and if I get caught this time, they'll put me away for good. I just got out of Florence, and I don't want to go back."

"Get yourself a bus ticket, and get up here, Bill!"

"Brad, I'm with a woman. Arianna has two kids …"

"Bring them, too."

And I did. Loaded with sleeping bags and suitcases, we drove straight to the U.S.-Canada border, and that's where we tripped on a new snag. I called Brad, depressed.

"Canada won't let me into the country 'cause of my criminal record. We're heading back to Phoenix. Thanks for everything, Brad."

"No, you're not. I'm sending you airline tickets. You need four, right? You'll fly out of Seattle. See you at the airport in Fairbanks."

When Arianna's other two children moved into our tiny house with the four of us, the Fairbanks winter seemed to stretch longer than all four seasons in Phoenix. Arianna was restless and drifted headlong into a heavier meth addiction; for me, my highs barely nipped the edge off a hopelessness that spread as far as the Alaska horizon.

And even while I fell back into serious meth addiction in my brother's hometown, I took my family to Friends Community Church, at least to instill some moral values in Arianna's four kids. In time, Arianna and her children moved away to Wisconsin amid a series of flare-ups in our marriage, resulting in our divorce.

I was a ship without a rudder, but a strong group at Friends Church, led by my brother Brad, stood like a lighthouse as I floundered toward a deliverance from drugs and immorality. The name of the church said it all: *Friends.* For the first time in my life, I felt like I could trust people — real, openhearted men and women who struggled with the same problems I did, yet had victory and peace through a personal relationship with God's son, Jesus Christ.

Other times Pastor Jeff preached about "deliverance" from addictions, and I asked pointblank: "God, are you going to deliver ME?"

I grew more and more regular in attending Friends, actually looking forward to associating with these honest-to-God Christians, though I smoked meth and lived a loose life when I wasn't around them. And always, my soul cried out, "God, what are you going to do with me?"

God's answers sometimes have sharp edges.

I slid closer to suicide than my worst days in prison. I called my meth suppliers and told them that I was done with drugs and NOT to call ever again. And that's when meth heads, as thick as a run of chum salmon, started ringing my phone.

"I know you said don't call, but, Bill! Man, I got some stuff that'll blow you away ..."

After months of teetering on this strange life or death seesaw, I told God one night, "The next guy that calls me about drugs, I'm going to kill 'im." Thankfully, no one called to test my sincerity.

The next week in church the pastor prayed for people who needed something special from Jesus Christ, and everyone was deep into it. I closed my eyes and begged God not to let me go to prison for murdering someone. And at that moment, I felt something begin to unwind like an internal steel spring. I knew that this Jesus had begun to set up shop inside me, and life around me appeared *different.*

I was being pulled in half: growing to love my church family, where Jesus touched me each time we met, yet *needing* meth to get me through the day. And just when I felt like I was ripping apart completely, God sent the next best thing to an angel to help mend my broken heart. At a sandwich shop, I happened to be watching a young woman slap meat on pieces of bread, her downcast eyes sorrowful.

"Don't get that sad on my sandwich," I quipped, and she smiled a little. The following day I barely remembered that I had asked her to go bowling sometime. She reminded me. Something about this woman — her inner strength, her gentleness — caught me off guard, and all my defenses soon lay at her feet. I told her about my meth habit, and instead of joining in, she said, "Don't ever let me see you using."

∝∝∝∝

got friends?

In a month, after meeting my Lisa, God completely delivered me from meth addiction — no sweats, no puking my guts out, no raging fever; yet, the grander miracle is crowned in Lisa and me. We're amazed that God's Holy Spirit can take two misfits — one a meth addict and the other a lifelong atheist — and shape them with life lessons into a strong Christian family with three wonderful little girls. Our marriage hasn't been without its freezes and thaws over the years, but together with the help of wonderful Jesus-inspired friends, we're strengthening each weak seam as we find it.

I sorrow over the wounded souls I left in my evil wake and must remind myself often that the blood of Jesus Christ has paid for ALL my sins, as heinous as they were. My Alaska daughters know their dad as loving, genuine, honorable, but my three older children still remember when prison guards, bulletproof glass and addiction separated us when they needed me most. This could add unbearable weight to the anguish I feel — if I hadn't experienced a pure miracle of mercy. Today, when I look into the eyes of my grown son and daughters, I see forgiveness and trust. Now they know me as "Dad," and it's as if *the addict never was.*

At times, I still wrestle with my past, but I'm learning to banish old memories with faith tempered in the pages of white-hot truth: My conscience isn't refurbished or repaired; my mind hasn't been honed or reshaped — I am completely REBORN. I'm dead to the old man I was and alive in Jesus Christ, *a new creation.* I can't explain how it happened, but I know HE did it when I decided to give my life to God.

I always say that salvation happened to me in *chunks*, and it seemed to be the same for Lisa. One day reality just broke through, and we both realized we needed Jesus to complete us and show us the path to eternal life.

God is rewarding Lisa and me with precious opportunities as we mature in our Christian lives, a Spirit-motivated team. I'm active in Celebrate Recovery, a program sponsored by Friends Church to help people heal from addictions. As I tell my story, my beloved prayer warrior has my back, praying in the name of Jesus for hearts to open and hear.

And whenever I'm called upon to visit a con in prison, he immediately knows I'm no "textbook" preacher — I *am* "him" a lifetime ago. After his story boils out, I tell him mine, and it's a humbling, exhilarating experience to place the keys of freedom in his hands — God's word.

high
The Story of Daniel
Written by Arlene Showalter

"Janelle, you gotta come and get me." I struggled to keep my voice firm, feeling the weight of my boss' eyes on me.

"I just dropped you off," she protested. "What's going on?"

"I'll explain when you get here," I said, clutching the phone with whitened knuckles. "Just come back," I said, tossing all my belongings into a single cardboard box.

"Don't touch that computer," my boss growled behind me. I fought to control my shaking hands and roiling stomach.

I clung to my box like a man clings to flotsam after shipwreck.

Janelle arrived, her eyes filled with questions. I climbed into the truck and slammed the door shut before she could fire off the first one.

"What did you do?" she cried.

"Go, go!" I ordered, control slipping from me like a snapped wire. Fear pushed tears, like twin geysers, from my eyes.

"I'm a goner," I blubbered. "I got fired."

My ship had wrecked.

Entangled

"Three cords twisted together are not quickly broken."
– Ancient Hebrew Saying

Dad moved Mom and my two older brothers from Washington to Alaska in 1972 to pursue his dream of farming.

He settled Mom and my two older brothers in Delta Junction, a tiny community 100 miles southeast of Fairbanks. He raised cattle, pigs, chickens, hay, grain and potatoes on 360 acres.

Four years later, I increased his crop of sons.

The 800-mile-long Alaska pipeline passes right through Delta Junction. In addition to farming, Dad took a job as an electrician at Pump Station Number 9. He worked seven days on, seven off.

After his 12-hour shift, Dad worked the fields until he fell into bed late at night. Mom and my older brothers worked with him.

Such long, hard labor took its toll on the family.

"Shhh, Daniel," Mom's voice soothed me as I lay cradled in her arms. I hid my face against her, trying to block out the sound of Dad's screaming and beating on my oldest brother. "You're safe. I'll take care of you."

I loved the Assembly of God church Mom took my brothers and me to. I'd sink back into the pew and absorb the music, the words — and the calm. *No yelling here,* I thought as I relaxed in God's presence.

46

high

Church and God became my refuge from the chaos at home. I gave my heart to the Lord at a young age. His reality soothed my young spirit, and I loved him.

Besides farming alongside Dad, Mom worked as a nurse. Tons of unsupervised time and a 10 year old's curiosity led to consequences that plunged me into a whirlpool of depravity for the next 20 years.

I found my brother Dom's forbidden, hidden treasure — a *Penthouse* magazine.

I gawked and stared, then hid it in a new place so I could visit my find as often as I wished.

After he'd learned of my discovery, Dom offered to share his porn videos. I became a quick and eager study. He flipped through the pages of *The Joy of Sex*, while I digested the titillating sights rolling from the video he put on for me.

Our common interest drew us together in a sordid, smutty bro-pact.

An oppressive force braided the first cord — and smirked.

࿔࿔࿔

I smoked my first bowl of weed with one of Dad's farmhands in my sophomore year. My parents shrugged off Dom's and my porn perks, but held a different view of marijuana. I knew I had to hide it and hide it well.

Weed need sprouted from that same graft. Soon I

smoked weed on the way to school, during my lunch break and on my way back home. I loved the high.

Yet, neither porn absorption nor weed consumption affected my drive for success. I had grown up in 4-H, showing pigs at the local fairs.

"Second place for showmanship goes to Daniel Brown," the fair announcer called. I stood proud and tall next to my prize-winning pig before taking a lap of acceptance about the arena. Once again, I put the pig through its trained paces, touching it now and again with a little crop.

Along with 4-H, I joined Future Farmers of America and shot straight to the top. I showed steers at the fairs now, sometimes bringing in $1,000 a head.

By the time I graduated high school, I had reached the level of state officer, served as president of the local chapter of FFA and ran the local meetings.

I took every Agra science class our high school offered. I was going places and fast.

❧❧❧

Leaning against the locker, I chatted with my friend Will. "You know," he said, "Janelle wants to go out with you."

I shrugged, feeling like the cool cat of high school. "If she's got the guts to ask *me*, I'll do it."

She did.

I did.

We did.

I also took every metal shop class at school and was offered a job as teacher's assistant in my senior year. One day, Mr. Brown and I were building metal racks for hydroponics gardening. The word is Latin and means "working water." The science of hydroponics is learning how to grow plants without soil by supplying all their nutrient needs through their water supply.

I cut triangle-shaped metal wedges to brace up the new shelving, then carried them to the grinder to smooth out the sharp edges.

In the middle of my grinding, somehow my thumb got caught in the wheel and ground it to the first knuckle. I stared at what was left, seeing only clear fluid rather than blood.

Surely I've lost all my bone.

I glanced at my other hand, black with oil. *What now?* I wrapped it, grease and all, around what was left of my thumb.

"Mr. Brown," I said, "I just ground up my thumb."

"Okay," he replied. "Lemme get you a Band-Aid."

"Uh … I think I need more than a Band-Aid."

He looked up. All the color in his face drained south. He rushed me to the local clinic.

They shot me up with pain medication and called my parents. The shock of seeing my usually absent father almost matched that of losing my thumb.

Drugged Depression

"You need to get your son up to Fairbanks ASAP," the doctor informed them. "We're not equipped to handle a case like this."

One hundred miles later, medical personnel cleaned up my thumb and prepared me for surgery the following morning.

"Hello, Daniel." Dr. Banks stepped into the cubicle. "I'm going to level with you."

My heart sank.

"We have three options," he explained. "One, we can cut off the tip of what you have left and sew some skin over it. Second, we can take a piece of skin from your arm, with the blood vessels still attached, and sew it to the thumb. There's a 30 percent success rate with that procedure." He paused.

"The third option has an 80 percent success rate. We take your thumb and sew it into your chest for one month. This gives it time to grow its own blood vessels. Then we cut the skin off of your chest and sew it to the other side of your thumb and rebuild the thumb through plastic surgery."

I still wonder if I am the first person in history to graduate high school with a thumb stitched to his chest.

Legal drugs charged through my body to dampen the constant pain in my right hand. I added tons of weed to ensure success.

high

I hunkered down in the back of the bus the day before my high school graduation.

"Have a swig of this," my friend Steve said.

"What is it?" I asked, reaching with eager fingers.

"Mushroom tea." He grinned. "You'll like it. Guaranteed."

His guarantee sufficed. I tipped the bottle back and chugged it down, not knowing — or caring — about its contents. The next day I learned I'd ingested peyote, a hallucinogenic similar to LSD.

Drugs came easy in our area. Sort of like finding snow in Alaska.

Crowds of 60s hippies moved to the area, bringing their habits with them. My buddies and I attended local bluegrass festivals where acid dripped like dew in the morning.

Restlessness and an incomplete thumb, requiring multiple surgeries and a nonstop flow of drugs, spurred me to visit Janelle.

"I don't want to be stuck with one person," I blurted. "I gotta see other chicks." She cried.

I shrugged, leaned over and kissed her. "That's our last kiss," I stated and walked away.

I hooked up with Cassie, because even at 13, she had a reputation for being easy. I decided to cash in on that.

Cassie and I hung out, sexed up and strung out.

"I wanna go home," she said some months into our relationship.

"Home?" I asked.

"Uh-huh. I wanna go back to Washington, where I'm from."

"Your folks are here," I said, not understanding.

"They're not my folks. They're foster parents." She snorted. "Don't want to go to my folks. Been in foster care forever. I just want to go back."

"What will you do?"

She shrugged. "I'll be okay. Just get me to the airport; I'll take care of the rest."

Police met us there, after her foster parents notified them of her intent.

"You can't leave Alaska," the officer said. "You're still a minor."

We got back into my car. "Where do you want to go?"

"Not back with *them*," she insisted.

I drove her to a friend's house.

"You'll be safe here," I said. "He's cool."

"Okay," she said and melted from my life.

Janelle always stayed on the fringes of my existence by working my dad's farm and accompanying me on the endless rounds of medical appointments and surgeries. Even though I no longer shared my body, I continued to introduce her to every drug I met. After Cassie's disappearance, I allowed Janelle back into my tiny orbit again.

I needed Dad, and I hated him for it. The resentment planted itself on his absenteeism while I was growing up, fertilized itself when I watched, helpless, as he beat the crap out of my oldest brother, Richard, and blossomed with my dependence on his employment.

I couldn't get a job anywhere else because of the numerous thumb surgeries. After each surgery, I couldn't use my right hand for weeks. The possibility that my thumb would never be fully operational again hung over my head like a cumulonimbus cloud.

I needed more drugs as my dependence on Dad remained. I upgraded from acid to methamphetamines. Meth made me feel invincible. I, the thumbless wonder, ran for days on its energy.

☙☙☙

I straightened my back after hours of sorting potatoes and looked around.

I can always work the farm. Dad'll always give me employment. My shoulders drooped. *I don't want to work the farm.* I clenched my fists. *I don't want to be dependent on Dad.*

Helplessness increased my resentment. Pain increased my sense of helplessness.

I needed drugs. I needed invincibility. I had to be in control.

Meth met every requirement. It got me through 12 surgeries. It bolstered and sustained me.

The dark force, the enemy of my soul, plaited the second cord — and chuckled.

Same Sex Saga

Richard owned a house nearby. While out of town, my younger sister, Naomi, house-sat for him. Some friends and I, including Janelle, decided to visit her and party down.

After I got the booze flowing through my bloodstream, I staggered over to Janelle with an important question on my mind. I navigated myself down on one knee. "Will you marry me?" I slurred.

She turned up her nose. "Gotta think about it."

I stared at her in my drunken stupor. She's turning me down? *Me?*

A week later she relieved me of my misery.

"I've thought about it. I'll marry you."

We married on Independence Day, 1996.

I was anything but free.

We fed our new marriage a steady diet of pot, acid and meth. Weed laid the porn obsession to rest, but several months before our wedding, it resurfaced. I discovered when I indulged in porn, the high I got matched that of weed.

Hey, this is cool, I thought. *Same high for free.*

Richard's homosexual friend left some gay porn magazines laying about his house. Never one to miss an opportunity to pollute myself, I ingested their entire contents.

I fantasized about man-sex. I had to have man-sex. Before I married Janelle, I hinted I might be bisexual.

"We'll deal with that when we get there," she replied, steady love reflecting in her eyes.

❧❧❧

A few months into our marriage, I booked a room at Alaska Psychiatric Institute (API) for nursing suicidal thoughts.

"Son, you just need to work on your self-esteem," the experts told me and handed me discharge papers.

The depression of continued surgeries, coupled with the anxiety of spending the rest of my life on my dad's farm under *his* thumb, drove me hot with unrestrained anger.

I hit Janelle. That won me a trip to the Fairbanks Memorial Hospital mental ward. They reduced my boil to a simmer, further encouraged me to work on my self-esteem and sent me home.

Two weeks later, Janelle and I got into a big fight. I head-butted her forehead and punched her shoulder. When she attempted to leave, I restrained her.

She broke free and jumped in her car. I chased her down in my truck, finally forcing her to pull over.

"I have to get out of here," she cried.

"No!" I yelled.

"Yes, I do," she insisted, hitting the accelerator and speeding away.

I returned home, thoughts of eternal dependence and endless surgeries joining forces in my head, mocking me. I locked the door behind me and pulled out my shotgun.

It lay in my trembling hands. *I can't do this.*

I stumbled to the kitchen and got a knife. *No dinky wrist slits for me. I gotta ensure success.*

I tried to cut the full length of my forearm. I pushed the knife down and in. Nothing happened.

Janelle and my parents arrived. Someone pounded on the door. I pushed harder.

"I'm gonna end it now!" I screamed.

"Please, can we talk about this?" Mom pled through the locked door.

"No use." I pushed *harder.* The knife refused to cut.

I stared at the futile red streaks marking my arm and threw away the knife, disgusted. I opened the door.

"I'll go back to FMH," I said, shrugging my shoulders in defeat. We discovered a small snag upon arrival: Fairbanks Memorial was booked up.

"Do you want to call the cops?" the admitting clerk asked Janelle.

She shook her head.

"Well, we can't send him back home. We can fly him back to API in the morning, but he'll have to spend tonight in jail."

The cops came, slapped on cuffs and hustled me down to the local jail. There, they stripped me down and dressed me in an anti-stab-self suit and escorted me to the drunk tank.

Drunks peed on the floor. Others babbled to no one. A few snored.

high

I scowled. *I don't belong with these low-class losers. No way.*

A few hours later, an officer came and moved me to my own private metallic quarters — metal bed, lidless toilet and sink.

"Breakfast." The officer slapped down a tray of bacon and eggs. *I don't suppose one person here gives a rip that I'm allergic to eggs.* My empty stomach complained with me. *This frosts me.*

A state trooper drove me to the airport in handcuffs, escorted me to the back of the plane and sat beside me. After we deplaned, a special van took me to the Anchorage jail.

We passed through the narrow corridors. Each door behind us closed before the door in front opened, taking me from locked compartment to locked compartment, deeper into the bowels of the facility.

Next, troopers shackled me to five other people; we shuffled back into the van and drove to a different airport to pick up another offender. The six of us had to shimmy out of the van, shackled by feet and hands, to receive the latest partner in our strange Congo line.

We returned to the jail. The troopers unbound us and then ushered the others into the jail. An officer drove me, alone, to API.

Nobody seems surprised to see me.

They blocked access to drugs — legal or otherwise — and put me in a room filled with crazy people.

The lights came on, dimly at first, but gradually brightening until reality slapped me in the face.

I couldn't smoke cigarettes or weed. All my crutches remained at home, 400 miles away.

I stood at the window and watched more crazy people playing in the yard.

I don't belong here. I'm not crazy.

"There's nothing wrong with you, so we are discharging you to go home," Mr. I've-Earned-My-Degree-in-Mental-Health-Issues informed me soon after my arrival.

"I'm gonna drive this fist into your face!" I screamed, bunching my fingers into a tight ball. "You have the nerve to tell me there's nothing wrong with me? Why did I try to kill myself?" I jumped to my feet — livid. My voice ratcheted up to the height of Mt. McKinley. "Why do I keep hitting my wife?"

Two beefy attendants grabbed me by my armpits and carried me down the corridor while I kicked and screamed. They tossed me into a padded room. I punched the walls and kicked and screamed some more.

I kicked at the metal strips reinforcing the windows. *The diamond shape is like two triangles fused at their base.* The thought filtered through my rage. The trinity of anxiety, depression and anger had fused with my threefold addiction — porn, drugs and sex. The first fed the latter, which further fueled the first, sucking me into the vortex of a vast dismal abyss.

The beefy guys returned with a nurse, who offered me

an antipsychotic medication. I swallowed it. After it kicked in, the rehab nurse returned to talk to me.

After seven days in lockdown, API released me for the second time. A year of psychotherapy followed.

"You self-medicate with weed," the therapist intoned.

Duh.

"I recommend you find an anger management class," she counseled.

Whatever.

Janelle and I had been attending a tiny church near Delta Junction, along with my mom and occasionally my dad. The pastor worked as a counselor and taught an anger management class in a little room tucked away in the church.

I completed the course. Depression lingered, but keeping out of the company of crazy people kept the rage at bay.

Five months after our wedding, I drove to North Pole, Alaska — not to visit Santa Claus — to indulge in my latest quest for sexual satisfaction.

I visited a porn shop. The vendor happily introduced me to homosexual sex. The high I experienced topped sex with a woman, weed, meth, acid and poppers. It hooked me in and swallowed me whole.

That North Pole shop offered homosexual highs 365 days a year. *Three hundred sixty-four more than Santa.*

৵৵৵

I enrolled at the University of Alaska Fairbanks and excelled in my classes. Janelle moved with me. Life hummed.

At last! No dad, no farm and no more surgeries.

I majored in computer science. Not the best choice for a porn glutton. Like a pedophile studying early childhood development.

In the blink of an eye, I discovered the treasure trove of online porn, downloading porn, incestuous stories and eventually hard porn. I fed my addictions with the toxic kerosene of Internet-accessible porn.

Porn developed a need for meth. Meth fed on porn. Hard porn, hetero-sex, homo-sex, meth, acid for a change of scenery and lots of weed.

I grasped harder and harder.

The dark enemy twisted the three cords together — and laughed.

∾∾∾

At the end of my first year of college, I returned to Delta because of difficulties and had to ask my dad for work once again.

The following fall, Janelle stayed behind in Delta Junction, and I tried going back to UAF. I lasted four weeks without her, returned home and crawled to my dad for a job. Down deep, I knew he loved me, even though we fought. Janelle worked for him as well.

A year later, I got a job at Fort Greely. Two years after

that, the Labor Union Hall accepted me into their apprenticeship program, and I returned to Fairbanks with Janelle, this time as a family.

Finally I'm making good money — on my own — without Dad's help.

The illicit hungers lured me, drove me and left me ravenous.

I gotta know if there's something I'm missing out there.

I had affairs with women, even girls Janelle knew, and sex with men. My computer smoked day and night, cranking out the satiating-but-never-quite-satisfying articles and photos of hardcore porn and homosexual porn.

Like a raging forest fire, it consumed everything in its path and demanded more. Janelle and I discussed divorce because I thought she failed to satisfy me. Other women disappointed me as well.

Quick trips to town for a loaf of bread lasted two hours while I visited the local porn shop.

Greedy, grasping, gasping at the cornucopia of desire. I couldn't stop.

Infernal Inferno

"Daniel!" Janelle screamed into my cell phone. "The house is on fire!"

I bolted to my truck and rummaged around under the seat for my blue emergency light I had on hand as a former captain of a volunteer fire company; I slapped it on top and raced home.

I *had* to get there before the cops because I had my own farming enterprise going, and it wasn't hydroponics — or legal. Marijuana plants filled my second-story rooms. *Why buy what I can grow for free?*

Fear compounded the urgency. *Alaska cops turn their heads at a few plants, but 26 aren't a few. I'm in deep trouble.*

I squealed into the yard. *Too late.* A cop had my hysterical wife cornered, questioning her.

"How much you growing up there?" Cop No. 1 asked, pointing to the grow lights showing plain as day from the upstairs window.

"Just a couple," I lied.

"Yeah, right," the cop growled, reaching for his cell. He punched speed-dial.

"Got us another," he said into the phone. "Yep. Okay. Drug enforcement's on their way," he announced to me.

A few of my drug pals showed up.

"Get Janelle out of here," I ordered. Our two dogs lay dead on the porch. She was out of her mind with grief. They complied, leaving about the time "Officer Drug Enforcement" pulled up.

"What've we got here?" he asked as he exited his pickup.

"Just a couple of plants," I insisted.

"You got a Medical Card?" he asked.

"No."

high

"Shall we take a tour?"

The officers harvested my shotgun and rifle from the first floor, placing them in my custody while they searched the rest of the house. They confiscated my wife's pistol, which she kept beside her bed.

Dad arrived. Richard pulled up a few minutes later.

The family trio watched officers tote out bags of evidence.

"We got us a felony case." The officer's smile held no warmth. "That wasn't a *few*, kid, that was a whole farm."

I hired the best lawyer in the state. He got the felony charge trimmed to a misdemeanor. My enterprise burned up a large chunk of our insurance money, required a year of unsupervised probation and affected my career in the Labor Union.

Before the trial, I'd been offered a job as a union organizer. The company flew me to Seattle for training. I zipped over to the local porn shops for man-sex.

After the trial, more training sent me to Vegas. Again, I haunted local porn shops, ever seeking but never quite alleviating the appetite for man-sex.

∾∾∾

"Sit down, Daniel," the union administrator said as he ushered me into his office. "Your computer savvy impresses us." He smiled. "How would you like to be our Internet technician?"

"Yes, sir!" I grinned. "I promise to give you my best."

"Good," he replied. "The job's yours."

"One thing, though," I said. "High-speed Internet would triple my productivity."

"Granted."

For the next three years I swirled further into the vortex of the devil's triangle, spinning deeper and deeper into hardcore porn. I added bestiality to my coarse diet.

I downloaded it at work and consumed it at home. I ignored Janelle, mother of our new son, in every respect.

I met people online, just as crazed as myself, and a network of trading sprang up. I witnessed the dark side of the moon in the porn industry — and reveled in it.

A divine voice poked through the mist of my cyclonic self-gratification. *Daniel, what are you doing? Why are you watching stuff that degrades women? What are you teaching your son?*

I brushed it off, an easy accomplishment after 20 years. I continued the madness, with one minor concession. I stopped smoking pot around my son. I balanced that sacrifice by growing it again.

Down I spiraled.

Ten computers stood at my disposal on the job. They obeyed like well-trained soldiers, spitting out whatever I commanded. I utilized them all.

Holy Ambush

That divine voice, what I call the Holy Spirit, stopped poking me in April 2009. He laid me out.

high

I came into work, humming. *Life is good. I can do anything I want, whenever I want.*

I sat down and punched my computer on.

"Hey, I need access to my computer," I complained to the manager. "Someone's locked me out."

A day later, I had to talk to the new incoming computer technicians.

"I'll let you log on, but I'm telling you now, bud, we found some porn. You need to get rid of it."

"Really?" I played stupid. "I don't know how it got there."

I logged on. My hands shook.

What should I do? I panted like a caged animal. *What should I do?* To erase even one perverted visual without backup sent waves of nausea through my body.

But what if I get caught? Cold chills swept over me. My thoughts raced, stalled and canceled each other out and raced again. Sweat dripped as I erased, bouncing from computer to computer to computer.

I had arranged to have lunch with Janelle that day.

D***. If I break this date, she'll be leaking questions. So will the manager. The sweat thickened. *I don't want him poking around here, wondering why I'm working through my lunch break.*

I stumbled through lunch. *Gotta keep cool,* I pep-talked myself, forking tasteless, nameless food into my mouth.

I watched Janelle drive away, turned and walked into the building.

I sat down in my office, and the manager quickly said, "Come to my office."

I sauntered down the hall.

The gig is up.

"Yes, sir?" I stepped in the manager's office.

He looked right through me. "We've found porn on your computers."

I scratched my head, trying to look nonchalant. "Haven't a clue how it got there."

He waited.

I pushed down puke, but feigned surprise.

"We're going to confiscate every computer and have them investigated." He stood up and escorted me to my office. He watched, arms crossed and leaning against the door, as I packed my personal items.

I dialed Janelle's number. She returned to get me.

"They found porn on my computer," I choked. "I'm done for."

The next day I called the same hotshot lawyer. He wouldn't say *get rid of the evidence,* but he told me I'd better have a squeaky clean house when the cops came calling. I had to confess all to Janelle.

She helped me destroy every shred of evidence in the house while our 1-year-old son toddled about. We smashed my laptops and hers. My addiction had metastasized to her property, too.

I gathered up all my bootleg DVDs, every scrap of porn stashed in my house. We moved in frantic panic-mode, like we were fleeing the devil himself.

high

We yanked up all my new marijuana plants. I made several trips to the dump, freaking out each time, fearing someone would see me unloading all the filth.

Janelle and I were still scouring the house for stray evidence when someone beat on the front door.

"Open up — police!" the male voice barked. My hands froze, while my heart thumped percussion so loud, my ears picked up the beat.

Janelle and I looked at each other — helpless.

I dashed upstairs and peeked through the curtain.

Thank God! It's just my sister and her goofy husband.

Relief weakened my knees as I returned downstairs, opened the door and forced a smile.

"Something's wrong." Naomi scrutinized my face. "Very wrong."

Finally, finally, finally, I came clean.

"They found porn on my computer at work," I confessed, with tears in my eyes. "Janelle and I are getting rid of everything."

Naomi gestured at my pipes and other drug paraphernalia sprawled out on the table. "Seems to me this would be a good time to quit smoking," she said.

"I agree," Janelle said.

"And get back to church," Naomi added. "There's a really cool one not far away, called Friends Church." She smiled. "I think you both would like it."

☙☙☙

Janelle and I smoked our last bag of weed.

Then we went to Friends Church.

As I listened to Pastor Jeff's message, I felt like God had downloaded my life into his computer. My thoughts tumbled over themselves. *I'm going to jail. My job's gone. Janelle's gonna have to support the family. My life is over.*

God, I am so sorry for the mess I've made of my life. For ignoring you all these years. I sank my head into my hands. *Forgive me.*

That day I ran to God as fast — no, faster — than I had run after sex, drugs and porn. I ran and ran, straight into his outstretched arms.

"We 'Celebrate Recovery' here at Friends Church," Pastor Jeff announced. "Come and join us on Thursday night." He invited all to a class designed to help conquer hurts, habits and hang-ups — and hardcore addictions.

I went. Janelle stayed home. After a meeting, one man in the group confessed to having sex with his daughter. He told how God had forgiven him.

If he can overcome his addictions, I can do the same. Hope flickered in my heart.

I approached him. "Dude," I said, "I need to throw myself into those steps you're talking about — ASAP." I drew a breath. "Will you be my sponsor?"

"Sure. You're well on your way." He smiled. "You just completed Step 4!"

"What's Step 4?" I asked.

"Confessing your sins one to another."

I grinned. "I feel better already."

high

We sat down while I poured out my story, the whole sordid, smelly, obnoxious mess. As it oozed from me, God's cleansing spirit flowed in — a cleansing, purifying, satisfying, authentic *high*. Halfway through the Celebrate Recovery's 12 steps, Janelle began working in childcare for parents attending the program.

One of my accountability partners asked me if I wanted to join his marriage group. I talked to Janelle about it. Then we jumped on it.

"Janelle," I said as we drove to another meeting, "you're going to see me throw myself 100 percent into this new life. Every Monday and every Thursday meeting. I can't afford to go back to the old ways." I inhaled. "Not in the least."

God soaked me in love, grace and mercy. No cops ever came to my door. No warrant for arrest.

What's going on, God? I read the papers and saw how other people got busted for the same things I'd done.

Daniel, I promise you that if you keep doing what I want you to do, I'll protect you. I'm much, much stronger than your strongest addiction.

Before I fled back to God, I had begged, *God, if you would burn down this porn shop and remove the temptation, I promise I'll do anything — anything.*

Nothing happened.

"Did you know the owner closed down that porn store?" a guy in our group asked me.

I stared — dazed, stunned, before understanding dawned.

Okay, God, you knew I had to hit the bottom of the bottom of the pit to change forever, didn't you?

❧❧❧

I realized how much the porn had affected my marriage: It allowed me to grow numb toward my wife and her feelings.

"Janelle, I want to apologize for all I've put you through," I told my wife after one meeting. "I don't know why you ever stayed with me."

Her eyes teared up. "I always knew the sweet, funny guy I fell in love with was still inside the torn-up you," she explained. "You always made me feel special back then. I couldn't just dump you. I never stopped loving you."

I wrapped my arms around my beautiful, faithful wife.

Thank you, Lord, for such a treasure.

Janelle and I began building a marriage that honored God and respect for one another. We began raising our son with God's principles. Soon after I completed the 12-step program of Celebrate Recovery, my sponsor approached me. "You've done well," he said, clapping me on the back. "How about leading the next group?"

Huh? You want me to be a leader?

"Give me a little time to think on it," I stammered.

God Rush

When an evil spirit leaves a person, it goes into the desert, seeking rest but finding none. Then it says, "I will return to the person I came from." So it returns and finds its former home empty, swept, and in order. Then the spirit finds seven other spirits more evil than itself, and they all enter the person and live there. And so that person is worse off than before. That will be the experience of this evil generation. – Jesus of Nazareth

"Men," I began, "if you try to clean up your life without God's help, these are the results you can expect. You can't remove major addictions in your life and leave a void. If you do, the enemy will find something to fill it, and you'll end up worse off than you were before." I scanned the faces before me, some closed, others questioning and a few hopeful.

"You have to fill that void with God," I explained. "You have to fill your time with God." I turned a few pages in my Bible. "Jesus says, 'If your right hand leads you to sin, cut if off and throw it away.' The Internet helped my descent into sin, so I cut it off. I only have it on my phone." I paused.

"I realize that I left a huge void in my life when I turned my back on sexual deviancy, drugs and porn. I have to keep that void filled with God, or I'll go back. I don't want to go back because I know 'The payment for sin is death, but the gift that God freely gives is everlasting life found in Christ Jesus our Lord'" (Romans 6:23 GW).

Several men in the group sat up and leaned toward me.

"I lived dead for years. Now, I prefer to live life. God promised me in Philippians 1:6 that he has begun a good work in me, and he will carry it on to completion in Jesus

Christ. He first touched me at camp, when I was 11. He never gave up on me in all the years I chose to do my own thing and go my own dark way."

I grinned. "He's not going to give up on any of you, either."

our pieces of power
The Story of Roger and Audrey
Written by Richard Drebert

Audrey

Before autumn yields to the grievous Alaska winter, the bush greenery smells of heavy moldering vegetation. Every breeze carries ferment as birch and willow, alder and cottonwood leaves give up their struggle to *cling* — and I was about to give up as well.

My yearning to reclaim the husband I had trusted was dying. He had been a different strain of man before the cocaine: decisive, caring, worthy of my respect, but as I stood at the kitchen window, the season before me seemed the bleakest I had ever known.

Once, as a young mother, I had divorced a man who chose addiction over me and my infant son; I faced the same insecurity now, except this time a Counselor cautioned me to be patient. My Counselor's wisdom spanned eternal seasons, and the winter might bring a fresh beginning if I could somehow brace a little longer ...

જ-જ-જ

As a 5-year-old girl, I hadn't been dressed for the bitter storms my mom and dad conjured when they divorced.

got friends?

Mom left for Fairbanks; my dad stayed in Anchorage working as a telephone system installer. They each remarried and started their lives afresh, while I divided my troubled love between the two. I visited Mom for the summers and lived and attended school in Anchorage, where my innocence frayed to pieces during adolescence.

I fastened my self-worth to other girls my age, "friends" who offered themselves to thoughtless boys and smoked weed. I wrapped myself in their acceptance against the chill of a dysfunctional family.

One day my dad made a deal with his little daughter. "If you stop smoking pot, I'll give up drinking ..."

I loved my dad, but how could I surmount the pressure of being "included" by my school chums? A few months after breaking my promise, I showed up on Mom's doorstep in Fairbanks, a waif with a suitcase. After an angry kerfuffle with Dad and my stepmom over smoking pot again, I had decided to move north and start over. The same kind of crowd, with different names, opened their arms to welcome me on the streets of Fairbanks.

I was 14.

At school I maintained a strong C-average in academics, but an A+ in partying. Looking sexy in my clothes mattered more to me than preparing myself for college, and I burned the midnight sun down to embers on the weekends, with barely a word from my mom and stepdad. The streets of Fairbanks shaped my character as I grew to womanhood, and by 18, after graduation, I moved into an apartment with a boyfriend who said he cared for me. After a couple years of living together, I married Reggie, hoping that a written promise of trust might magically help our relationship last.

I was 22 years old when we married — street smart, but naïve. Reggie loved cocaine more than he loved me.

I partied with his friends and mine, and cocaine became my poison, too. We were weekend warriors, using about a gram or two that soaked up our paychecks like cat litter. I might have been lost forever in the seductive web of drugs and alcohol except for my desire for more in my life. I woke up one day and decided to quit drinking, drugging and smoking. A year later, I got pregnant, and our son came to us, a true gift.

And I decided that I *would* live — without drugs in my life. Reggie said I was growing more difficult to live with — I wasn't the same party girl he married. A maternal instinct had caught hold of me, and I felt like I had a future after all. Mom took care of my son while I was at work. Reggie couldn't stay awake during the day, often dragging himself home in the early morning after parties.

I made a choice: It was better to be lonely than to violate my son's future.

"Give up the cocaine or get out, Reggie."

I divorced this child/man who refused to give up vices to rear his son. And I persevered in my vocation, with the help of a supervisor and friend who had no motives except to see me succeed.

≈≈≈

"Oh, come on, it'll be fun! High school reunions don't come 'round that often, and you'll see old friends." Dina meant well, and I didn't have the heart to tell her that most of *my* old high school friends would likely be stoned somewhere the night of the reunion.

"I'll go, but don't expect me to stay long."

And I didn't. Like I expected, these were the jocks and girls I had laughed at in school — and they had ignored the likes of me. I was polite, feeling out of place, and I left after a few obligatory drinks of punch.

My marriage to Reggie had lasted four years, and one year had gone by since my divorce. I filled my time with advancing in the payroll department at Fred Meyer and making a child-friendly home for my 2 year old. At times I wondered if I would meet a man I could trust and finally dismissed the possibility — perhaps some kind of a nonbinding relationship, but marriage?

Then I got the call.

I wracked my brain to remember what Roger looked like at the class reunion two months before. He asked me to go out for dinner, and for some strange reason, I said yes.

"Uh … you don't know me, and we haven't met. We haven't even spoken, that I remember, but we went to high school together about 10 years ago …"

Are you that desperate for company? I asked myself. My girlfriend's eyes grew wide when I told her about Roger. It was so out of character for me to take a chance on a guy I hadn't *inspected …*

our pieces of power

Roger

I'd seen her across the room in her blue skirt, a little out of sync with the whole "reunion thing" going on around her. In fact, she melted away before I could get close enough to ask her name. But I didn't leave until I found out it was Audrey. Days after the reunion, her face (and such) never left my mind. In the following 60 days, I picked up the phone to call Audrey over and over — but I hung up, worried that I wasn't ready for any kind of relationship. But Audrey's brown eyes just wouldn't leave me alone. My own divorce was about a year old, and after four years of marriage, I still smarted from the suddenness of my former wife's rejection.

"I've met someone, Roger. And I have an apartment. I'm leaving..."

Somehow I forgot about the excruciating angst of that painful day as I sat down to dinner with Audrey the first time. We were both 28 years old, each married for four years and we had graduated from the same high school — totally ignoring one another until now. We had come from broken homes, and neither of us wanted to be married again. Audrey seemed genuinely interested in me, and I poured out my story, salve upon my wounded memories.

I had traveled across Canada on a few occasions from Fairbanks to Wisconsin and back again in my years as a youth and as an adult. At 17, I had graduated early in Fairbanks to work on the North Slope's Prudhoe Bay, where oil flowed through the Alaska pipeline to the coast at the Valdez terminal. My father was a welder, supervising multimillion-dollar jobs and seldom home, whether in Fond du Lac (where I grew up) or in Fairbanks, where we moved when I was a sophomore. Mom kept the home fires burning, but led a lonely life with my brother and sister and me.

"I love sports; wrestling, baseball, football ..."

"Not me." Audrey chuckled a little.

"Well, I don't play anymore, anyway," I said. "Just a little softball these days. Bum knee ... three operations. Hurt on the Slope ... I work for Wonder Bread now. "

When she told me about her life, I knew I wanted to see her again. She seemed to fill the emptiness in my heart, and after two months and several dates, I moved into her house, taking part in raising her 2 year old, still with no real notion of marriage. I just needed to be close to someone who I hoped I might grow to trust — after betrayal. And if it didn't work out, no harm, no foul, right?

But our relationship grew complicated. At first our arrangement proceeded like a well-organized bread route, but in time each of us felt married — responsible, accountable, needed — and our expectations reached toward deeper commitment. I was spending too much time with my friends; Audrey worried that I was breaking trust, and her nagging sent my blood pressure soaring.

I wasn't like Reggie!

Arguments grew more heated. We tried to stick it out, amid stamping feet and screaming opinions, but we finally decided to take a breather from one another after nearly two years of searching for that "happy place" that some couples find. Strangely, we actually talked out our differences over the few months we were apart. We agreed to give one another more room to be ourselves, and we even talked about moving into a new house and investing in our future together.

Neither of us had noticed the subtle shift in my appetites during this time of new decisions. Beyond my relationship with Audrey, I gravitated toward people who were heavy drinkers and drug abusers. I met co-workers at a local watering hole after my shift, and I took hits of cocaine from time to time. Later my "friends" offered it free of charge. I enjoyed it so much that sometimes I began asking for it, and soon they were selling me coke when I *needed* to get high.

Audrey had no clue it was happening, and I pursued the same selfish "code" that I had followed as a young man: *If it doesn't hurt anyone, I can indulge in it.*

I didn't realize that I stirred up waves that would swamp the dreams of everyone close to me.

My Alaska friends that I'd known since high school never thought I would actually marry Audrey — we had such a history of clashes. But on New Year's night I fumbled with an engagement ring and pulled it out of my pocket to show my boyhood pal, Tom. Tom and I had partied together, played sports together in school and now I included Tom and his wife, Janet, in my decision. They were special people.

Tom's jaw dropped, but he shook my hand. And his father, a minister and friend, performed our wedding ceremony months later. No more "living in sin." We were doing the right thing, and I hoped that a marriage contract could resolve the trust issues we struggled with, once and for all.

No one plans to ruin his family with drug addiction or alcoholism. It happens in stages, like rainy spring, sweltering summer, frigid winter — and the road you've been traveling is suddenly heaved and impassable. I had trundled through the best years of our lives in a Wonder Bread truck, while Audrey 10-keyed her way to better positions at Fred Meyer. Routine took the place of communication, and when we did talk, it usually ended in personal sniping or sullen fuming.

Demands at Wonder Bread stole more and more of my time away from home, and my coke-head buddies finally netted a full-on addict to add to their cooler. Adept at dodging Audrey's impromptu "searches" in my personal life, I developed an artist's flare for lying about my whereabouts and activities. And she wasn't shy about her accusations.

"Roger, the truth. Are you doing coke?"

In her eyes I could see anguish and finality.

I looked properly exasperated and hurt. "NO!" I said, and she chose to ignore her misgivings, while my secret grew heavier to bear for both of us.

I don't recall exactly when Audrey began attending a women's Bible study with Tom's wife and a few others. All

our pieces of power

I knew was that when she was away, I had more time alone to indulge in cocaine. I'd become too paranoid about going to jail to snort anywhere but my garage or a few other very private places. I lived in a world divorced from Audrey inside my head, numbed to reality sometimes by alcohol and more often by cocaine.

On the very few days of the month that I wasn't high, I shuffled through credit card statements on accounts that I hid from Audrey; my debts were mounting. My self-serving "code" had lured me onto thin ice, and I felt it cracking beneath my own weight.

One day, after Audrey's coaxing, I finally admitted that I was using cocaine, and I promised to quit. It was a coldblooded, calculating lie that I stood upon, slowly spidering beneath me. I was no longer in control.

Audrey

Denial was over. My husband was a drug addict; I recognized all the signs: extreme mood swings, internalizing, bursts of anger, isolation, paranoia ...

I prided myself in being the wife I envisioned Roger wanted, entering into our marriage with the same moxie I had when I quit partying: *determined.* The least Roger could do was meet me halfway, but it wasn't happening. His drift away from our promises enraged me.

I attacked him verbally to shove him into my way of thinking, but nothing worked. He lived in an alternate universe, and I knew he must be using. At first I didn't want to ask, until I remembered how I behaved when I was coked up.

I badgered him into admitting that he was snorting cocaine, while I clung for dear life to the last knot at the end of my rope. Reggie's doped-up face came to mind, then Roger's — it was happening all over again.

When my friends invited me to their Bible study, I pondered the "lucky" timing, and I accepted, desperately hoping that I could trust them. Our discussion focused our hearts on the words we read together in the Bible; it started to change me, little by little. I discovered that this big book was full of durable truth — apparently *God's* truth — that I could apply to my situation.

One day it finally sunk into my relenting conscience: Roger wasn't my real problem. God wanted to forgive *me* unconditionally, for every immoral, wrongheaded act I had knowingly or unknowingly done. My jagged edges and messy choices were against God; he took it very personally, and I sensed a mountain of remorse in my heart.

At home on hands and knees, tearfully I asked Jesus to wash away my guilt and sin once and for all. I felt him come into my presence, and somehow, into my life, spreading through my being like warm fireweed tea. Jesus took up residence in my heart, a TRUST that I could depend upon forever.

I redoubled my efforts to change Roger for a while. I tried to pray a miracle into him, and after months and months, I was getting desperate again. Our marriage held together on delicate strands of hope alone, and I confided my feelings to my women's Bible study group who had been praying with me. We considered an "intervention" of his friends who might insist that Roger get help, but my new Counselor, Jesus, alerted me to wait patiently for God to act.

I was keeping a journal, and I wrote about my sense of helplessness:

> *I cannot do this. I cannot fix it. I cannot help our marriage, and I am giving it over to you [God]. I am putting my marriage in your hands and Roger in your hands.*

Next month was Christmas, and I had failed. I could pray from outside of his universe, but God himself must pierce Roger's shell of addiction. Somehow I had to hang on …

Roger

I hated when Audrey was right. A depression gripped me whenever I wasn't high, and I wanted to shut out the world for good. When I read the flyer tacked on the bulletin board at the Wonder Bread warehouse, I jotted down a drug counselor's phone number and finally decided to call him. It had been four months since Audrey had stopped haranguing me and seemed almost contented to watch me fall apart. My scheme was to get help without setting off alarm bells all over Fairbanks. No one needed to know that I had a "problem." I could get my life under control and simply go back to my Wonder Bread life.

But God never deals in half-measures, and my drug counselor spoke bluntly. "You are addicted to cocaine and are an alcoholic, Roger. You need to get out of the state and get rehabilitated. I know of a 30-day program in Kirkland, Washington ..."

A week later he called and let me know a bed was opening up in the program. I packed, but the drug rehab center called back to say the bed had suddenly filled ...

Party time.

A bed didn't open again for two weeks! As I came down after a cocaine high, I felt as if the ice bearing my weight had suddenly shattered. Despair covered me, and I prayed to drift off in cold eternal sleep, while Audrey silently rejoiced, praying a very different prayer — for my rescue.

I made a profound decision before I left for rehab.

I drove around to the homes of those who had respected me, to those in my family, to those I worked with. "I ... I'm heading to the Lakeside-Milam Recovery Center to get help. I'm a drug addict." My cards were on the table for everyone to see.

My wonderful friend Tom boarded the plane and flew with me to the Seattle-Tacoma International Airport. We shook hands before he re-boarded for his return trip to

Fairbanks, and I stood alone at baggage claim with my suitcase, searching for my ride.

The doors are never locked at Milam; patients can walk out anytime they want. A convenience store is just down the street, and I could have bought a fifth of Vodka to deaden the self-hatred I felt.

But I had promised Audrey and my friends that I would submit to the rehab for 30 days, and I had to follow through.

I stared at the old brick hotel-turned-rehab-center and followed my driver up the steps. After check-in, an attendant ushered me to "detoxification," where patients stayed until withdrawals grew less painful — and messy. The walls and floors, beds and furnishings were constructed of materials easily hosed off and sterilized. Mercifully, I never experienced the slightest withdrawals associated with cocaine addiction, and the techs moved me to my own room after an introspective four days.

A broken 42-year-old man moved into his new off-white-colored cell, agreeing to lay aside all "will" to decide his own agenda for 26 days. I slept in a bed with plastic sheets and pillow, smelling slightly of Clorox, and was roused from bed at 7 each morning. At 7:45, technicians served breakfast to a cafeteria full of recovering addicts, primed for their daily 14-hour marathon of psych evaluations, classes and group sessions.

The main thrust of Milam's inpatient program was to help me *"recognize that ... addiction is a ... disease, rather than any manifestation of moral consequence, character weakness or psychological dysfunction ..." (Lakeside-Milam Recovery Center Web site).*

I wrestled with this narrow secular insight, happily trying to un-tether my addictive behavior from the "moral consequence" I was living, but it was no use. I knew how corrupt I was inside, even without cocaine, and no one could sugarcoat the reality. After 15 days of the inpatient program, the counselors encouraged me to attend meetings geared to my particular addictions: AA (Alcoholics Anonymous), NA (Narcotics Anonymous) or CA (Cocaine Anonymous).

I chose CA, and our sessions always included a few war stories about how horrible "I used to be." Addicts referred to a "higher power," distant but watchful, who somehow aided in decisions to keep sober. This Entity had no name and no personal distinction and stayed just out of reach, as if he might offend someone if he introduced himself.

Harry was an outsider who sat in our CA sessions, and as with other former addicts, he was encouraged to add a fresh perspective on recovery. Harry hadn't spoken much before he stood up one evening, and he seemed to command an audience far beyond the walls of Milam. You could have heard a pin drop.

"For those of you looking for some higher power ... it's GOD you need. If your higher power is not big enough to keep you sober — come break off a piece of mine ..."

I grasped exactly what he meant. God was reaching out to ME; I had seen him change Audrey and Tom and Janet back home. Peace showed in their eyes, and the truth in

Harry's words slammed my conscience like connecting for a homerun.

That day I asked God to forgive me of the "sin" residing in my character — my sin had resulted in *moral consequence* (addiction) and obvious *psychological dysfunction* (perverse thinking).

I spoke to God like he stood in my room, telling him that I would no longer serve my own ambition, and a mountainous weight lifted from my shoulders. I couldn't wait to tell Audrey about my experience, but I faced a confounding communication problem at Milam: one payphone with a long line of weepy addicts, including me. Letters could barely express what I was feeling, and when I read Audrey's, her tone seemed less than sympathetic. What would I face when I got back home? I pleaded with God to give me another chance with Audrey and my wonderful little son.

By the time I left Lakeside-Milam Recovery Center, I could feel my self-serving arrogance vaporizing like a Fairbanks mist. I could never hope to kick my addictions without God's help — and I knew he was flying home with me.

Audrey

My husband quit his job after 12 years, and the benefits of seniority and insurance vanished. I didn't balk when he told me; I knew why. The old Roger would have stayed, rubbing shoulders with other cocaine addicts — but my man was a new creation.

Old things were gone, the "NEW" had come. It was time for him to cut the line and let the old lure drift downstream for good.

We began attending Friends Community Church regularly. In fact, the week after Roger returned from rehab, on my birthday, I was baptized by Pastor Jeff, with my beloved husband smiling encouragingly. Emerging from those waters, I was publically proclaiming my own "newness" and willingness to follow Jesus. It was a gift I'll cherish as long as I live.

I never dared hope that my prayers would touch our lives in such a material way, but I live with the proof of God's generous, extravagant love every day — as we laugh and play card games with our friends or roast marshmallows over the campfire together.

Roger has discovered the same Jesus who hiked in Galilee with his disciples. He follows him and works twice as hard these days (with two jobs) as he ever did in his previous life. And we've both learned what it really means to trust one another. Our confidence is in God, and our daily commitment to *him* creates a shatterproof bond between us.

I still meet with my girlfriends to study God's word, and sometimes women with broken marriages or addictions join us. We point them to the Counselor, Jesus, as we study the Bible and watch … expecting the next miracle.

Roger cooks dinner for the Celebrate Recovery guests every week, and when asked, he tells his story. He has served as co-leader and leader of a CR 12-step program, sponsored by Friends Church. Our marriage is a work in progress, and we tackle nitty-gritty issues every time God shows us one to address.

Alaska peaks set in azure sky can never be captured in the telling, and so it is with the fulfillment Roger and I know today. Morning and evening, my husband takes my hand in his, and we pray for the needs of family and friends. As we grow older and *closer*, we shall never forget the long cold winters behind us.

"Lord, for my Audrey, this day …"

"Jesus, for my Roger, tomorrow …"

As we meet — often bedraggled from the storms of life — we verbalize aloud what's on our hearts for the other to hear, and we accept comfort. No corpse of tangled secrets hides our struggles anymore, and we trust God to protect our precious union, knowing that he is answering our deepest needs.

Often in our community we see people fall out of "romantic" love, and we truly know their grief and confusion, but through hard-won experience, we have learned that Christian love is far more powerful than mere emotion.

It's a devotion that *stays.*

crown royal to royal crown
The Story of Gabriella
Written by Arlene Showalter

"Some Christmas present," I muttered, clutching the steering wheel of my friend's truck. I peered out at the bleak Alaskan sky. *As full of "holiday cheer" as I am,* I thought. My shoulders sagged.

I pulled into the Wal-Mart parking lot and stepped into the store, dragging my wide-eyed daughter, stumbling past harried shoppers, pushing carts pregnant with toys, tricycles and other Christmas treats, on my trek to the manager's office.

"Ms. Leland," he began, with a sneer. "It would seem you need to inform your child that our store policy of holiday generosity does *not* include shoplifting."

"No, sir," I mumbled. "I promise it won't happen again." I hurried my daughter out the door. Garish Christmas lights and holiday music blaring through the intercom assaulted my senses.

The exit doors came into view. I stepped up the pace. Moments from freedom, an officer stopped me.

"Ma'am," he said, gesturing for me to stop. "We've received a call from an employee here …" he paused to lean in and sniff, "suspecting that you are under the influence." His smile held no humor. "Looks like you're in for a holiday filled with good cheer — in jail."

got friends?

Roots of Rebellion

Mom met her first husband, Philip, at a church camp. She learned that his parents served as Assembly of God ministers — as did hers. She hated the moral boundaries imposed in the home — as did he. They capitalized on this one common bond, got pregnant and married.

God blessed them with two daughters: Tami, and three years later, Cara.

Having nothing but determined rebellion to bind them soon proved a brittle glue.

They divorced.

Mom bounced into a second marriage long enough to gain a son, Robby.

She divorced again.

Then Mom met my father, Evan, in Arizona.

They married.

"You were my only *planned* child," she often told me. Producing children was one thing, providing guidance another. She passed me off to my sister, Cara.

At 5, I attended a Lutheran kindergarten. My daddy taught Sunday school there, and my sisters, Tami, 13, and Cara, 10, sang in the choir. Robby joined the scouts.

We looked quite put-together on the outside.

Sundays were for church. Thursdays — BBQ and liquor. My parents hosted dinners every week, while my sisters were at choir practice and my brother at scouts. Too young to be involved elsewhere, I remained with them at home.

92

crown royal to royal crown

They had an older friend who worked in a Greek restaurant. Along with his love of good ethnic food, he also seemed to favor young flesh.

"Hi, cutie." Mr. Gropes' smile matched his oily hair. "Come and sit on Uncle Georgie's lap."

I scooted behind my mom.

He followed.

"Come on," he coaxed, "don't be shy." He reached around my mother and scooped me into his brawny arms, laughing as I struggled against his probing clutches.

Awareness of my distress never registered in my parents' booze-saturated brains.

Liquor flowed through our home like an amber river. Each person paddled through it in his or her own flimsy boat — desperate to avoid capsizing.

Tami secreted herself in her room after experiencing a rape Dad blamed her for.

Robby retreated to the shadows, shamed by phantom inadequacy.

Cara flitted here and there, frantic to make and keep peace at any cost.

Climbing Combat

I played with my dolls in the driveway while Mom and Dad worked together close by. They had constructed some blinds and were assembling them to hang.

"I told you that piece wouldn't work," Mom suddenly snapped.

93

"You told me no such thing," Dad retorted.

"Yes, I did! You can't do anything right!"

"No?" shouted Dad. "I'll get *this* right." He yanked a dowel rod from the bottom of the blind and swung at Mom.

She grabbed another one, and they began beating each other. Through panicked tears, I saw those rods chopping and slicing against a backdrop of matching shirts.

Matched shirts. Mismatched hearts.

I screamed and tried to pull them apart with my baby hands.

Operation Failure.

Exhaustion closed their battle.

Apprehension sprouted in me.

When Mom and Dad divorced, Phil swooped down and swept us all out of Arizona and into California. Mom married him a second time and then nursed the resentments birthed in their first marriage.

The three older children fended for themselves. Cara continued to look after me.

Addled Adolescence

I whistled as I approached the corral. My mustang, Cherokee Bill, nickered his response and moved toward me. I saddled him up and stroked his face and laid my cheek against his.

"Why is it that when we're together, I feel so happy?" I murmured.

He pulled back to study me with his large brown eyes. Then he reached out to nibble at my shoulder.

I laughed in pure joy and hugged his neck.

He bobbed his head as if to say, *Don't we have a date?*

I hopped onto his back and rode from nightmare to paradise — if only for a few hours. Love cemented our hearts.

We moved on to an upscale neighborhood in a nicer town. But Mom and Phil divorced again. She couldn't support us there, so we moved again, to a place where I couldn't keep my beloved companion.

"We'll have to take Cherokee to your father," Mom said, oblivious of my distress.

To Arizona? Sorrow swallowed me whole.

I loaded Cherokee Bill into his trailer with leaded hands and heart. Mom and her friend refreshed themselves with an endless supply of booze while we sat, hour after hour, in heavy traffic.

My horse stood the entire 12-hour trip without food or water.

"Come on, Cherokee," I coaxed after we arrived at Dad's place. "Come out and stretch your legs a bit."

He staggered out of the trailer like a drunk. I hid my dismay as I fed and watered him. We walked around until he became steadier on his feet.

"Let's go," Dad shouted, waving his beer bottle, "it's getting late." We still had to go to where Cherokee Bill was to board.

I led him to the trailer.

He refused to get in.

Dad tried to beat him into submission with a broom while tears ran down my face.

My friend, my faithful, faithful friend, my heart sobbed. *You've done nothing to deserve this.*

Cherokee Bill still refused to get into the trailer.

Finally, Dad let me ride my horse part of the way. The rest of the time, Dad let his 9-year-old daughter drive his truck, while he held Cherokee's lead rope from the passenger side — and drank.

Dad left Arizona a year later to work on the Alaskan Pipeline. Cherokee Bill returned to California and boarded near El Toro Air Force Base, outside Irvine, California.

Joy returned with our cherished times together. My friend Jeannette often joined us with her own mount. We served as trail guides for visitors to the area, while the Blue Angels screamed overhead, practicing their stunts.

Jeanette's family mystified me. Her mother ran a daycare. Her father trained animals. They discussed everything together in calm, rational tones.

I observed open communication, outward displays of love and genuine happiness. It all seemed quite peculiar to me.

Tami and her boyfriend moved in with us and started a career selling weed. When they upgraded to coke, Mom asked them to leave.

Cara left for Sweden, having been accepted into a yearlong foreign exchange student program.

Dad invited us to visit him in Alaska.

Mom accepted. Robby and I accompanied her.

We stayed.

My old friend, Cherokee Bill, deteriorated when we didn't return to California and died of a broken heart within the year.

When I learned the news, I locked myself in the laundry room for three days and taught my new furry companion, a husky-shepherd dog named Tonsina, how to run an obstacle course. The work took my mind — but not my broken heart — off my loss.

I had learned at an early age to appreciate animal love. My pets never complained, loved me unconditionally and listened to everything I had to say.

They never judged me or abused me. I came to lean hard on their accepting affection when human love failed.

My parents returned to their previous relationship — alcoholics who slammed down to make up, only to slam down again. They thrived on violence. It bloomed and spread, like a nuclear cloud, in our one-room cabin on the lake.

I stood in front of our cramped home one day and inhaled the panorama surrounding me. I felt miniscule against the backdrop of jagged, towering mountains and the massive Gulkana Glacier. The lake captured their images, doubling their mass.

Who am I? I wondered, shrinking into myself. *I'm 11-year-old Gabby, but who am I, really?*

I searched my memory, like a secretary thumbing through a file cabinet. Mythical tabbed folders rose up.

got friends?

Victoria. I open the file in search of the memories within. Mom-who-makes-no-time-in-her-life-for-me. I shoved it back and reached for the next folder.

Evan. Father-who-beat-the-crap-out-of-my-horse. I threw it from me.

Cara. Caregiver-of-necessity-who-abandoned-me-for-Sweden.

I felt my heart dropping into a mist-saturated void. *Even my memories don't tell me who I am, only what others have done to me.*

Construction workers swelled the population of Paxson, 180 miles south of Fairbanks, from 50 to 3,000, as the Alaska pipeline project inched its way from Prudhoe Bay on the North Slope south to Valdez on Prince William Sound.

I worked the counter at the Tangle River Inn. One day, as I sold an old drunk some cigarettes, clad in ditto pants with a low-cut waist, wide bottoms and a tube top, he reached across the counter and touched my bare belly with one finger.

Dad walked into the lobby at that moment.

"I'll teach you not to touch my kid!" he roared, grabbing the old coot by the back of his neck.

He dragged the man out the front door and pulverized his face on the mud grate outside. "She's only 12!"

My life consisted of duo dads. Sober Dad protected me, taught me many things — including construction — and took me fishing and berry picking. Unfortunately, Drunk Dad superseded Sober Dad most of the time.

Drunk Dad hooked up with a hippie bartender, Ruth. A rumor rumbled about town that she dug heroin.

Mom retaliated by transforming herself into a party girl and hanging out with the most happening men around.

My parents split again. Mom, Tami, Robby and I moved and moved again — this time in with Mom's sister in Juneau.

Mom and Tami shared a room, while Robby slept on the floor of our cousin's room and I slept on the couch. We had to board Tonsina at the local animal shelter.

Mom and Tami took bartending jobs, while I tried to adjust to life in a public school. I spent all my leisure hours at the local animal shelter, visiting Tonsina and surrounding myself with many loving furry friends.

Robby started a drug business and succeeded well enough to get him shipped out of the clutches of Alaska's law enforcement and back to Phil in California.

We moved again into our own trailer in Mendenhall Valley. Tonsina came home to my welcoming arms and heart.

And I gained what I had coveted for years — an identity of my own.

The first time I got singing-puke-producing drunk was before my 7th birthday. Over the years I'd learned to handle my booze. I had great role models — my parents.

Now, I, Gabriella, became known and admired at Floyd Dryden Middle School as the "cool party girl." I had only to flick out my thumb in the morning to catch a ride to school and again to return home. My generous chauffer generally had a joint ready to relax me on the way in and a beer handy to further relax me on the way back.

At 13, I had found my way, baby, and I was *on* my way.

Dad bought me another horse, Chris Miss, a beautiful strawberry-roan Tennessee Walker. My heart galloped with joy.

I jumped into work to pay for her board. A state trooper I'd known in Paxson had relocated to Juneau. His wife owned a t-shirt transfer store. I worked for her and babysat their children.

Trooper Brown introduced me to his co-workers as a reliable babysitter. He watched over me like a big brother and helped me haul hay and shavings for Chris Miss.

I also worked as a housekeeper, cleaning for a group of guys living near my horse's barn. The young entrepreneurs excelled at drug dealing and theft.

One night, as I relaxed on their couch next to one of the guys, the door slammed open, and the DEA burst in. A miniature mountain of cocaine sat heaped on the coffee table.

Only my trooper friends kept me from getting busted. I was underage, and they had mercy on me.

But their influence couldn't keep Floyd Dryden Middle School from kicking me out when a teacher discovered alcohol in my locker. That began the slow and easy downward slide of a lifestyle filled with drug dabbling and alcohol swigging.

On top of that, I began understanding the benefits of my own sexuality.

Just before my 15th birthday, Mom shipped Chris Miss, my belongings and me back to Dad and his new wife, Ruth, in Paxson.

"Hello, Gabriella." Ruth pushed her heavily pregnant body off the couch and waddled over to give me a hug. "Welcome home."

Ruth, only 12 years older than I, strove to be both stepmother and friend. We chatted over hot chocolate while we waited for her first baby's birth.

"Last year I gave my life to Jesus," Ruth began. "He changed me and helps me every day."

"In what way?" I challenged. *Anyone crazy enough to marry Dad needs all the help she can get.*

"He guides my decisions through prayer and reading the Bible," she explained. "Wouldn't you like Jesus to help you with your life, too?"

"Sure." *If he can protect me from Dad's drunken rages, I'm in.*

Ruth led me through a prayer and gave me *The Way*, a modern translation of the Bible. She tried hard to guide me.

I read *The Way* twice, but little penetrated my understanding at the time. Three weeks after my arrival, Ruth gave birth to Amanda, then plunged into a crevasse of postpartum depression and never regained her footing. I became Amanda's surrogate mama — a relationship that continues to bless me to this day.

Cara returned from her year in Sweden and got a job at one of the local lodges in Paxson.

Just about the only families in town were those who ran the lodges, so I hung out with all the "lodge kids." One of those kids, Zach, and I became good friends. We zipped up and down the hills around Lake Summit on snow machines. As we marveled at the beauty, we shared our hopes and dreams.

I graduated at 17 and moved to Fairbanks to attend the University of Alaska and find a job. *Fairbanks should be far enough from Dad's temper.*

Zach drove from Paxson every weekend, keeping our friendship alive.

I lived in a travel trailer on Dad's property and collected an assortment of needy friends. *If I can't help myself, at least I can help others.* They stayed in tents until winter came — and then abandoned me.

It got too cold for me as well, so I relocated to a cabin. Juggling work and full-time school proved too hard, so I pared down my classes and started driving a school bus.

Lost in Loneliness

Dad couldn't stay sober, and Ruth's mental state oscillated from unsteady to unstable. I kept their growing family of children in my home for months at a time.

Zach moved in with me and my quasi-family. Our long friendship had budded into intimacy and then blossomed into pregnancy.

"We should get married," I told Zach.

"Yeah," he agreed.

"We should marry in a church," I continued.

He shrugged.

"Just doesn't seem right if we don't," I explained.

"You want to start going to a church and find a preacher you like?"

"I don't know about actually *going*," I said. "Just want to be married in one." *Church folk are different,* I thought. *We don't fit in with good people. But we have to be married by a preacher or I won't feel married.*

We contacted a minister and married in a church in the spring of 1986. Six months later, our beautiful daughter, Jewel, was born, and 18 months after that, our son, Zach, Jr.

Dad and Ruth decided to give their marriage one last shot, collected their children and stumbled to Wisconsin.

Goodbye, Amanda. Goodbye, Josh. Goodbye, Jake. My fractured heart mourned as Dad's car sped away, shrinking and shrinking, until the distant horizon swallowed it up.

Zach and I decided to improve our life by "getting ahead." We worked hard and rewarded our efforts with hard parties.

"You go out too much," I complained.

"I need some down time," Zach retorted. "I work hard so you can stay home all day with the kids. Stop whining."

He left to go zipping around Summit Lake on snow machines — like we used to — with his buddies.

Resentment seeded itself in my heart, wrapped its sinewy arms around it and squeezed.

If that's the way he wants it, I raged, slapping peanut butter on the kids' sandwiches, *I'll show him what it feels like! I'll make myself scarce around here, too.*

I got a job and created a life separate from his. Our hot love cooled to tolerance and heated to divorce.

I refused financial help from Zach. Instead, I found more needy people, a single mom with kids, and took them into my care. That freed me up to work in a bar, where I met my second husband.

Loren attracted me because he never stopped smiling. We exchanged light chit-chat while I worked. I learned he grew up the way I imagined all perfect childhoods should be: with the white-picket-fence-with-stay-at-home-mom-baking-chocolate-chip-cookies sort of childhood.

"I brought something to show you," Loren said, his perpetual grin lighting the dim bar. He shoved a book of Christmas letters across the polished counter. "My mom took 30 years to put this together."

I fell in love — with the book *and* the man. *This is it. Loren has it all — education, money for a real house, he's fun loving. I'll finally have security — forever!*

Loren worked for Alaska Fire Service, which meant he spent most of his time out in the bush, patrolling for and fighting fires.

The kids and I followed him, camping for weeks at a time, and enjoyed the novelty of our new life and adventure. But as the children got a bit older and extracurricular activities filled our days, we opted to stay home while he worked.

Another baby further tethered us.

"Where am I supposed to put my drink?" Loren glared at the coffee table, littered with toys. I rushed over to clear them away. "Every time I come home, the house is a mess," he grumbled.

Marriage and three little ones achieved the unachievable — the cessation of his endless smile. Now, his brows stayed knit in frown mode whenever he visited home.

If I could just do things good enough to please him and love him more, I know he'll change and love us back.

Loren stumbled down the hall, inspecting every bedroom. "This place is a disaster," he roared. "It looks like a bunch of pigs live here."

Our lives separated before we did.

A Ponzi scam Loren had sunk a lot of cash into collapsed. We took our children's savings to settle legal fees.

I returned to work.

He turned to his co-workers for comfort.

I turned to another man.

We divorced.

I drifted about my house, wandering from room to empty room. Zach had picked up Jewel and Jr. for the weekend, and Madelyn was with Loren.

I stumbled into the kitchen and pulled three ornate bottles from the fridge, along with a rock glass from the cupboard. I set them down and began mixing the concoction I needed to fill the stillness.

First, I poured golden Crown Royal, straight up, as my base. Next, I mixed Jägermeister and Goldschläger to make a shot of *liquid cocaine*. The 56 herbs in the Jägermeister and real gold leaf floating from the Goldschläger mesmerized me, but not enough to halt the questions.

"Who am I?" I whispered in the deafening silence. Thoughts that had slumbered for years awakened to torment me. "Why am I here?"

Without my children to distract me, reality loomed up and challenged me.

I scooted to my bedroom for drugs and out to the local bar for an available man — anyone to escape this black void called life.

I have purpose again, I thought, bustling about the kitchen, after once more filling my home with needy people and more animals.

A Significant Other moved in. *Now I won't have those black-hole moments when the kids are gone.* I smiled. *Life is good. I'm good.*

A snake slithered out of the shining morass.

"I need a garage," Significant Other whined. "Why don't you build one?"

"I don't have any extra income," I protested. "The only money I have is my retirement fund."

"You can rebuild it," S.O. insisted. "Think how much a garage would improve your property."

I listened, withdrew the money and hired someone to build it.

He split — with another woman — and the garage stands unfinished to this day.

I anesthetized and desensitized myself with my three faithful crutches: drugs, alcohol and nameless men.

Deepening Depths

In 2005, Ruth returned to Alaska after finally divorcing my dad. She secured a degree in accounting, a good job and an apartment. *She's finally got her act together,* I decided. *Still acts peculiar, but that's just Ruth.*

Months later, the phone rang.

"Hello, Fairbanks Police Department. Is this Gabriella Leland?" the officer on the other end of the line asked.

"Yes. How can I help you?"

"Are you the oldest child of a Mrs. Ruth Leland?"

My mind scrambled. *Yes … no … why is he asking that?*

"Uh … yes."

"Then, ma'am, we have to ask you to come down to the Wal-Mart parking lot."

What? "Why?"

"We need you to identify her body."

I drove to the store, numbed by a new substance — shock. But first, I swung by Aurora Motors to pick up Ruth's son. He rode with me but refused to go into the parking lot.

"Let me out here," he insisted as we approached.

"Why?" I asked. "She's your mother."

"Don't want to see it ... her. Let me out."

I complied and then inched my car toward the police cruisers and yellow tape.

Ruth had carried all her legal documents with her, which identified me as her own child. She had stepped into Wal-Mart to purchase 11 bottles of Sominex and a bottle of rubbing alcohol. She returned to her van, climbed in the backseat and ingested everything.

My mind spun at this new darkness — a cosmic vacuum of barren desolation.

Only my yet-unknown-friend, Jesus, would remove it.

Five months later, my 13-year-old daughter was caught shoplifting at the same Wal-Mart. The hole deepened. I needed fortification before driving down to get her.

An employee smelled alcohol on my breath and called the police.

"Ms. Leland." The officer scowled. "You understand this is your second DUI in three years?"

"Yes, sir," I mumbled.

"You know what that means?"

"Yes, sir."

"One more and you're going to jail."

My head drooped like wheat in a drought, and my heart plummeted to the bottomless bottom. "I understand, sir."

Fears of jail time and a desperation to find a way out of

my hopeless abyss caused me to wander aimlessly for the next few years. My kids drifted into their own separate universes.

"Why are you acting like this?" Jewel screamed. "You're just like your parents! How many times have you whined that you didn't want to end up just like them?"

I climbed on the carousel of no-hope-make-ends-meet-keep-the-house-going-maintain-dead-end-job-while-fighting-to-get-driver's-license-reinstated-to-find-better-job, but never quite grasped the brass ring.

It screeched to a distinct halt the moment an officer handed me a third DUI in less than 10 years. According to Alaska law, Gabriella Leland was now an official felon.

I sat in jail and realized I was at long last stick-a-fork-in-me-I'm-done done.

"God," I cried out to the one I'd ignored or avoided all those years, "help me!"

I discovered a group of women who met daily for prayer and reading the Bible at the jail. God began pouring his healing balm into the broken shards of my heart.

I faced the sentencing judge two months later.

"Ms. Leland." The judge glowered down at me. "You are well aware of the consequences of your actions?"

"Yes, Your Honor, I am." My heart pounded loud enough to be heard in the Lower 48.

"I'm prepared to offer you two options. Jail or ..."

I dared to look up.

"Wellness Court."

"Wellness Court," I answered decisively.

"You don't know the implications yet."

"I'll do it," I insisted, struggling to keep my voice steady.

"It's no picnic," he informed me, ticking off the requirements. "Adult probation with supervision, constant drug and alcohol testing, intensive counseling and full accountability to a recovery group. A sponsor and 30 hours of community service or employment per week."

"I'll do it," I repeated, a flicker of hope warming the tip of my frozen heart.

"Furthermore," he continued, "you will have to lodge at the local Rescue Mission or a dry cabin."

"Dry cabin," I responded, without hesitation. *This girl's used to roughing it.* Dry cabins offered no modern conveniences, including plumbing or electricity.

Christ Connect

One morning, as I left the cabin on my bike, I looked at the gorgeous mountains all around me. Mt. McKinley stood like a proud soldier in the distance.

"God," I cried in the chill morning air, "please help me. I can't do this on my own. I have failed," I choked. "Failed miserably."

"Hi, Gabby!" My friend Diane popped in the coffee shop where I worked. Her husband, Roy, was Zach's brother. I had hung out with him in Paxson, and we two were the graduating class of 1982. "How're you doing?"

I shrugged and poured her coffee. "Not good, not bad. Trying to maintain."

"Our son, Alan, has found a church he's really excited about," she said. "I think you'd like it."

"Um … church … I don't know …"

"Roy and I have gone a few times. I promise you won't feel out of place."

I doubt that.

"Come on," she coaxed.

Shame and guilt clouded my thinking, but desperation drove me.

"I need a refuge … some place I feel safe," I admitted. "I'll go."

"Good. We'll swing by and pick you up next Sunday."

"This is Rosemary." Diane introduced me to a lovely lady at Friends Church. She smiled and extended her hand.

I hesitated and then put out my own. Her warm hand covered mine.

"I'm pleased to meet you, Gabriella."

She seems genuine, I thought. *I'll soon know, I'm sure.*

"Thank you." *Does she know what I really am?*

"Diane tells me you live up by me," she continued. "I live just beyond you, up at Rosie Creek. How about if I pick you up for church from now on?"

She can't be for real. I bit my lip. *Doesn't she know why I live up there in one of those dry cabins?* We became fast friends fast. Rosemary showed me the love of Jesus with her total acceptance of me — and all my baggage. I inched my way toward trusting those "church people."

Soon after I started going to Friends Church, Pastor Jeff announced a new program: Celebrate Recovery. The base of the 12-step program is the eight Beatitudes, or blessings, Jesus spoke about in Matthew, chapter 5.

I'd like to do that, I thought, *but am I ready to bare my soul in front of strangers?* Shortly after that, I stood up in the group to share my story. I took a deep breath. *Reveal to heal,* I thought and plunged in.

For the first time, I experienced the cleansing release that comes when one gets everything out into the open.

Rags to Restoration

In 2002, doctors had diagnosed my mother with oral cancer. She moved from Juneau to live with Tami in Southern California and underwent aggressive radiation treatments.

In 2009, her right jawbone had deteriorated from the radiation. Doctors took bone and skin from her lower leg and grafted it onto Mom's face.

"She looks like she's been hit by a truck," Tami sobbed into the phone, two months later. "The graft won't heal."

"I'll fly down and help," I offered. "I have lots of experience with extensive wound care."

"Oh, good," she said.

"Don't worry," I assured her.

"I'm so glad," she said, sounding relieved.

Before my third DUI in 2007, I had worked as a home health aide, caring for a young man with spina bifida. Manny, paralyzed from the chest down, required total attention. He'd also been severely burned as a child and needed special skin care.

Besides his other handicaps, Manny communicated through a soundboard. He typed in words, and the machine spoke them. He used sign language, too.

Manny appreciated my every effort in caring for him. He showed unconditional love to every person in his life. God used him to touch my heart.

I sat by Mom's bed, gently swabbing away soft dead tissue, thankful for Tami's warning of her appearance. Her face lay gaping open. Each day I checked my tears at the door before entering her room.

Her physician, Dr. Kim, cleaned out the large chunks of dead tissue on his morning rounds.

"A wound of this sort has to heal from the inside out," he explained before allowing me to participate in her care.

Like my life, I mused as thoughts of my troubled past marched across my heart.

I studied Mom's damaged face. *My heart is like this,* I thought. *I covered up years of un-mourned losses and woundedness with foolish pride, not realizing I had to heal from the inside out.* A tear gathered in one eye, lost its footing and dropped.

The graft failed. Next, the doctors tried titanium screws. That failed as well, forcing them to implant a permanent feeding tube in Mom's stomach.

❧❧❧

"Gabby." Cara phoned me in April 2011. "Mom tried to kill herself." I heard the panic in her voice.

"Why?" I asked. "How?"

"You know she's had pneumonia twice in the last three months."

"Yes."

"She's been very depressed about it," Cara explained. "Yesterday I went into her room to check on her." She stifled a sob. "She seemed to be sleeping so peacefully, I went to clean her bathroom."

"And?" I prompted when she paused.

"I discovered three empty bottles of methadone."

"What?!" I cried.

"She had poured them through her feeding tube," Cara said. "The doctor told me that in her condition and taking that much methadone, she should be dead."

"Why?" I clutched the phone in both hands.

"She left a note saying she was done and wanted to be with Jesus."

"Jesus?" I all but screamed.

"Yes, Jesus," Cara said. "She's been turning back to God."

I arrived in California, and Cara picked me up at the airport and drove me to the hospital. Her eyes mirrored exhaustion.

We sat together and waited for Mom to awaken, chatting about where life had taken us and how we each got back to God. We shared how much he had changed us.

Aunt Jean, Mom's sister from Portland, flew down with her husband and was there when she awakened.

"Victoria," Tom said, after a few minutes of small talk. "Remember how we were raised that if we didn't do the right thing, we'd go straight to hell?"

Mom nodded.

"Well, it's not true," he went on. "Jesus loves you and wants to show you all the love and grace he has for you."

Tears pushed up from Mom's eyes and trickled down her damaged face, soaking her pillow and cleansing her heart.

"I'm going to rededicate my life to him right now," she said. We leaned forward to hear her declaration. "I'm going to live whatever years I have left completely for him, and I'm going to show all my children just how much I love each one of them."

"Mom," Cara said one morning. "The doctors want to release you to a rehabilitation center."

"If only I had a friend who could stay with me, I could go home," she said.

A nurse named Grace stepped into Mom's room.

"I overheard what you said, Victoria," Grace began. "I could stay with you. My background is clean, and if they'll give me benefits for your care, I'll do it."

Mom smiled.

This is too good to be true, I thought.

"What made you say that?" I asked.

"The Holy Spirit," Mom responded.

"You mean to tell me the Holy Spirit told you to say that?"

She nodded.

"You hear from the Holy Spirit?"

"Yes."

I shook my head, incredulous.

Mom changed dramatically — both physically and spiritually. After so many years of doing what she wanted to do, Mom began speaking words of encouragement and gentle truth over all her children, speaking the word of God into every situation.

Although the plans with Grace as caregiver fell through, it seemed like God used it to lead us to Horizon, a beautiful place filled with wonderful staff, and we made arrangements for Mom to move there.

As she left the hospital in an ambulance transport, she noticed her attendant was wearing a wedding ring.

"You're married?" she asked.

The man nodded.

She opened her mouth, and words from the Bible poured from her lips. She blessed him, his wife and their marriage.

I met Lesa, a leader of Stephen's Ministry at my sister's church, The Bridge.

"Do you think you could help me?" I asked. "I love my mom, but we have some issues that need working on."

"No," she replied, smiling. "But I know who can. Give Bobbi a call." She paused to scribble down a number.

"She's director of Whitestone Counseling Center."

"Uh … thanks," I said.

"It's faith-based counseling," she added.

I brightened.

"I'll definitely call," I said.

જીજીજી

"Gabby," Bobbi said after ushering me into her cozy office. "I want you to remember a few things."

"Okay."

"When you leave, you just be the best Gabriella you can be. Don't you worry about meeting anyone's standards, except God's."

I nodded. *I know he loves me just as I am.*

"And another thing," she continued. "Leave your mom's stuff on her side of the fence. Keep trusting God that *he* will take care of her. Remember that she belongs to Jesus."

She smiled. "Go home and set some boundaries — and stick to them. Agreed?"

I held out my hand. "Agreed."

જીજીજી

I got a job at the Barista Coffee Shop in Fairbanks. Between mixing cappuccinos, lattes and making gourmet sandwiches, I chatted with our customers.

Our clientele ranged from mental health patients to tourists to the wealthy. I learned that *everyone* carries heartache, no matter what the condition of his or her mind, heart or bank account.

I pulled a letter, written by a former co-worker, from my mailbox and was surprised at what I read.

"Dear Gabriella," Miriam wrote. "Thank you for being such an example to me." I gasped.

A WHAT? I stared at the words. *This girl has her act together. She's got a good home, good family, she's a Christian leader in her high school.* I shook my head. *She's writing to thank me?*

"You don't know what an impact you have on others' lives."

I felt the Holy Spirit's smile.

"I don't get it, Lord. How can a former drunk influence anyone for good?"

You can, and you do, he answered.

ॐॐॐ

The Spirit of the Lord is with me. He has anointed me to tell the Good News to the poor. He has sent me to announce forgiveness to the prisoners of sin and the restoring of sight to the blind, to forgive those who have been shattered by sin (Luke 4:18).

Thank you, Jesus, for using my brokenness to touch others. Guide my words this evening. Amen.

I take a deep breath and scan my audience. Eyes in varying stages of boredom, apprehension or belligerence stare back.

"Hello. My name is Gabriella." I smile. "I'm 46 and the mother of three. I have one beautiful grandchild, and … oh, yes … I'm a convicted felon."

Some eyes roll. Others challenge me. A few folks stifle yawns. But some — some sit a bit straighter, eyes lighting with a momentary flicker. Hope.

I go on to share my story. "I'm here to tell you that you all are headed where I once was, but you can be where I am." Warmth fills my heart for those watching me carefully.

I understand. I've been where you are.

the long and winding road
The Story of Charity
Written by Laura Florio

"He's coming!" I jumped up and ran to my brother Rob's room. Rob told me to wrap myself in a blanket and lie down by his bed.

We listened breathlessly as my father confusedly stumbled through my room, tried my sister's door and then made his way down the hall to Rob's.

"Where's your sister?" he bellowed. Rob and I knew that he could see my outline perfectly.

"She went out," Rob coolly replied.

"Well, then, where's your other sister?" my father persisted.

"She's spending the night with a friend."

There was silence for a brief moment, and then I heard him slink down the hall and up the stairs. The sweat poured down my face as I let go of the blanket, my heart beating loudly in my ears, and caught Rob's relieved glance.

❧ ❧ ❧

I was 8 when I first remember my father touching me inappropriately — although I believe he started when I was 4 or 5 — and he kept it up until I was 17. At 13, I confided in a friend that I thought it was normal that fathers "broke their little girls in."

"What?"

"Doesn't your father —"

"Ugh and never! That is so gross, Charity!"

Then she laughed and changed the subject.

My father trained in the Air Force, and when he drank, he became promiscuous. Having been a part of the Fairbanks community for years, I am still unsure how people, above all my mother, failed to understand that he was sexually abusing me and one of my brothers. Or that my brothers were, in turn, having sex with me and my sister. I really don't know how my mother didn't hear my father's drunken lumbering down the basement steps to the room where I slept. I've previously described her as wearing rose-colored glasses, but perhaps blinders are a more appropriate description. She stayed in the relationship with him, even after she learned the truth — a decision that deeply pained me and the rest of the family.

Weight gain was the byproduct of my abuse. Once I understood that my father was unnaturally attracted to me, I put on the pounds to try and keep him at bay and perhaps to numb myself from his advances. By sixth grade, I weighed 175 pounds. I stopped weighing myself in ninth grade, when the scale tipped to 300 pounds. By then, I took to smoking pot, which eventually morphed into a cocaine addiction. My brothers also shared these pastimes with me.

the long and winding road

❧❧❧

After Rob hid me that night when my father came home drunk looking for me, my father never tried to touch me again because he knew that other people knew. After more than 10 years of suffering, the sexual abuse was finally over, but I would experience the repercussions from it for years before I started to heal.

After the abuse stopped, I knew I desperately needed something to fill the gaping void in my life. Tom introduced me to a more personal God when I was 27. Tom worked at a tanning salon that my sister and I frequented; he was very good-looking, believed in God and wasn't bothered by my antics.

I always maintained that God existed, but Tom challenged me on what exactly I believed about him. He told me pointblank, "The devil believes in God — you have to have faith in him." Through Tom, I started going to a local church.

A few years later, with the help of the church I attended, I recognized that I needed some counseling to work through the consequences of the abuse. I went to my father, rather ironically, who grudgingly gave me $360, saying that if that wasn't enough money for counseling, I would have to figure something else out. He was really just afraid I would tell my mother.

Later that week, one of my brothers came in for a haircut and divulged that my father also abused my oldest brother. Oddly enough, this was new information, and when I heard it, something broke inside of me. I called my brother and told him I was coming to see him, and then I got on a plane and flew to Anchorage. When we met up, I explained what our father did to me and then asked him whether or not our father ever abused him. He admitted, yes, it happened, but he also insisted that he had dealt with it and did not want to keep reliving the nightmare by talking about it.

I returned home, and when I saw my mother, I knew I had to tell her. With the help and prayers of the pastor from the church I attended, I asked her to meet me at a lookout point in town. I felt so afraid. She came late, and I remember thinking, *Is this her ultimate rejection?* We had a tumultuous relationship at best, mostly because my family deemed me their strength and the one that kept everyone cared for and together, instead of her. When we finally sat face to face, the truth poured out of me in a torrent of tears. My father abused me, as well as my brother, and my brothers abused me and each other.

After that, my mother left my father. For about two weeks. Then she went back to him, saying that we were all grown up, and the abuse was no longer an issue. Somewhere in her spiel, she also mentioned that, financially, it was more convenient for her to remain married to him. I was devastated, but the support of my brothers and sister, along with the acute need for love from my mother, kept me in a relationship with her.

Life went on. That same year, the church I attended split, and I was left without a community. I tried going to other churches, but none of them ever really clicked. And then one Sunday, I knew distinctly that God wanted me to attend church. I heard about one church through a few of my customers at the hair salon. So I went. After a few songs and announcements, the pastor took the podium and began his talk.

"Today, I want to tell you a story about the beloved younger son of a very wealthy man. The son completely disrespects his dad by demanding his inheritance before his dad's death, leaves town with the fortune and squanders it on parties and prostitutes. Eventually, when the money runs out, he works on a farm where the pigs eat better than he does. He comes to his senses and decides to go home. Maybe, he thinks, his dad will allow him to work as a hired servant since he no longer has his inheritance rights. When the son approaches the house, his dad sees him, and he runs to welcome his son back into the family. Then the dad throws a huge and costly party in the son's honor."

The theme of grace that saturated the story floored me, and the next Sunday, I was back for more. The pastor talked about a woman that a group of religious leaders caught in bed with a married man. Back in that day, the punishment for such a deed was death by stoning, but one of the men, Jesus, challenged the others with this: "Let him who has no sin cast the first stone." Then Jesus approached the woman, who couldn't even look at him because she was so ashamed, and gently told her that she was forgiven and not to do it again.

Involved in an extramarital affair at the time, I thought that story a little too close for comfort. I felt content in the relationship, and since no one aimed a stone at me in condemnation, I walked out of the church, knowing that I would not return for some time.

প্রপ্রপ্র

Then one Sunday a few years later, I felt another unusual urge to attend church. It struck me as a bit strange.

"Okay, Lord, I am going, but you must be gentle with me. Last time really scared me off."

I slid into the gymnasium-style church a few minutes late, just to keep a low profile, the back row being a favorite of mine. I mused — a bit nervously — through the singing and announcements about what God would have to say to me this time.

Time to face the music: I was a 37-year-old hair stylist with a weight problem and a penchant for married men — I was, in fact, involved with two married men.

Basically, I built myself into my own fort — a bulwark against a very unfair and cruel world. If God was going to get to me, he would have to be good. Very good.

"I don't know why, but I feel the Lord is telling me to preach gently today," the preacher said. I swallowed. It was like he was reading my mail.

After the service, I made my way up to the front. The pastor greeted me, and I started crying. I asked him if he did any counseling. "Yes, certainly." He invited me to come in that Monday, which happened to be my day off.

From the first, I was truthful to the point of bluntness. Yet my brazen comments never caught the pastor off guard. Whenever I said something scandalous, he asked if he could pray for me. We prayed a lot.

I left my first session knowing that I needed to end my adulterous affairs. However, I did not have a clue how to go about it — affairs made up the entirety of my romantic relationships with men, and I really did not know that I could be anything but the "other woman." I felt unworthy to be anything else.

Still, something had to be done. But it wasn't anything *I* needed to do. God now led me, and he orchestrated everything perfectly. Every time I was supposed to meet one of the men I was involved with, something came up, and the tryst couldn't take place. It bordered on the comical. And when I reported all these things to the pastor, he merely smiled and said, "God is protecting you." I was still leery, but after experiencing that protection, I began to realize my worth in Christ. It was during these sessions with the pastor that I counted the cost and asked Jesus to come into my heart and save me.

During the three weeks following my first session, every man that I ever had an affair with, or even wanted to have an affair with, contacted me. I rejected them all, saying that I was no longer interested in being "the side order." I wanted commitment and love. The fear of male rejection lost its hold.

A few months later, a woman came up to me after church. "Have you ever thought about going on a missions trip?" she asked brightly. "Two people canceled for the upcoming trip to Mexico, and when I prayed about it, your name came to my mind."

My friends had asked me the same question a few days before. My answer the first time was, "Never!" However, I now thought I should reconsider.

"I'll check my schedule," I said, confident it would be full and thus impossible for me to attend.

Oddly enough, the trip occurred on a week with no scheduled hair appointments, something that usually never happened. As a longtime hair stylist, my weeks were usually very full. My clients gave me money, and my brother provided my plane ticket. I knew I was meant to go.

I have never experienced a more intense spiritual transformation than that trip. Observing toddlers playing in the streets with no shoes opened my eyes to a level of poverty that I never knew existed. Their lack of worldly goods revealed my own emotional and spiritual poverty, and understanding that level of need, I poured myself out to them in love.

The men on my team showed me how daddies are supposed to love their little girls. One of my team members would become my spiritual mentor and one of my dearest friends. I even quit smoking marijuana. At the end of the week, I was voted "Most Changed" by my group.

Something else happened in Mexico. On the drive from San Diego across the border, I felt the Lord urge me to have the group pray for my father. He was ill and not responding to the treatments the doctors gave him. Of course, I resisted. The last person I ever wanted to pray for was my father. But it's very difficult to argue with one's Creator, so I relented and told my group.

The next morning the man who I watched so intently because he loved his family — especially his daughter — so well prayed for my father. I never witnessed a prayer so passionately or sincerely uttered in my life. He knelt with his hands clasped together so tightly that his knuckles went white. The words that spilled out of him were not eloquent, but they were filled with an all-consuming compassion — I think he prayed from his toes.

"Father, you and you alone are the one that heals, so we are asking you to rescue Charity's father from the clutches of death. We know he's made bad choices and that he is far from you. But we also know your love for him. We know that even though he is a sinner, you sacrificed your beloved and perfect child so that he could be your son and have a relationship with you. We know your love is stronger and more powerful than his pain, his sickness, his mistakes. We believe you can not only heal his body, you can heal his heart and his mind and give him the peace for which he longs. So we pray for your mercy. In Jesus' name, Amen."

His prayer forged a path toward forgiveness and healing — both my father's physical healing and my emotional healing. My father, much to the surprise of the doctors and nurses, recovered.

I returned to Mexico four times, once with my mother. During one of the church services the team held, a young girl received Jesus as her Savior. I saw my mother standing at the back of the room, watching the girl receive the love and grace of her heavenly father. My mother knew that, despite having attended church her whole life, that was something she missed, and shortly after the trip, she realized her need for a Savior and accepted Jesus into her heart.

I have always treasured the fact that I played a part in her exciting new beginning.

After the first Mexico missions trip, I attended a revival at Toronto Christian Airport Fellowship. It seemed like God's Spirit was doing some amazing things there, and word reached our church in Alaska. I arranged for several friends to go with me, but at the last minute, everyone backed out, and I was left to embark on an adventure I never thought I possessed the courage to do by myself. It was at that revival that I experienced a marvelous outpouring of the Holy Spirit. It was like wading deep into an intense and genuine love that has no end. It's hard to explain, like so much about God, but that encounter with the Holy Spirit has been very helpful in my healing process.

෨෨෨

Church became a huge part of my life. I made a lot of friends there. I got involved wherever I could. I gave financially whenever there was a need.

Then I accidentally signed up for a class based on a book called *The Wounded Heart: Hope for Victims of Childhood Sexual Abuse* by Dr. Dan Allender. I say "accidentally" because as soon as I signed up for the class, I wondered why I did it and wanted to rescind my agreement to attend.

When I went for a brief interview with the instructor, I relayed my feelings.

"Charity, several years ago I was praying for you," she told me. "And God showed me that you were a sweet little bird inside a cage. The door of the cage was open, but you would not come out. When I asked God why, the little bird lifted its wing and revealed a large hole in its heart. You have a wounded heart, Charity, and this class was made for you."

Indeed, the class was made for me! After 15 years of searching for healing, I found it. God not only healed my heart, he healed my relationships with my mother and siblings.

God revealed to me how he grieved over the fact that my father sexually abused me, and I forgave my father. He also opened my eyes to the many, many people who experience abuse. The need for such a class is so great. Although I did not realize it then, God planted a vision in my heart to bring healing to other victims through this course.

I finally fully forgave my mother one evening at dinner. A friend was supposed to join us, but didn't show. Dining alone with Mom didn't exactly thrill me; there was still so much tension between us, and lately her blatant declarations of love for my brother during our cell group exacerbated those issues. I did not understand why she was able to love him so much but harbor such resentment toward me.

So during dinner, I asked her. "Why don't you love me? You easily express your love for my brother, but I never hear you say you love me. I need to know why." Feeling the sting of her rejection flush my cheeks, I pushed my food angrily around with my fork.

She put her hands to her face and took a deep breath. "I never really thought you liked me. You always seem so angry with me."

"Um — yeah. That's what happens when someone acts like she loves everyone else but you."

"No, honey. This has been going on for a long, long time. Since you were little, you had this chip on your shoulder toward me, and I never understood why."

"What do you mean?" I asked, my heart softening toward her. "How long have I seemed angry at you?"

My mother traced the pattern in the tablecloth with her finger as she thought. "I think it started when you were 4 or 5."

"Wait … that's about the time he started abusing me."

My mother hung her head.

"It makes perfect sense." The realization suddenly hit

me. "Especially since he always tried to keep you from finding out."

We passed the rest of the evening in thoughtful silence, but both of us knew a breakthrough in our relationship happened during that conversation and a more affectionate understanding of one another took root.

More breakthroughs occurred, making it a watershed year for me. I built my first home. I thought renting perfectly fit my lifestyle, but then my roommates moved out of the rental we shared, and the opportunity arose to buy property and build.

It was during this time that I first recall allowing myself to receive from other people. Previously, I refused to take anything from anyone, because I learned early in life that there were always strings attached — usually sexual. So I gave to everyone, but received from no one.

The building of my house changed that. The contractor built my home and then sold it back to me, so that I could pay a lower financing fee. A fellow from church *volunteered* to construct my deck. I only paid for the materials. Another friend transported the five truckloads of dirt I needed for the yard for free. My brother Rob did the landscaping at no charge. People randomly stopped by and dropped off reams of plants and trees for my yard. It was truly amazing, and I received it all with a joyous heart!

Three years later, I decided to undergo gastro-bypass surgery for my obesity. I had prayed about doing this several times before, but it never worked out. It was a big ordeal. I traveled to California, and the doctors told me that my recovery required several weeks. The surgery went fine, but I wasn't healing as the doctors promised. It turned out that I needed to have my gall bladder removed. Because I recently underwent the gastro-bypass surgery, most doctors would have refused to operate on me again so soon. But several of my customers at the hair salon were doctors or knew doctors, and they pulled some strings.

That surgery also went fine, but it required a five-month respite. Along with a large amount of weight, I lost a few clients, but the majority of them, along with my friends at church, supported me with lots of love, grace and encouragement. They also supported me financially. One woman even gave me $10,000 — $2,000 every month for the five months I couldn't work — just so I would not lose my house.

The weight loss has freed me to eat smaller amounts of food and to do ordinary activities, like take a walk or work in my garden. I savor these activities even more, knowing that I wasn't able to do them for so long. The weight loss also started me on my journey toward recovering my femininity. Part of my "protection" was to dress in a very masculine way. Now I wear dresses.

❧❧❧

When my father died, I experienced yet another level of freedom and forgiveness. I walked away from his grave with the realization that my father lived a life without peace, and for the first time, I wanted him to have that peace in his death.

As I was taking those steps to my car, I turned back and said, "In the name of Jesus, I forgive you." The weight that I carried from that relationship finally lifted.

~~~

I told my mother half-jokingly that she owed me at least five years of a solid loving relationship to make up for the ones that had been tainted by the abuse. I wanted a new beginning for our relationship, and I believe she did, too. She laughed and promised she would do her best. We indeed had some lovely times together, but she passed away a little less than two years later. Two days before she died, I felt this impulsive prompting to call her at 7:30 a.m. and tell her I loved her. I am so thankful I acted on that!

Several important events happened surrounding my mother's death. The first was that I got an idea to cut homeless people's hair. I called this inspiration Hair for the Homeless. After my mother died, I realized I needed to act on that idea. I saw a news story about a rescue mission and called them up to tell them I would like to cut hair for the veterans who came there. I went a few times before realizing that this was an opening for later leading a wounded heart class, not so much about cutting hair. I decided to meet with my church leaders to ask for guidance on how to proceed. I had since switched churches and was now attending Friends Community Church.

I set up an appointment with Pastor Jeff and Pastor Floyd. As our meeting began, I asked them whether they knew about the book, *The Wounded Heart.* They did not, so I briefly explained that it was about healing from childhood sexual abuse. As I spoke, Pastor Floyd interrupted me and told me that he felt this was a green-light idea and that the church should really support me in this. It turns out that the church had recently asked people to pray for someone to come along and address this very issue!

We decided that I would lead a class based on the book as part of Friends Community Church. I am not a Biblical scholar, despite having an incredibly intimate relationship with the Lord, so I knew I needed to find a co-facilitator that was. I asked them to pray for the Lord to bring another facilitator into the picture, and God did just that. A woman who participated in the wounded heart class that I took a few years back agreed to lead this new class with me. Besides having a solid Biblical scholarship, she is also an Alaskan Native, which has brought a lot of people from that culture into the class.

In my preparations for the class, I reviewed my old workbook from my first experience with the class 10 years prior. The changes God had wrought in me since that time made me weep.

Dear God, I had written, *I really want to be more kind, gentle and compassionate toward others. I try so hard to be those things, but I come across all wrong ...*

In another place, I wrote about wanting a relationship and wanting to believe that I was beautiful. I stared down at the pages, the writing now smeared with my tears. All the prayers I uttered during the course of that class were now reality. I was more kind, gentle and compassionate. I knew I was beautiful. And I had recently started dating. God truly healed me and transformed me.

෨෨෨෨

When each participant comes to class, they are carrying the shame of sexual abuse. As they tell their stories, the bond begins: It is such a relief for them to know they are not alone. We talk about how we've been affected, how we feel and why we feel the way we do. We get to the root of the problem. Everyone experiences respect in the class. They leave with hope and an understanding of what love really is, which gives them the freedom to give and receive love. They are equipped to recognize who they are in Christ and, in the process, become more compassionate and loving toward themselves and others.

A dear friend of mine, Anne, signed up for the class. She's an upstanding member of the community, she has a wonderful marriage and family and she has a profound relationship with the Lord. I felt very nervous about leading my good friend through this journey of healing, so I prayed. *Lord, I know she is one of many others who will do this, but she is the first, and I have no clue how this is going to work out. Help!* In the end, God chose the perfect person as my first friend/participant.

Anne questioned why she was taking the course — why she wanted to open up old wounds and dig up those horrible memories. It was not an easy journey for her. But she persevered, maybe even more out of respect for me than a desire to finish it. In the end, she brought me flowers and a card. Tears glistened in her eyes as she handed them to me.

"You have no idea what you've done for me."

I gave her a big hug. "Yes, I do. That's why we do what we do here, so that you can stand before me and say exactly what you just said."

Our second class recently ended. The healing I have received through facilitating and witnessing others receive healing from the stronghold of sexual abuse is beyond description.

I have found my calling.

The second important event that happened right around the time my mother died was a romantic relationship. The day after her death, I was asked out on a blind date. The guy actually initiated the date four months earlier, but postponed it for various reasons. Despite our tumultuous relationship, I always viewed my mother as a source of support. I was single without a boyfriend, but she was around. At her death, I realized I desired an intimate relationship with a man.

My blind date turned into a two-and-a-half-year relationship, through which the Lord changed me. He opened my heart up to be able to love again. My boyfriend was kind and gentle and patient. He tolerated my eighth grade behavior because I had never really dated. I didn't know how, yet he was so patient.

On several occasions after going to the movies or shopping at Fred Meyer, he would hold my hand to keep me safe from the ice in the parking lot.

One day, we went to a Montgomery Gentry concert — a remake of our first date. I knew I needed some intimacy in our relationship, and I had prayed for God to make that happen. As the band played the music, my boyfriend reached out and took my hand. He not only held my hand, but his warm arm snuggled around my shoulder gave me goose bumps. I was so happy!

Though the relationship did not last forever, it taught me how to feel beautiful and respected by a man. He taught me to be the "one" instead of the "side order."

Now, at 51, I eagerly anticipate a future of intimacy and love. I am finally and completely ready to embrace a full life that includes friendship, the possibility of a committed relationship, leadership and Christ. God has used the long and winding road of my life to draw me and many others to himself.

That path is straightening, and the best part of my journey has just begun.

the long road home
The Story of Corey
Written by Karen Koczwara

I can't keep running anymore.
I have known this for some time.
I have known that someday I will get caught.
And someday is today.

I glance in the rearview mirror and hardly recognize myself. The pale, gaunt cheeks, the hollow, sunken eyes that stare back like a stranger's. Inside my worn pants pockets, two guns rest against the fabric, reminders of my past, my present and my future. My white-knuckled hands grip the steering wheel as the familiar road comes into view. I am almost home. The sirens will sound any minute, I know.

I don't know what I'll say when I get there.
I don't know what I'll do.
I just want to lay down and rest, sleep for days.
Weeks, maybe. I know I must surrender.

❧❧❧

Grants Pass, Oregon, is a sleepy little town, one a tourist might breeze through with a passive glance out the window at the Rogue River that rushes through it. It was the place my two older brothers and I called home for the first 10 years of our life. And it is where my story begins.

I was born on October 29, 1985. From the time I was young, I was an active, angry and sometimes aggressive kid. The rural Southern Oregon terrain was my playground, but when I was just 10 years old, my father announced we were moving to Fort Greely, Alaska, so he and my mother could find better work.

The idea of moving didn't thrill me. I had my friends at school and my routine at home. We had family in town and church folk who often stopped by with food when the fridge was empty. I grew angry as the moving truck pulled out of the drive and we made our long journey up north. I was too young to understand about survival, to understand that my father was only trying to provide for our family. Moving felt like the end of the world.

I was even less happy when we arrived at my uncle's house in Fort Greely that fall. He lived in a small place on the military base with his four children; our brood only added to the chaos.

"We'll stay here only temporarily, until I find work," my father assured us.

"Temporarily" turned into six months. With little supervision or direction, we grew restless under the small roof and began to search for ways to fill the long, dark days. One day, my older brother beckoned me into the back room.

"Try this stuff," he whispered, handing me a bottle.

I took a whiff and made a face. "What is it?" I asked cautiously.

"Just a little booze I snuck from the cupboard. C'mon, give it a try. Just take a long swig, like this." He demonstrated and then passed the bottle back to me.

I took a few sips, shuddering as it went down. "How do you drink that stuff?" I asked, grimacing. "It's nasty!"

"You'll get used to it." He winked, as though to let me know this wouldn't be the last time we'd touch the booze.

Within no time at all, I began drinking with my brother. What started as a few sips became a few beers that no one seemed to notice went missing from the fridge at night. I grew accustomed to the taste and liked the way the booze made me feel … lighter, happier, able to forget my troubles for a moment.

When a friend of mine pulled out a joint one night, I took a hit without hesitating. "This gonna get me high?" I asked, eyes wide with excitement.

"Maybe. Depends how much you smoke." He laughed. "Just make sure your dad doesn't catch you and give you a good whoopin'."

I doubted my father would notice. He'd found construction work in Fairbanks and now commuted more than 100 miles each day to his new job. My mother was busy, too, looking for work in town. Days went by without much more than a good morning "hello" or a "goodnight." I decided that if I was going to be on my own in a new town, I'd just do whatever I liked.

ప్రోప్రోప్రో

"Hey, Corey, what you lookin' at?" a kid sneered one day after class.

I whirled around and glared at him. "I ain't lookin' at nothin'. What are you lookin' at?"

Something rose inside of me, like a fire being rekindled, and I took a swipe at him with my fist. For the next few minutes, we scuffled on the ground, until blood painted the concrete and the teachers came running with their whistles.

"You've got to stop behaving like this, Corey," my teacher said sternly as she marched me down to the principal's office. "You can't go around picking on kids and throwing out swear words. Doesn't your mother soap your mouth at home if you say bad words?"

I shook my head. My parents were good folks, but they were so busy these days, I doubted they'd notice if I spouted my mouth off. I sulked in the principal's office as he droned on about the proper school conduct and the consequences of fighting and cussing on campus.

"I won't do it again," I promised.

After tiring of the long commute to work, my father moved us to Fairbanks. This meant more change for me and my brothers — another school, new friends, new teachers to pick on us. Within no time, I was back to fighting at school. The minute I got home, my brothers and I slipped out back to share a joint or down some booze. We took turns sneaking into the cupboards to grab a bottle or two; somehow, no one ever seemed to notice.

One day in sixth grade, a new friend sidled up to me after school. "Hey, Corey, you get your hands on the new Green Day CD yet?" he asked.

I shook my head. "Don't have money for that kind of stuff."

"I know where to get some CDs," he said, snickering. "Come with me."

A few minutes later, I stood next to a rack of CDs, shiny in their plastic cases on a shelf inside a local gas station. The cashier was busy ringing someone up and didn't even glance up as my friend and I shoved a couple CDs up our shirts and slipped out the door.

My heart raced with adrenaline as we ran behind the building and pulled the shiny discs out of our shirts. "Whew, that was crazy!" I laughed. "I can't believe we just got away with that!"

"I do it all the time. It gets easier and easier," my friend said, grinning. "Enjoy your new tunes."

As our family grew more distant at home, I grew more daring with my new ventures. I returned to the gas station a few more times, always pretending to pick out a soda or candy bar before I sauntered over to the CD section and shoved one under my shirt. My blood pumped each time I slipped out that door; the thrill and the challenge of not getting caught was beginning to grow on me.

One day, however, my luck ran out. I was halfway out the door with a CD under my shirt when the cashier flew from around the counter and grabbed me by the arm.

"What do you think you're doing, young man?" he demanded.

I gulped hard. "Um, nothing?" My voice came out as a squeak.

"I saw what you just did. Now hand it over. I'm calling your folks."

My hands shook as I repeated my phone number to him, and he dialed my parents. My father's disappointed, angry eyes said it all as he drove me home later that night.

"I can't believe a son of mine would do something like that," he said, deploringly. "If I ever catch you stealing again, young man, you're going to be sorrier than sorry, you hear?"

I nodded from the back seat, temporarily paralyzed by fear. I knew my dad meant business, and I really didn't want to see his wrath. I decided to stay far away from the gas station from then on and stick with the pot and the booze.

≈≈≈≈

In 1998, just days before I was to start seventh grade, I set out on a bike ride with my friend. We had been drinking all morning and planned on hitting the booze again when we got back home. As we sped down the rural road, my friend called out to me, "Hey, Corey, wanna switch bikes?"

"Sure!" I hollered back. I liked his bike better; it was bigger and went faster. I hopped off mine and onto his and was just pedaling back into the street when a truck barreled around the corner at high speed and struck me. I crashed to the pavement and lay there in a daze, my legs throbbing, my head pounding, blood trickling onto the ground.

The next few hours were a blur of foreign smells, strange sounds and new faces as the doctors and nurses rushed around me at the hospital. I heard the words "broken femur" but was in too much pain to piece my injuries together. My parents arrived, their faces stricken with panic as they hovered around my bed.

"Corey, thank God you weren't hurt worse!" my mother cried, stroking my face.

I tried to move my mouth but was too tired to speak. Instead, I lay back on the pillow and drifted off to sleep. I spent the next week at the hospital on morphine and prescription painkillers. As I became more coherent, I realized that I'd already missed the first day of junior high.

Six weeks after school began, I was finally able to attend. I limped onto a new campus that first day with pins in my leg, a pair of crutches and a gnawing anxiety in my heart. This wasn't the way I'd planned to make my big junior high debut.

"Hey, why you walk so funny?" A kid next to me sneered as we slid into our seats in math class.

I tried ignoring him, determined to stop picking fights now that I was a big seventh grader. But when the taunting continued in the halls, my blood began to boil.

"I got in a bike accident, okay? Now leave me alone!" I

snarled as kids snickered beside their lockers. It was hard enough finding my new classes and catching up on school work, much less having to deal with those stupid guys!

I grew depressed and began popping a few extra painkillers to numb the pain in my leg and in my soul. I liked the way they made me feel — as though all my problems were floating away. I met a boy across the street whose friend had accidentally shot him in the face when playing with a gun one day. He was also on painkillers and slipped me a few extra Percocet here and there.

"Gotta numb the pain, right?" he said as he popped a pill and took a swig of booze.

"That's right," I replied. I glanced across the street at my house, a pang of sadness hitting me inside. My parents were working late again, and my brothers had wandered off to goodness knew where. The kitchen table would sit empty again, a reminder that our family was drifting apart. I wished we could all go back to Oregon, where things were simpler and happier, where we were together. But wishing wasn't going to change anything now.

During this lonely time in my life, my brother met a family who attended a local church. They invited all of us to attend the youth group, and I began going. I had been to church off and on in Oregon; the kind folks at our church back home had taken care of us when things got tight around the house. I had been introduced to the basic Bible stories, like Daniel in the lions' den and Jonah and the whale, but didn't really understand much about God.

As I sat in the pews of this new church and listened as

the band sang about God's love, I wondered if that love could really be for me. I wanted to believe it could, so I went along with everything the pastor said, reading my Bible and praying all the right prayers.

"Are you going to get baptized next week, Corey?" my brother asked. "A lot of the kids from the youth group are doing it."

"Yeah, that sounds cool." I had just begun to understand the basics of the Bible and this God that everyone talked about, but baptism seemed like a logical step for a boy my age. I joined in with my peers the following weekend when it came time for the ceremony.

It would be years later, however, that I would truly know what it meant to have a real relationship with the Lord.

🙠🙠🙠

In 2001, toward the end of my freshman year, I began selling marijuana. It was easy to buy and sell a few ounces here and there, as I knew all the right people to buy and sell to. I enjoyed the extra cash in my pocket and hoped it would keep me from having to do time at the fast-food joint down the street like most teenagers did.

Painkillers like Percocet and Vicodin became a second best friend to marijuana. I enjoyed the high I got from them and often trudged across the street to my neighbor's house to see what he had in stock in his medicine cabinet. I also dabbled with 'shrooms. I told myself these things were all harmless, that I wasn't doing *real* drugs like those strung-out guys on the street.

Little did I know that my harmless habit would one day spiral out of control, and I would mirror those guys.

Though I was smart and got decent grades throughout high school, I continued getting into trouble and skipping classes. Most days, I came to school high, looking for someone to sell an ounce or two of marijuana to. The administration caught on to my reckless behavior and kept a close eye on me. Eager to get out from under their watch, I decided to take correspondence classes toward the end of my senior year and graduated a semester early.

At last, I was free to do what I wanted.

❧❧❧

In 2003, I moved out of my parents' house and was introduced to two more friends: meth and coke. The high I got from coke was completely different than the high I got from prescription meds or pot. I was literally soaring on coke; I felt I was on top of the world. Suddenly, I wondered what I'd been missing out on all this time.

One day, a guy asked me to be his middleman on a drug deal. When I caught a glimpse of the hefty profit, my eyes lit up. Maybe there was something to this selling business!

Selling a few ounces of pot to a friend was one thing, but selling coke was quite another. I was in the big leagues now. I started by purchasing a half-ounce of coke, and within six months, I had made so much money that I turned it into a half-kilo of coke. I began selling grams and then 8-balls, doing $100 to $200 deals at a time. The little game was quite simple: The more money I invested, the more money I made. Dollar signs danced before my eyes, and I hoped that my days of scrounging for food in the fridge would soon be far behind me.

When I was 19 years old, I bought my first kilo of coke. In the drug-selling world, this was quite an accomplishment. I now had a full-time job. The illusion of power sucked me in; I loved that I had something other people wanted to get their hands on. I purchased fancy things, from guns to nice cars to flashy jewelry. Every night was a party, and every day was another opportunity to rake in the dough. As I cruised the streets in my expensive cars and blasted my rap music, I felt like a king with the world at my feet.

By 2005, I was using coke daily. I tried to keep my use on the down low with my family, but they knew I was selling. Physically, the drugs had taken a toll on me. I had lost weight and the deviated septum in my nose caused frequent nosebleeds after I snorted coke. "I hate what you're doing, son," my father said with a weary sigh one day. "I wish you'd just get out there and get a real job like everyone else. You can't do this forever, you know."

My father had always worked hard with his bare hands, and I knew he thought I'd taken the easy way out. But it would be hard to give up such a lavish lifestyle at this point. If I was this "successful" at age 20, I could only imagine the houses, cars and jewelry I could snatch up by the time I reached my father's age.

One of the disadvantages of selling drugs was trying to hide from the law. I never stayed in one place long, moving from apartment to apartment to avoid suspicious neighbors. People came to my house at all hours of the day and night, wallets and hands open as I gave them what they wanted. Word quickly spread, and there was never a lack of clientele.

To increase my productivity, I decided to "hire" a few part-time helpers. These guys did the dirty work, selling the smaller stuff for me so I could focus on buying and selling the bigger stuff. Before long, my little system was working quite well, and the money was better than ever.

My drug usage was now out of control. I woke up snorting coke or meth and went to bed doing the same. Often, I didn't even need to go to bed and stayed up for days at a time, which left many more hours to sell and make money. If I needed to come down from the drugs, I popped a few Vicodin, Xanax or Percocet, and the painkillers offset the high.

Everything seemed so easy, but in truth, I was in for the hardest ride of my life.

❧ ❧ ❧

One night, an older guy came to my door. He had bought from me a few times before, and I knew just what he wanted. As I put his package together for him, he pulled out a needle. "You ever shot up, man?" he asked quietly.

I stared at the needle. "No." I flashed back to the days with my brothers, taking my first sips of booze and my first hit on a joint. Then came coke and meth, the next step "up" in the drug world. Still harmless, I managed to tell myself. But shooting up? That was a whole other ballgame.

"The high is outta control," he said with a laugh, showing me how to shoot up. "You in?"

I was already high from earlier that day. As I sank onto the couch, I took the needle and shot the coke into my arm. Within a few minutes, just as he'd promised, I was flying. The room spun and took on a completely new dimension, and again, I wondered how I'd missed out all this time.

Shooting meth and heroin launched me into a whole new world. The high from shooting was 100 percent more powerful than the high from snorting. At times, my stomach lurched, and I wondered if I might die when I shot up, but this didn't stop me from doing it again.

I was literally hooked, unable to quit.

While I had once been the life of the party, I now grew reclusive, paranoid, edgy and even suicidal, sometimes not leaving my apartment for days at a time. I kept my guns close by my side at all times and purchased a bulletproof vest, just in case I ran into trouble. I felt I could trust no one, even myself at times. When the loneliness began to creep in, I simply shot up again to keep from feeling anything. And for a while, the numbness seemed to work.

One night after shooting up, I began gasping for breath; it felt like someone had dumped hundreds of bricks on my chest. I lay on the floor, the room spinning before my eyes, wondering if I really might die. After what felt like days, the feeling subsided, and I began to regain focus. Terrified that I was losing control, I took a step and called up an old friend.

"Man, I gotta tell you something," I confided. "I'm shooting up now. I didn't want to start, but now, man, I can't stop."

My friend also used drugs but had never experimented like I had. "Man, that stuff is bad. Real bad. You gotta stop shootin'. Get help," he said. "I'm worried about you."

"I'll be fine. Just gotta get my head together," I replied.

I knew my friend was right, that I needed real help. Part of me wanted to reach out, but I was so invested in the lifestyle that I hadn't a clue as to how to do so. Instead of heading for rehab, I decided to quit the coke and focused solely on meth and heroin, slipping in a few painkillers here and there when I wanted to come down from my high. I kept selling the coke to fund my habit and told myself that everything would be okay. If I just kept busy and stayed high, the loneliness that gnawed at me would never surface and stare me in the face.

My parents grew more and more concerned. My mother stopped by one day to visit. "Mom, you can't be here. You gotta get out of here," I hissed, ushering her to the door. I hated shooing away my own mother, but I couldn't risk her being here if the cops or a buyer came to the door.

"Corey, I really just wish you would stop all this." My mother's eyes were weary and sad, and though it pained me to see her hurt, I didn't have what it took to quit my lifestyle. I watched her walk away, shoulders slumped, and breathed a sigh of relief when I closed the door.

My older brother, who I had been especially close to at one point, had moved to Arizona after joining the military a few years before. I flew down to visit him and my other brother one weekend, showing up with lavish gifts that I hoped would ease the awkward distance between us.

"Look at yourself, Corey," my brother pleaded one night over dinner. "You're a total mess. You think you can come down here flashing all this expensive stuff, but we see right through it. You're wasting away there, barely eating, hardly functioning as a human being. You look like death. If you don't quit, we're going to intervene because we love you. You hear us?" He was crying now, tears spilling down his cheeks as he gripped my bony shoulders.

I nodded, my heart sinking as I stared at his tear-streaked face. I knew how much he cared for me, and deep down, I wanted to change, but I just didn't know how to climb out of the hole.

"I can take care of myself," I replied with a defeated sigh. "I'll be okay."

By 2006, I was shooting up meth and heroin multiple times daily. Every relationship in my life began to deteriorate as I traded my drugs for those I cared about most. I became increasingly paranoid and moved out of my friend's house and into a place in south Fairbanks where drugs ran rampant. There, I figured, I would blend in better.

"What' goin' on with you, man? You never come around anymore," an old friend said when he bumped into me one day.

"They're after me, man," I replied, patting my pants pocket. I now packed two guns every day, just in case the cops or someone else caught on to me. In my trunk sat a kilo of coke and a large wad of cash. "I gotta lay low," I added, giving my friend a knowing look.

He raised an eyebrow. "You sure you're cool, man?" he asked skeptically.

"Yeah, it's all good. Just gotta lay low." Even as I said the words, I glanced around skittishly, afraid a cop or two might jump me if I didn't stay on guard.

My behavior became more erratic. To my friends, I was more unreliable than ever. I became convinced that someone was recording my every move, and I spent my days hiding in random places around town. My new friends were the "tweekers," or meth users; other gaunt-looking guys covered in sores, greasy hair and dirty clothes. A few of these tweekers passed away, and while it rattled me momentarily, it didn't stop me from shooting up the next day. The moment I felt myself start to come down from my high, I shot up again. My mind was spinning out of control and so was my life, but I wasn't ready to surrender. Yet.

To remain incognito, I stayed in hotels, often jumping from one to another to avoid the people I was convinced were after me. One evening, I grew so paranoid that I took all the dope I had on me and headed to a friend's house, where I unloaded my bizarre concerns on him.

"The cops are after me, man. I just know it. They're gonna show up, and we're gonna have a shootout. I gotta lay low at your house for a few days, if it's cool, okay?"

My friend agreed to let me stay. I curled up on his couch and tried to fall asleep for the first time in days. My matted hair clung to my gaunt face, and I reeked from going days without showering or changing my clothes. Yet even my own filth did nothing to jar me out of my terrible state. To my friends, family and the world, I was "gone," a shell of a person running around town like a mad man. Yet even at my lowest, someone was still fighting for my soul. And the battle was about to get intense.

One night, I headed out with some friends to score some dope. We were already high when we pulled up at a guy's house and marched up to his door. The minute he let us in, we pulled out our guns and waved them in his face.

"Give us all your dope!" I ordered, nudging the pistol into his cheek.

The guy's eyes grew wide with panic as he tossed me his dope. "Take it easy, man," he stuttered.

"This all you got?" I demanded.

"Yeah," he insisted, trying to keep cool as I nudged the pistol further into his skin.

157

"You believe him?" I asked my friend.

"Yeah, man. Let's get outta here." He grabbed the dope, and we ran for the car. In the background, I heard the guy calling the cops, and I knew my time was running out.

I had envisioned this moment a thousand times in my head, what it would be like to finally get caught. I'd pictured violent shootouts with the police and car chases worthy of a high suspense action movie. But as I climbed in my car and tore off down the road, I only wanted one thing. To rest. To surrender. Deep down, I was relieved that the cat and mouse game might finally be over.

Instead of going home, I took a detour and drove up to my parents' house. Our relationship had been strained for the past few years, as I shut them out of my life and tried to hide my dark secrets from those I loved the most. I knew I'd hurt both my mother and father, as well as my brothers. Yet there's something about coming home that always makes sense, that feels familiar, right and safe. Home was where I needed to be.

"What are you doing here, son?" My father looked surprised to see me when I showed up at the door.

"I need to come in." I brushed past him, weak with fatigue and headed straight up to his room. Just before I crashed onto the bed, I pulled my pistols out of my pockets and handed them to my father. "I'm done," I said wearily. "I can't do it anymore."

My father took the pistols and stared at me, a mixture of sadness and relief spread over his face.

"Glad you're home, son," he said with a half smile.

Moments later, I heard sirens. Looking out the window, I saw state troopers surrounding the house, their rifles aimed. Just as I'd suspected, they'd come for me.

"I'm sorry, Dad," I whispered. I felt terrible that my parents had to be in the middle of such chaos. They certainly didn't deserve it. Slowly, I stood to my feet. I knew what I had to do.

☙☙☙

The irony about going to prison was that I finally realized I'd been in prison long before the doors shut behind me. The world I'd created had been closing in on me for some time, and at last, I'd been compressed to the point of surrender. Now here I sat, facing my past, dreading the present, the future only a blip of uncertainty.

I began to have terrible delusional thoughts in prison as I came down from my high. As I lay on my bed, my bone-thin body wracked with shivers and sweat, my mind played crazy tricks on me. Everyone around me was suspect; I didn't even trust myself. The days ticked by like one long nightmare I could not wake from.

One day as I walked back from the dining hall, a guard pushed on me. Anger boiled inside, and I lost control of myself; I spun around and elbowed him with force.

"Hey!" he shouted, grabbing me as hard as he could. He called for backup security, and later that afternoon, they threw me in solitary confinement.

Solitary confinement is the lowest rung on the prison ladder. In many ways, prison was a social scene, complete with basketball games, TV and card games when it got dark. But solitary confinement was truly the loneliest place I'd ever been in my life. For days, I sat on a tiny metal bed and stared at four blank walls without a soul to talk to. Outside those walls and outside that prison, life went on for everyone else. It was February now; Christmas decorations had long since come down and those on the outside talked of spring camping, hiking and boating. But for me, there was nothing. Nothing at all.

As I stared at those four walls, day after day for six long, terrible weeks, something stirred inside of me. My mind became more clear, and I began to reflect on the last few years of my life. Suddenly, I realized how fake it had all been. The friends I thought were friends really weren't; they only wanted my drugs. The people I'd imagined were after me really weren't; paranoia from the meth could explain that. The flashy cars, the jewelry I flaunted, the women I pursued — that, too, was all fake.

My life had been one horrible, giant lie.

My parents had sent me a Bible while I was in prison, but up until now, I hadn't been able to touch it. One day, I had a sudden urge to read it and picked it up eagerly. I pored over the pages, reading many of the stories I'd heard growing up, as though reading them for the very first time. The pages came to life as I flipped them; I was devouring them like a fine meal after a long period of starvation. And that's when I realized how truly starved my soul had been.

Deep down, there had always been a longing for more, for the truth. I hadn't understood it all as I'd sat in church all those times, but now, sitting here, it suddenly all made sense. God's word was the truth.

Lord, I get it now! These words are real! The Bible is wisdom!

I wanted to shout it from the mountaintops, but there was only me and God in this tiny room. And it was there that he met me when I cried out for him, when I bowed my head and began talking to him like an old friend. It felt strange at first, but the more I read the Bible and continued to pray, the more alive his Spirit became. The blinders had finally come off, and in that dark room, I finally saw the light.

The rest of my days in solitary confinement were filled with a newfound joy as I pored over the scriptures and memorized Bible verses. I no longer felt alone as I sensed God's presence right beside me, comforting me as I read his words. It had taken 22 years, but I finally understood the greatness of the gospel. The good news that Jesus had come to earth to die on the cross for a rotten sinner like me was unfathomable, but I believed it was true at last.

"Lord, please forgive me for what I've done. I know it's a lot, but I also know from your word that you are faithful to forgive those who come to you and repent. I promise to stop using drugs when I get out of here. Please help me to stay strong as I find a new life in you. I want to be a new man and put the old one behind me once and for all," I prayed through my tears. In the stillness of that room, I felt him there; my surrender had led me straight to his arms.

I walked out of solitary confinement six weeks later a changed man. As I strode down the corridors, my homies called out to me from their cells. "Hey, Corey, I got some dope. You wanna smoke it later?" one guy whispered.

"Nope, I'm good, man," I replied, keeping my eyes straight ahead.

My homies stared at me like I was crazy. "Dude, what'd they do to you in there?" one said, laughing. "Since when don't you want to smoke dope?"

But I just kept walking, a content smile spreading across my face. I had something way better than dope — I had the Holy Spirit. Getting thrown in that lonely room turned out to be the best thing that ever happened to me.

❧ ❧ ❧

During the next few months, I spent time with a guy named "Hop" who sat in the cell right across from me. Hop had been thrown in prison for assault in the first degree and kidnapping charges. A former coke user, he had given his life over to God once entering prison.

"Hey, man, that's so awesome you gave your life to Christ!" Hop told me excitedly when he learned about my recent commitment to the Lord. "I tell you, I'm never goin' back to that old life. God is the God of many chances, and I'm just so thankful that he's given me one. Even though I got a few years in here, I'm still gonna make the best of my time and try to serve him." He went on to explain that he was starting a Bible study two times a week for the other guys in prison. "You in?" he asked with a smile.

"Definitely," I assured him.

Hop's Bible study was a blessing not just for me, but for many other guys in the prison. During the study, he shared scriptures that had spoken to his heart and prayed that God would heal our wounds and give us the strength to trust in him.

I met several other guys who were seeking Christ as well; like me, they'd had some sort of background with church and God but had never truly committed their lives to Christ. We shared our stories with each other and found we all had one thing in common: We'd been trying to fill an empty hole with drugs, booze, money, power and other worldly substitutes instead of filling it with the only thing that could truly satisfy us — a relationship with Jesus Christ.

శ్రాశ్రాశ్రా

After eight months in prison, I was finally released in September 2007. My final charges were assault with a deadly weapon; since I had ironically robbed another druggie, the prosecution could form no other charges. I learned that one of my co-defendants, a guy who had been with me during the robbery, had been shot in the head after the incident. I was so thankful to be alive, so thankful that God had given me a second chance. I could hardly wait to get out and start serving him.

I moved back with my parents; they were happy to have me home and quick to forgive me for my past. We spent time talking about the pain I'd caused our family, and I promised to never go down that path again.

"I'm not the same guy anymore," I promised.

Promises hadn't been one of my strong suits in the past. I'd promised to love and cherish girls, only to cheat on them and leave them a week later. I'd promised to show up somewhere or do something for someone, only to get high an hour later, grow paranoid and bail on my friend. But this time was different.

I was determined to keep my vow to God and my family and stay clean.

A few weeks after being out, I ran into some old friends. They invited me to party with them, and in a moment of weakness, I agreed. As I hit the booze and smoked the dope, a horrible feeling hit the pit of my stomach. *What am I doing? I'm not this guy anymore!* Repulsed, I went home that night and cried out to God, "Please help me, Lord! I don't want to be that man anymore!"

From that moment on, I never touched anything again. I realized that the Holy Spirit had convicted me in my moment of weakness and would help stop me from going down that dark road again. I knew in my heart that God was real, that his word was the truth and that the Holy Spirit was powerful, as I had never been able to change for anyone else in my life before. What a feeling of freedom that was!

Being an ex-drug dealer is a humbling experience. Sometimes, as I walked down the street, my former homies who had once revered me laughed at me instead. I no longer had what they wanted, so I was now worthless to them. The temptation to return to the lavish lifestyle of power, money and fame snuck up on me, but I quickly reminded myself of those dark days in solitary confinement, when I'd cried out to God for a fresh start. The road ahead may be filled with a few bumps and unexpected turns, but I was never, ever turning back.

Slowly, my mental health was restored, as well as my physical health. My once-emaciated frame regained life and color again. I praised God for taking such good care of me, for bringing me back from the brink of death, both spiritually and physically. I was truly a new man.

Living with my parents was humbling; the guy with the flashy cars and fancy jewelry was now unemployed with not a dime to his name. Just as I began to grow discouraged, my brother's girlfriend invited me to go to church with her.

I eagerly accepted the invitation.

෴෴෴

Friends Community Church of Fairbanks was a large church, brimming with life, love and laughter. The moment I walked through the doors, I felt right at home.

got friends?

Many people my age came up to greet me with a warm handshake and a smile. There was a genuineness about them that was so different from the guys I'd hung with on the streets. I knew I'd come to the right place.

God filled my life with more than I could have imagined or dreamed of the next couple of years. He blessed me with a great job as a welder, as well as a wonderful girlfriend who completely supported me in my new journey with Christ.

My girlfriend and I had dated sporadically before I'd gone to prison, but she had since given her life to Christ as well and was eager to walk down this new road with me. We attended a small group at Friends Church together and met many other awesome people who were also excited about their new relationship with Christ.

God also restored my relationships with my brothers and brought our once-distant family closer than ever. I knew they had prayed hard for me over the years, and God had faithfully answered those prayers by restoring my life and our relationships.

Not long ago, as I sat on my bed reading my Bible, I couldn't help but praise God for his abundant faithfulness in my life.

A thousand words danced inside my head, and in an effort to give God the glory for everything good, I pulled out a pen and scrawled these words:

the long road home

Lord, I give you all the compliments I get
for my accomplishments
You made a life of confusion all make sense
You saw me through dark days and even scarier nights
Thank you, Lord, you showed me the light.
Through it all you have taught me knowledge,
wisdom and understanding
Your love and grace are the only reasons
I'm still here standing
You took me for who I was
Right where I was at
And upon the cross you erased my sins
Just like that.
You took away every heavy burden
All those prayers through the years
I know you truly heard 'em.
You love us all more than we truly know
If we could stop long enough to listen
You'd tell us the way to go.

As I set down the pen, a smile crept over my lips. God had indeed told me the way to go, and though the road had been long, I'd finally come home.

love story
The Story of Rocky and Cathy Pavey
Written by Karen Koczwara

Once upon a time.

It's how most love stories start, isn't it?

Perhaps the story begins with a shy glance, a shared laugh, an awkward moment, a smile.

Then there's the middle part, the ups and the downs, the uncertainty, the heroes and villains, the question of whether or not love will stand the test of time.

And then there's the end. *Happily ever after*, as some fairytales read.

Our story began like all the rest, but it's the middle part you need to know about.

The middle part is full of tears, laughter, hope and despair. There were moments when I, Rocky, wondered if it might be the end. Moments when I could not see beyond that hospital room, the doctors' sullen faces and the dark, quiet mornings that bled into dark, quiet nights. Moments when I thought the tears would never stop.

But even then, I held out hope for the happily ever after. I had to believe in tomorrow.

This is our love story.

෴෴෴

"And now, folks, for the limbo contest!" the DJ announced.

The pretty brunette next to me smiled. "You gonna try it?" she asked.

"Sure, why not? But you go first," I replied, laughing. It was hard not to stare at her … big brown eyes, gorgeous smile, long brunette hair that danced along with her to the music in the club. Our friends introduced her as Cathy, and I quickly took note of her name. I never forgot a pretty girl's name.

"Oh, I don't know if I can go that low!" Cathy laughed as she arched her back and ducked under the limbo stick.

"You're a pro!" I cheered her on. "And you're gonna make me look like a fool."

By the end of the night, I wound up with a crick in my neck and a phone number in my pocket. It was just days before Christmas 1989, and winter held its usual chill in Fairbanks, Alaska. Yet Cathy and I were just getting warmed up.

At 26 years old, I was still holding out for Ms. Right. Cathy was a single mother; I quickly grew fond of her 9-year-old son, David. Cathy explained they were a "package deal," and I couldn't have been happier. When I asked her to marry me, she eagerly accepted.

Cathy and I desired more children after we wed, but we were devastated when she got pregnant and miscarried.

"We'll try again," I assured her. "We have plenty of time." Cathy got pregnant three more times, but each pregnancy resulted in a miscarriage. After losing a baby six months into the pregnancy, the heartache was too great. We had tossed around names, shopped for little clothes and discussed paint colors for the nursery. Through many tears, we chose to accept that we were not meant to have more children and focused on David, our wonderful son. David loved all things motorized, including motorcycles, snow machines, jet skis and tractors. Cathy and he were best friends, confidants and competitive Parcheesi opponents. I enjoyed stepping into the role as his father and taking him on outdoor adventures.

Cathy was no stranger to hardship. She had lost her mother at age 9, her brother to a drunk driver when she was 19 and her father in 2006. Despite these tantamount losses, Cathy faced life courageously, living and breathing in each moment with a contagious air of peace about her. Little did we know there was greater loss to come.

Since age 19, Cathy had worked for the Fairbanks School District in the student records department. I was a heating contractor and began my business, Rocky's Heating Service. On the weekends, we focused on David and enjoyed the outdoors. And once in a while, we attended church.

I had gone to church most of my young life while growing up in Oklahoma. I had never been a big fan of church; the whole idea of God and religion seemed a bit stifling for a rugged, outdoorsy guy like me. I loved hunting, fishing, hiking, boating and joking around with the guys. Sitting in some boring church service when I could be tearing up a dirt road or tossing my fishing line in the water didn't seem like much fun.

Cathy had first come to know God at 13. She was baptized shortly after, a way of publicly showing her church that she intended to follow the way of Jesus, but throughout high school, she fell off track and returned to partying. We both agreed it would be good to start attending church again once we married, but I still struggled to find its relevance in my life.

After David graduated high school, he moved to Washington and enrolled in the rigorous Construction Management Program at Washington State University. We were sad to see him go but excited for his new adventure. Cathy and I began attending services at Friends Church in Fairbanks; Cathy joined a Bible study and started reading the popular *Purpose-Driven Life* book by Pastor Rick Warren. I continued to take it all in from the sidelines, still convinced that truly giving my heart over to God would mean an end to my rough and tough manly ways.

❧❧❧

In May 2004, David called us from Seattle; he had graduated from the university the previous year and was working in Seattle. "Just calling to say hi. I'm on my way home from a party!" he announced.

"Are you on your motorcycle?" Cathy asked with a sigh. "Please, be careful on that thing, David."

"I will, Mom. I always am," David replied cheerfully. "Love you. I'll talk to you soon."

"Love you, too," Cathy replied, hanging up. She shook her head. "I really hope he's careful on that thing."

Early the next morning, the phone rang again. This time, it was a police officer's voice on the other end, somber as he said our names. "I'm afraid I have bad news. Your son, David, has been killed in a motorcycle accident."

There are no words to describe the way a parent feels when losing a child, no label to put on the moments between hearing those horrible, life-changing words and planning a funeral. Cathy and I waded through the following week in a daze, crying until it felt like the well inside our souls would dry up. We had lost our only son, the only child Cathy would ever have. It was devastating.

David's death was not just an incredible loss for us, but for the whole town. He was well loved by everyone; on an average day, his phone rang 200 times from friends all over the United States just calling to say hello. His goofy, loving spirit had touched many, prompting me to write "Fairbanks Lost a Son" when I penned his obituary.

David's friends gathered together at our home the week before the funeral and spent hours putting together a musical video tribute of our son. They stayed up all night, scanning photos into the computer, laughing and crying and reminiscing about the boy who impacted their lives.

We held David's funeral service at Friends Church. The outpouring of love and prayers from neighbors, friends and church members was overwhelming. The sanctuary held 500, but it was so packed that people poured into the foyer. As the 40-minute slideshow played, I glanced around and caught people laughing and crying as they remembered the tall broad-shouldered boy who brought so much life wherever he went. As I glanced back up at the front of the church, the coffin sitting on the steps jarred me out of the surreal setting. Tears streamed down my face as I tried to wrap my head around the fact that our once-vivacious son was lying in there. It was too painful to process.

During that dark time, something stirred inside of me. I had always believed in God, but suddenly I felt his presence, real, like never before. It was undeniable, as if he had reached his arms straight down from heaven and wrapped me in them.

There seemed to be no other explanation for the peace and strength that got me out of bed each morning. I didn't know quite what this feeling was all about, but I knew I wanted more.

As Cathy and I grieved, we began attending Friends Church more regularly. I leaned forward in the service, hanging on every word the pastor said; his messages resonated with my heart.

"He makes being a Christian seem exciting," I told Cathy one day after church. "I always thought it was this legalistic thing, full of a bunch of rules, but I really believe there's more to it. Maybe there is room for a 40-ish outdoorsy guy like me in the church."

love story

The hole in our lives where David had once been was glaring. We returned to work and continued attending Friends every week. In February 2005, I attended an evening class on the Holy Spirit. The pastor spoke about the intimate relationship we could have with God, and at last, the pieces finally clicked. God's Spirit was what had carried me through this dark time! It made such perfect sense. Christianity wasn't about a bunch of rules and regulations, but about a true and living relationship with God. *This* was what I wanted.

After the class ended, I bowed my head and prayed the prayer that would change the rest of my life. "Lord, I've known about you for a long time, but I truly want to know you now as my Savior. Please come into my heart. Forgive me of my wrongdoings, and please help me to follow you from this day forward."

As I drove home that night, praising God for the work in my heart, I realized something quite stunning: God had sent his only son, Jesus, to die on the cross for our sins. It had taken the death of my own son to point me back to Christ. My heavenly father and I had something in common.

Cathy and I threw ourselves into Bible study and other activities at church for the next few years. Cathy was growing in her own relationship with Christ; we were both excited to share our newfound faith.

శాశాశా

In early 2010, Cathy woke one morning feeling strange. "I'm weak all over," she complained. "I can barely move my arms."

I thought this was odd, but I wasn't too concerned. We continued with our day, but as the weeks passed, Cathy's symptoms grew worse. One evening, we sat down for pizza and began chatting. As we laughed, I noticed only one side of Cathy's face turned up in a smile. "Cathy!" I cried, alarmed. "What's going on with your face?"

Cathy looked at me with her big brown eyes, confused. My pizza stuck to my throat; I knew we had to get her to a doctor.

Through God's amazing provision, we got an appointment with world-renowned neurosurgeon Dr. Sekhar. Most people wait months to see this doctor, but we were able to land an appointment within the week. An MRI confirmed our concerns: Cathy had something wrong with her brain.

"A cavernoma, to be specific," Dr. Sekhar explained. "Basically, a massive blood leak, or hematoma, that is putting pressure on part of the brain and causing swelling. We need to go in and map out exactly where this hematoma is coming from and what parts of the brain it's affecting before we operate."

I swallowed hard. *Cavernoma* was a big word. So was *hematoma*. And *operation*? I squeezed Cathy's hand tightly and tried to take a deep breath. "It's going to be okay," I whispered. "God is in control." I reminded myself that we were in great hands, not only with Dr. Sekhar, but with the creator of the universe. God would take care of my bride.

The doctors performed a battery of tests to map out the cavernoma before surgery. "They're going to put half of your brain to sleep," I explained to Cathy. "In other words," I added with a chuckle, "they're going to turn you into a man."

After reviewing the tests, Dr. Sekhar called us with the results. "I consulted with my neurosurgeon partner, and we have decided to access Cathy's cavernoma through the top of her head. This will greatly reduce the chances of affecting the other parts of the brain. We would also like to perform the surgery while she is asleep rather than awake as we originally thought, thus cutting down the operating time from eight or nine hours to five or six hours. We'll need to remove quite a large portion of the skull in surgery, so when we replace it, we'll secure it with small titanium plates."

Whoa. Lots of information.

My brain was on overload, but I was confident in Dr. Sekhar's plan of action. I relayed the latest news to our good friends Jim and Misty Nordale. "So they're going to have her only use half her brain *and* make her hardheaded? They really *are* going to turn her into a man!" he joked.

It felt good to laugh in the midst of such serious circumstances. The Nordales insisted that I stay with them during Cathy's surgery and recovery, which would take place at Seattle Harborview Hospital. I was grateful for their offer, as I had a hunch we'd be away from home in Fairbanks for some time.

Just before we left Fairbanks, our friends Jeff and Gena Barney prayed with us. Jeff pulled out his Bible and read perhaps the most comforting words in the entire scriptures from Psalm 91: "Whoever dwells in the shelter of the Most High will rest in the shadow of the Almighty. I will say of the LORD, 'He is my refuge and my fortress, my God, in whom I trust.' Surely he will save you from the fowler's snare and from the deadly pestilence. He will cover you with his feathers, and under his wings you will find refuge; his faithfulness will be your shield and rampart."

I loved the image of God sheltering us with his wings, like a mama bird watching over her young. I trusted that God would take care of my bride and restore her to health.

The night before the big day, 11-year-old Hanna Nordale handed Cathy a manila envelope. "Each kid in my class made you a card," she said with a shy smile. "Hope you like them."

Cathy smiled as she pulled each card from the envelope and read them with delight. One student had drawn two fish on a card and scrawled, "To Cathy Pavey, I hope your brain surgery goes swimmingly." We all chuckled, joking that Hanna's classmate might have a future at Hallmark.

The morning of the surgery, Cathy shared another Psalm that had spoken to her heart. "I woke up thinking of Psalm 23 this morning," she began. "The LORD is my shepherd, I lack nothing. He makes me lie down in green pastures, he leads me beside quiet waters ..." (Psalm 23:1-2). As she quoted the rest of the passage, I realized it was the one we had had engraved on our son David's gravestone marker. How thankful we were to have the comfort in God's own words during this time.

Cathy and I arrived at Harborview Hospital at 6 a.m. on April 13, 2010. Her brother, Dave, and his wife, Toni, arrived a few minutes later. Dr. Sekhar came in to meet with us and said a prayer; I was immensely comforted by this. After he left, I pulled out my Bible and re-read Psalm 91. Friends and family had been writing and texting us with Bible verses the past few days, and I was so grateful once again for God's words.

"Rocky, please pray for God to comfort all of our friends and family who aren't here; I don't want them to be too worried about me," Cathy requested in her soft, sweet voice. I was amazed that just moments before a harrowing surgery, my wife thought not of herself but of our loved ones instead.

Around 7:15 a.m., the nurses came to wheel Cathy into the operating room on the gurney. I planted a big sloppy kiss on her mouth, and she returned the affection with a wide grin and a thumbs-up sign.

"If you get worried, just repeat these words: 'Thank you, Jesus, Thank you, Jesus, Thank you, Jesus,'" Cathy whispered, mustering a sweet smile. Even in her gown and cap, she looked beautiful, like an angel, not like a woman about to go have brain surgery.

I trudged into the waiting room and grabbed a cup of bad hospital coffee to settle my nerves, musing that it didn't seem right to find a bad cup of coffee in Seattle.

My mind immediately turned to Cathy, my beautiful wife, and as the tears came, I gave them all to the Lord.

Seven long hours later, Dr. Sekhar called from the operating room. "The most critical portion of the surgery is over," he said. "We're in the process of sewing Cathy back up. To be honest, it was a very difficult surgery. We had to go in pretty deep because the cavernoma had grown so much. As of now, Cathy's motor skills seem to be intact, but we're not sure about her verbal skills just yet. We'll keep her sedated for another 24 hours to regulate her blood pressure and swelling."

The post-surgery ICU room was terribly dark and depressing; there were foreign-looking machines, with tubes and alarms that beeped intermittently. Nurses hustled about in the dim light like green-clad ghosts, whispering in hushed tones. I inched my way toward Cathy's bed and took a deep breath. She was still woozy from the anesthesia and hooked up to more machines and IVs than I'd ever seen in my life. Her chest rose and fell as she lay there, the same woman who just hours before had sweetly told me to pray if I got worried. Nothing could have prepared me for this difficult, dark moment. The nurses grew concerned when she was hardly able to respond to verbal and physical prompts.

"She's not coming around as we expected," the doctors said. "We're going to take her in for an MRI to make sure she hasn't had a stroke and isn't hemorrhaging."

Please, God, let her be okay. I collapsed onto the plastic hospital chair and played the waiting game once again. It was a horrible feeling to see my wife so helpless while I sat helpless as well, at the mercy of doctors and nurses. I reminded myself God was in control, that he held Cathy in his loving hands.

"Good news," the doctor reported when he came back into the room. "The MRI didn't show anything alarming; most likely she's just suffering the lasting effects of the anesthesia."

Over the next few hours, we all studied Cathy carefully. Occasionally, she wiggled her left hand or slightly opened her eyes. I grew anxious, just wishing she'd hop off the table, laugh and maybe even do the limbo for me. It was more difficult than I'd imagined to see my normally vivacious wife nearly lifeless on that bed, and for the first time since that morning, the tears flowed freely.

As the morning progressed, Cathy still could barely move her right side. "She may be having seizures, which is common after this type of surgery," a doctor explained. "The cavernoma was in a critical part of her brain that affects verbal skills, sleep motor skills and cognitive functions. It's not terribly surprising that she's having a difficult time coming around. Physical rehab is a high possibility in her future."

My head spun as I processed the information. It had just seemed so simple at first: go in and remove whatever was affecting Cathy's brain, and we could all get on with life. Now it appeared we might have to walk down a very long, difficult road to recovery.

As Cathy continued to make minimal progress with her movement, the doctors reviewed the post-op MRIs with me. "There's a whitish color on the right hand control area on the MRI that is very concerning," Dr. Sekhar began. "This can often mean a stroke, but there is also a strong chance it's just severe swelling on the brain. Either one could cause the symptoms Cathy's having."

I returned to my laptop and updated my Caring Bridge Web site, which I'd been using to inform friends and family about Cathy's surgery. "Since God likes us to be specific in our prayers, please pray it's swelling and not a stroke," I wrote.

Cathy made minimal progress that day.

"Cathy, can you wiggle your fingers for us?" the doctors asked when they popped into the room to evaluate her.

Ever so slowly, Cathy lifted her right hand and tried to wiggle her fingers.

"Good job," the doctor said, smiling. "That's what we like to see!"

I stood to the side, encouraged. Never would I have thought such little movements would prove so exciting.

Thank you, God, I prayed. *My girl is in there. I just know she is.*

I slipped outside and headed to the small park area behind the hospital overlooking the harbor. As I sat down on a bench, the tears flowed, and my heart ached. I wanted my Cathy back; this process was much more painful than I could have imagined. I was just entering into a really good pity-party when I noticed a woman striding toward me, a little Yorkshire Terrier on a leash beside her.

"Oh, you're an answer to prayers. I needed a little pick-me-up. Can I pet your dog?" I asked, wiping away my tears.

"Of course you can. Her name is Sugar." The woman stopped and smiled as I leaned down to pet her little dog.

"I have a Yorkie just like this back in Fairbanks," I told her. "My wife's beloved dog, actually. I can't wait to get back to her, but my wife's got to get better first."

"What's wrong with your wife?" she asked gently.

I told her about Cathy's surgery and that the recovery didn't seem to be going very well. "I'm very concerned for her long-term wellbeing," I admitted.

"I've had three brain surgeries. On the last one, they hit my verbal center, and I was in a coma for two weeks." She stepped back and waved her hands in front of her as if to say, "Look at me now!" Then she added, "My name is Nora, and I'll pray for you." She bent down and threw her arms around me in a long hug. "We serve a mighty God," she added with a smile as she pulled on her dog's leash. "Come on, Sugar," she called, and the two of them walked off.

New tears filled my eyes as she disappeared around the corner, tears of happiness this time. *Forgive me, Father, for my lack of faith. You have promised you would send your angels to hold us up so that we would not even strike our foot on a stone. You have said you would hear and rescue those who love you and who call upon your name. Thank you for sending this angel, Nora, to remind me of this promise.*

Back in Cathy's hospital room, I sat beside her bed, squeezing her hand as I broke out into Merle Haggard tunes. My singing always made Cathy laugh, and I hoped that it might stir up at least a faint smile today, but instead she slept peacefully.

"I'm so proud of you, baby," I told her. "We all love you, and so many people are praying for you."

As I watched Cathy's chest rise and fall, it occurred to me that my relationship with God could often be like this. While I sat anxiously over Cathy, waiting for her to "show up," God did the same with me. He sat at my side, waiting patiently, saying, "Why, hello, child! I've been missing you!" when at last my eyelids fluttered open. In that moment, God comforted me once again, reminding me that he had planned this to happen from the very beginning of time and that he was weaving it all together for good, using his faithful servant Cathy to bring others to their knees.

Later that afternoon as I peeked in on Cathy, her eyes suddenly fluttered open. I raced to her side as she tilted her head and gave me a long, vacant stare.

My heart soared as I stared back into her big brown rounds.

"There you are! So good to see you!" I cried. I pulled up a chair and laid my hand on her bed. Slowly, she picked up her hand, waved it around in a wobbly motion and then placed it firmly in mine and squeezed. I didn't move a muscle as I basked in the sweetness of the moment and her tender touch.

"I'm going to be here to hold your hand forever," I promised.

One huge tear appeared at the edge of her eye and rolled down her cheek. "Oh, Lord, she's in there!" My heart sang with joy.

My friend Dave Whitmer flew in that night to be with me. He and I sang renditions of "Amazing Grace" to Cathy and lulled her to sleep with our off-key music. A few minutes later, as I typed away at my laptop, Dave nudged me.

"Look at Cathy!" he cried.

Cathy's right hand, which had been resting on her stomach, now slowly climbed up her chest toward her neck. "I do believe she's trying to cover her ears because of our singing," I laughed. "Boy, am I insulted." Cathy's movements may have been slow, but her surgery certainly hadn't affected her eardrums!

Mornings proved to be hardest at the hospital. Cathy lay quiet and unresponsive, the halls were dark and quiet and I was growing tired of the stale hospital coffee. Mornings were when the devil seemed to taunt me with his old tricks and tried to discourage me.

One of the ICU doctors discussed Cathy's progress in frank detail. "In truth, we don't know what the future holds for Cathy," he said. "She most likely has a long road of recovery ahead."

Downtrodden, I trudged out back to the little park I had come to know as my Garden of Sorrow. There, Satan stepped up his game, haunting me with thoughts like, *Give up, it's useless. This whole thing is all your fault.*

But in that moment, God spoke to me, reminding me of his truth. I poured out my heart to him, telling him my fears and struggles. *Trust me. I am the Great Physician,* I heard him say.

Thirty minutes later, my wife's dear friend Linda Sather sent me an e-mail that pierced my heart to the core. She shared how she had gone through major brain surgery five years before and wrote in great detail about her journey to recovery. After hearing one doctor after another say, "We don't know exactly what will happen with Cathy; everyone's recovery is different," it was so comforting to read about Linda's journey and feel in my heart that Cathy was going to be okay. Linda's words were exactly what I needed at that very moment.

God's timing: impeccable.

❧❧❧

One morning, 11 days after surgery, I got a brilliant idea. I grabbed a bottle of lotion and began massaging Cathy's feet. As I moved from her left foot to the right, I said, "Cathy, if you want me to continue, you're going to have to pick up your foot." Ever so slowly, she lifted her little toes off the bed. Dave and I stared at her, wide-eyed with excitement. Movement from the right side meant her delayed progress was due to swelling in the brain, not a stroke. This was great news!

Dr. Sekhar confirmed this when he asked her to move her right toes and her leg. "Yup, it's swelling. She'll get better. It's just going to take a long time."

Later that day, Cathy's brother and his wife announced it was time for them to head back to Fairbanks. Toni leaned forward and kissed Cathy's forehead. "We're so proud of you," she whispered. "We will be back as soon as we can." Cathy's eyes filled with tears, and so did ours. My girl was still in there, fighting for her life.

Cathy's slow progress continued. One morning, the nurses entered to find Cathy had pulled her feeding tube out during the night.

"Look at you, making trouble again," the nurse teased as she proceeded to reinsert the tube.

Suddenly, Cathy rose up from her pillow and blurted out a string of curse words. "&*$*!" she cried out, her voice strong and confident as could be.

We all stared at her in disbelief for a moment, then burst out laughing. "Well, what do you know! My baby is back and cursing like a sailor!" I laughed.

Cathy just sat there with a coy smile, as if to say, "What? What's so funny?"

I laughed again. These weren't the particular words I would have chosen for her comeback debut, but we were so happy to hear her speak, it hardly mattered what she said. I sat down and took Cathy's hands. "I'm so proud of you!" I gushed. "We all love you so much. You're doing so well." Cathy looked like she had so much to say, but no more words escaped her mouth. Instead, we sat there, holding hands like two giddy high schoolers on a first date.

One evening, Cathy opened her mouth and began talking in a small, nearly inaudible voice. I knelt before her and said shakily, "Cathy, tell me what my name is."

She reached her wobbly left arm up, cupped the back of my head and whispered distinctly, "Turd."

"No, honey, tell me my real name. The name you use in public!" Inside, I was dying of laughter. Turd was the name Cathy had affectionately dubbed me at home. It appeared my girl's memory was indeed returning.

That night, as I sifted through the many e-mails our friends and family had sent, one in particular caught my eye. "Rocky, I read about your wife, Cathy. I'm so sorry to hear about her situation. I haven't prayed much in the past 20 years, but I'm going to start praying right now." Again, God reminded me that he was working all things together for good, weaving together a beautiful tapestry that he would one day reveal. *The fabric is the body of Christ, and I am using Cathy, my dear child, as the needle,* he said.

Cathy's progress: three steps forward, two steps backward the next few days. When Dr. Sekhar asked her where she was, she promptly said, "Seattle." She even used the words "Rocky" and "handsome" in the same sentence, which we all found baffling and amusing. But the next few days, her confusion returned, and I grew concerned. Was she experiencing seizures?

I decided to lighten things up with my famous singing again. I tried lulling Cathy to sleep with Merle Haggard tunes, and within no time, her eyelids grew heavy, and she drifted off to sleep.

As Cathy rested, I slipped out back to my Garden of Sorrow, which I'd recently renamed the Park of Praise. I sat down, lit a cigar and thanked God for Cathy's healing progress. My dear friend Jim Nordale had specially ordered my favorite cigars for me, and I was grateful for his kind gesture. As I prayed, I grew distracted and accidentally put the lit side of the cigar in my mouth.

"Ouch!" I yelped, jumping up as the hot cigar burnt my tongue. Reeling from the burn, I fumbled with the cigar and quickly wrapped up my prayer. I chuckled at myself as I strode back inside. Once again, God lifted my spirits with light moments like these.

∾∾∾

Almost two weeks after the surgery, Cathy progressed from a feeding tube to gooey foods like applesauce, yogurt, cranberry juice, milk and ice cream. I snuck the leftover ice cream sometimes, considering it a favor for Cathy and the doctors as I kept her blood sugar down.

In the evenings, when Cathy was more coherent, I tried joking around with her. Cathy continued to speak in a nearly inaudible voice, but it was often difficult to discern when she was making a joke because of her "flat face." As the doctors explained, Cathy's face muscles had not yet re-learned to express themselves, so she did not smile, raise her eyebrows, purse her lips or wrinkle her nose like one normally would. This made our conversations hilarious and a bit unnerving at the same time.

Two weeks after we entered that hospital, I wheeled Cathy outside into the Seattle sunshine for the first time. The Nordales had brought their new German wire-haired pointer puppy, Ellie, upon Cathy's request. We helped Cathy out of her wheelchair, set her on a blanket and let Ellie climb up onto her lap. Slowly, Cathy stroked her, an unsure smile slowly creeping onto her face. She seemed rather frightened of the dog, but we praised the Lord for that smile anyhow.

As we sat there, basking in the sunshine, Nora, my angel, and her dog, Sugar, walked up. "What a coincidence!" she said to Cathy. "I've been praying so hard for you, girl." In that moment, we all knew it was not a coincidence, but a divine appointment by God himself. What a wonderful day!

With some convincing from our dear friend Kathy Hughes, Cathy's therapists recommended her for the intensive live-in rehab facility on the fourth floor. This was a big deal, as there were only so many available beds for patients on this floor. We praised God for this "golden ticket" opportunity; Harborview was known for its outstanding rehab facility, and we felt much more comfortable having Cathy there than moving her to an outpatient facility.

Late one Monday night, as I typed another entry into the Caring Bridge site, God spoke to me about the difference between hope and faith. "Hope is born of fear and worry. Faith is born of trust."

I said two sentences out loud: "I *hope* she'll get better." There was worry in that. I tried it again: "I have *faith* she will get better." One sentence came from desperation, the other from confidence in Christ. In the moments when Cathy seemed to regress, my panic quickly returned, and I succumbed to worry. I had to live in faith, constantly seeking the Lord and trusting him.

"Oh, Lord, forgive my weaknesses," I prayed through tears that night. "Heal me, as you've healed my wife. I need your strength."

༺༺༺

On Thursday, April 29th, Cathy left the third-floor neuro care wing and moved on up to the fourth-floor rehab center. I shared the good news with Cathy's brother, who flew in that day. "It must be all the prayers from everyone," I said excitedly. "You should see all the hits the Web site has gotten. More than 10,000 to date! It looks like Cathy's gone viral!"

At that moment, a nurse walked in and happened to hear the last part of my sentence. She went into "Code

Red" mode and started poking Cathy with needles to pump her with antibiotics and IV fluids.

"I think there's been a misunderstanding," I tried to explain. "By viral, I meant …" I glanced over at Dave, and we cracked up.

Though Cathy still struggled with movement on her right side and often remained confused, talking about herself in third person, her sense of humor began to return. One day, after I returned from the store with some fresh fruit for her, she cocked her head back, stared at me and said, "And who are you?"

I began to shake, panic stricken at the thought that she might have had a hemorrhage or stroke. Just as I was about to lose it, Cathy gave a little snort and grinned. "I know who you are, Turd," she said. I had always been the jokester in our relationship, but now it seemed the doctors had activated the "funny" center in my wife's brain when they went in. I was going to have some serious future competition!

It felt so good to laugh again. God had put joy where there was once fear, peace where there was once worry, faith where there was once a shaky hope. Cathy and I exchanged jokes back and forth; thankfully, she seemed to have forgotten all my old ones, and I could recycle them again. As they say, laughter is truly the best medicine of all.

As Cathy settled into her new private room on the rehab floor, Dr. Sekhar came to me with her latest MRI results. "There's a small triangle-shaped piece of white material on the outer edge of the image, probably a tiny piece of the cavernoma left behind in surgery. At this point, it's nothing to be concerned about," he explained. "The good news is that everything else looks great."

I praised God once again for good news. As I did, he reminded me of a wonderful Bible verse, 1 Corinthians 13:12: "Now we see things imperfectly as in a cloudy mirror, but then we will see everything with perfect clarity …"

Some days, the picture was still fuzzy, much like Cathy's memory. But in the end, I believed God was working all things for good, still weaving that magnificent tapestry that he would someday unveil for all to see.

On May 1st, I witnessed one of the greatest acts of kindness in human history.

Tom Bartels, proprietor of North Pole's Coffee Roasters, sent me a care package with two pounds of "Black Gold" blend coffee. Real, authentic, delicious non-hospital coffee. For a guy who had spent the past few weeks drinking questionable, murky decaf coffee, this was simply a dream come true. It also worked wonders when bribing the nurses for a little extra attention for my beautiful bride.

On May 2nd, I witnessed yet another exciting event. Cathy asked to type something on the computer. It took her two whole hours, but she managed to eke out a few precious lines:

Hi, everyone, Big Rocky and my brother, Dave, are here keeping this thing going! Thank you, thank you for letting me ride along. Go, me, go. Fight, fight, fight! Cathy.

Encouraging responses poured in left and right, proof that Cathy's fan club was growing by the day.

That evening, we celebrated our wedding anniversary together. The Nordales picked up King Crab with all the trimmings from our favorite place, The Fisherman's Restaurant, as well as tiramisu and blueberry cheesecake from the Cheesecake Factory. They also brought a few extras to complete the romantic setting: white linens, real silver candleholders and two long dinner candles.

"This is absolutely perfect, isn't it?" I said to Cathy, serving her a bite of delicious crab. The nurses stopped by and seemed alarmed by the candles, commenting that the place might catch on fire. I reminded them that the hospital had an excellent burn unit should things go bad.

After dinner, I wrapped Cathy in a new quilt and walked her out to the park. We sat there for more than an hour, watching the sun descend and the lights flicker in the skyscrapers.

"I think this may just be the best anniversary we ever had," I told Cathy, squeezing her hand.

Back in the room, we admired the 25 beautiful handmade paper butterflies Emmi Nordale's class had made for Cathy. As we taped them up on the wall, I read each encouraging message to her. "Dear Cathy, we are praying for you. We hope these butterflies help you feel better." In no time at all, those drab hospital walls were cheery and bright.

❧❧❧

Cathy grew stronger the next few days; each feat was exciting, like watching a child take steps for the first time. She insisted on showering herself, curling and blow-drying her hair and putting on makeup. I resisted the urge to help her curl her hair and cringed when her weak right hand slipped and the hot curling iron touched her forehead. At last, I could stand it no longer and took over curling iron duties. This amused both Cathy, myself and Cathy's brother, Dave, who happened to walk in just as I perfected her bangs.

The doctors were amazed by Cathy's progress. Each time a new doctor walked onto the rehab floor, the other doctors brought him in and introduced him to Cathy. "This is the person we've been telling you about," the old docs said as Cathy beamed back. Once again, I knew the credit belonged only to God, the Great Physician, and, of course, to the many prayers from around the country and beyond.

Cathy continued working with the physical therapist every day, taking small walks and working on regaining her strength. Her speech and memory remained a challenge; she had a communication disorder called aphasia that made it difficult for her to start a conversation. "This is not something we can cure," the doctors said. "She just may never be as talkative as she once was." I bit my tongue to keep from joking, "And this is a bad thing *because?*"

The speech therapist encouraged Cathy to write in a journal to regain control over her fine motor skills and to work her memory muscles. The occupational therapist came, too, and helped Cathy with simple chores, like doing laundry. It hit me that she was re-learning everything again, like a child venturing off on her own for the first time. We still had a long road ahead, but Cathy was making remarkable strides.

Mother's Day rolled around, and the Nordales showed up at the hospital park with a trunk load of food for what they announced was the "First and Last Annual Harborview Get Well/Mother's Day Picnic." We enjoyed a spectacular day on the lawn; the weather was a perfect 70 degrees, the potato salad was delicious and the company was even better. It was a bittersweet day, however, as we remembered our dear son, David Alan. His brilliant smile and sweet, goofy spirit remained forever etched in our hearts, and we did not try to ignore the pain in our hearts on this Mother's Day. They say sorrow shared is halved and joy shared is doubled, and as we sprawled on that hospital lawn with our dear friends and watched the sun go down, we realized we'd had a little of both that day.

One night, Cathy and I sat together enjoying deli sandwiches with Toni, sent from our friends the Manzies.

"Who wants a little dinner music?" I asked.

Toni raised an eyebrow. "So long as you aren't providing it," she said with a laugh.

I borrowed a friend's iPod, and the beautiful Kutless song "Word of God Speak" wafted through the room. Halfway through the song, I glanced over and saw Cathy with her palms turned upward toward heaven, tears streaming down her face, singing along with the words. "I am so thankful," she whispered.

Later that night, Cathy told me, "When David died, I was so ready to go home and be with him. But God told me he wasn't through with me yet."

"That's right. He wasn't through with you yet," I agreed. God was still weaving that beautiful tapestry with a needle tempered with the fire of trials and faith. Someday, his majestic work will be revealed to our eyes.

❧❧❧

On May 11th, exactly four weeks after surgery, Cathy was released from the hospital. She still had a ways to go with her recovery, but we planned to resume rehabilitation with therapists back in Fairbanks when we got home. To celebrate, the Nordales cooked a New York steak, which Cathy devoured in no time. It took nearly five hours to pack up all her cards, gifts, pictures and personal items people had showered her with.

As we walked out toward the park that afternoon, an ICU nurse I recognized walked toward us. She introduced herself as Megan and seemed very excited to see Cathy walking and talking. "Normally, patients in your condition are in rehab for months and months. We never get to see their end results," she gushed. "You look great!"

Once again, I praised God as the realization that my wife could have been bedridden and incoherent for months hit me like a speeding train. My wife was a walking miracle, a testimony to God's amazing faithfulness and healing hand. And a testimony, of course, to the power of prayer.

Cathy celebrated her "great escape" with a plate of our friend Susan Sele's famous brownies and a trip to the hairstylist for a much-needed color and trim. She walked out of that salon a redhead, and I had to do a double take from the little coffee shop table where I sat. It would take some getting used to, but I was pretty sure the redhead thing would grow on me.

We returned home to a front yard full of balloons, yellow ribbons, posters, signs and lawn angels, all placed by friends, family and neighbors. The inside of the house was filled with goodies, posters, ice cream and a fridge full of delectable dinners. "Looks like just a couple people love you," I said with a wink, pulling my beautiful bride in for a hug. "Did I happen to tell you that I'm one of them?"

"Are you going to start singing Merle Haggard right now?" Cathy asked, laughing.

"Only if you do the limbo," I replied with a grin.

᧞᧞᧞

So that was the middle of our story. There was much more, of course, but you get the gist. God worked a miracle in our lives, replacing the losses and hardships with miracles, provision and healing. Today, a year and a half after her surgery, Cathy and I live a simple but happy life, and I am pleased to say I am more in love with my wife than I've ever been before. We enjoy long walks with the dogs, gardening and being outdoors when the finicky Alaska weather permits. I belong to a group called Wild-Hearted Alaska Men (WHAM), comprised of outdoorsy guys like myself who love the Lord and enjoy fishing, hunting, canoeing, snowmobiling and hiking. I purchased an airplane as well and am in the process of obtaining my pilot's license, which I think concerns Cathy just a tad. She may stay on the ground and wave.

Three months after surgery, her occupational and speech therapist met with her boss and co-workers to determine what they could do to get her ready for work again. But those she worked with wanted her to come back right away and said they'd help her. The job would be her therapy. Her boss, Janet, tailored Cathy's duties to her abilities and assigned someone to work right alongside her to help her remember things.

This was — and is — a huge blessing to Cathy and me. They are understanding if she needs to leave for a two-hour lunch break to take a nap. And several of the ladies Cathy works with started having prayer meetings for her when she was in the hospital, and some have come to visit Friends Community Church at different times.

"Cool!" one friend said one day when she walked into the sanctuary, greeted by so many genuine smiling faces.

We have received a continuous outpouring of support for Cathy at Friends Church. At last, I've found a place I can be transparent with other men who love the Lord and love to have fun. We feel so blessed to call this place our home.

This side of heaven, I may never know how many lives were impacted by Cathy's journey. I do know this, though: We serve a great and mighty God, and just as he promised in Psalm 91, he watched over my wife and brought healing and hope to our lives.

❧❧❧

"How was your day?" I asked Cathy when she came home from work one evening. Her eyes looked weary, and I sensed she'd had enough activity for one day. As much as Cathy loved her job, her "new" self wore out a bit more easily than the old one.

"I'm tired. I think I'm going to … go to the place … where I sleep," Cathy replied sleepily.

"Going to bed?" I asked, smiling. Cathy still sometimes fumbled for the right word when speaking.

"Yes, bed." Cathy laughed. "I love you, Rocky."

"I love you, too." I planted a kiss on her forehead and helped her down the hall to our room.

This may be no castle, and I may be no king, but I certainly feel like I've found that princess in my own fairytale, I thought to myself as I tucked my bride into bed with one last goodnight kiss.

… And they lived happily ever after? I like to think so.

conclusion

Did you find yourself sympathizing with the people in this book? I am certain that no one who reads these stories will be able to put the book down and honestly say that he or she has nothing in common with these storytellers. Despite our varied backgrounds, ethnicities, cultures, etc., human beings are amazingly similar. This is why it is called the human condition. These folks found relief and solace in the one place that could offer them real comfort and healing. That place, that shelter from the storm, is the foot of the cross.

If you find yourself battered by the world, enslaved by sin, shamed by iniquity or pained by loss, if you have tried to solve your problems with pills and booze only to wake up feeling more empty and hopeless than ever, why not try something new? Why not simply learn from the people who were happy to share their stories with you in hopes that you would not continue to rely on the things of this world?

Got friends?

If you have hit rock bottom or are just ready to stop digging and ask for help, like Sydney, Rocky, Cathy, Charity, Rita, Roger and Audrey, Gabriella and others in this book, loving friends in your community are waiting with open arms to show you the God who can give you true peace.

A new life is waiting for you; don't spend another day in your old one.

If you wish to be touched and changed by God's unfailing love, you can talk to God right now. He's right where you are and more than anything desires to transform your life.

How does this change occur?

Recognize that what you're doing isn't working. Accept the fact that Jesus desires to forgive you for your bad decisions and selfish motives. Realize that without this forgiveness, you will continue a life separated from God and his amazing love. In the Bible, the book of Romans, chapter 6, verse 23 reads, "The result of sin (seeking our way rather than God's way) is death, but the gift that God freely gives is everlasting life found in Jesus Christ."

Believe in your heart that God passionately loves you and wants to give you a new heart. Ezekiel 11:19 reads, "I will give them singleness of heart and put a new spirit within them. I will take away their stony, stubborn heart and give them a tender, responsive heart" (NLT).

Believe in your heart that "if you confess with your mouth that Jesus is Lord and believe in your heart that God raised him from the dead, you will be saved" (Romans 10:9 NLT).

Believe in your heart that because Jesus paid for your failure and wrong motives, and because you asked him to forgive you, he has filled your new heart with his life in such a way that he transforms you from the inside out. Second Corinthians 5:17 reads, "When someone becomes a Christian, he becomes a brand new person inside. He is not the same anymore. A new life has begun!"

We'd love to see you soon!

Blessings,

Pastor Jeff Wall
Friends Community Church
Fairbanks, Alaska

We would love for you to join us!

We meet Sunday mornings at 9 and 11 a.m. at
1485 30th Avenue, Fairbanks, AK 99701

Please call us at 907.452.2249 for directions, or
contact us at www.friendschurch.org or at
info@friendschurch.org.

For more information on reaching your city with
stories from your church, please contact
Good Catch Publishing at
www.goodcatchpublishing.com

GOOD CATCH
PUBLISHING

Did one of these stories touch you?
Did one of these real people move you to tears?
Tell us (and them) about it on our reader blog at
www.goodcatchpublishing.blogspot.com.